STEVE WAUGH

NEVER SATISFIED

STEVE WAUGH

NEVER SATISFIED

The diary of a
record-breaking
year

HarperSports
An imprint of HarperCollinsPublishers

Harper*Sports*
An imprint of HarperCollins*Publishers*

First published in Australia in 2000
by HarperCollins*Publishers* Pty Limited
ABN 36 009 913 517
A member of HarperCollins*Publishers* (Australia) Pty Limited Group
http://www.harpercollins.com.au

HarperCollins*Publishers*
25 Ryde Road, Pymble, Sydney NSW 2073, Australia
31 View Road, Glenfield, Auckland 10, New Zealand
77-85 Fulham Palace Road, London W6 8JB, United Kingdom
Hazelton Lanes, 55 Avenue Road, Suite 2900, Toronto, Ontario M5R 3L2
and 1995 Markham Road, Scarborough, Ontario M1B 5M8, Canada
10 East 53rd Street, New York NY 10022, USA

National Library of Australia Cataloguing-in-publication data:

Waugh, Steve, 1965 - .
    Never satisfied : the diary of a record-breaking year.
    1. Cricket captains – Australia – biography. 2. Cricket
    players – Australia – Biography. 3. Cricket – Australia.
    I. Title.
    ISBN 0 7322 6436 7.
796.358092

Front cover design: Blue Cork
Design and finished art: Brevier Design
Front cover photograph: Allsport
Back cover photograph: Steve Waugh
Printed in Australia by Griffin Press Pty Ltd on 100gsm Matt Art

6 5 4 3 2 1
03 02 01 00

CONTENTS

Acknowledgments

As always, I am extremely grateful to a number of people who helped and supported me in the making of this book. First up, I must thank my wife, Lynette, and children, Rosalie and Austin. Without their love, help, guidance and support nothing I have achieved in cricket would have been possible.

Special thanks to:

- My teammates, for letting me write about the on and off-field events, and also for letting me intrude with my camera into our dressing room and beyond.
- Pat Farmer, a truly inspirational Australian, who, while he was only in our dressing room for one afternoon, certainly made his presence felt. His rousing words stayed with us for the rest of the season.
- Dave Misson, for allowing me to use the poetry he often produces before a day's play, and also for kindly permitting me to use two of his essays — one from Sri Lanka and one from South Africa — that are absolutely spot on.
- Errol Alcott, who has offered enormous support to me and the team over many years and who also generously used my camera to take a number of the photos that appear in the book.
- Rupert McCall, for the effort he put in to write — with just 24 hours notice — a very special poem for the team. Rupert has kindly allowed me to reproduce that poem.

As has been the case with my previous tour diaries, a large proportion of the photographs in *Never Satisfied* are from the superb files of Allsport. I am very grateful to all their photographers and staff — their skill, diligence and patience have been magnificent throughout the development of this book.

Thanks to all my sponsors who supported me throughout the year of cricket covered in *Never Satisfied*. And also to all the managers and support staff of the Australian teams, the Australian Cricketers' Association, and the officials and staff at the Australian Cricket Board.

I am very grateful to Geoff Armstrong — who has now worked with me on each of my eight books — for his dedication, professional attitude, commitment and skill. I am looking forward to working with him again on future projects.

I also appreciate the help of the following group of extremely creative and patient people:

- Everyone at HarperCollins, for their enthusiastic support and patience.
- Jake Causby at Blue Cork, for the cover design
- Kylie Prats at Brevier Design, for designing and then producing the final pages
- Sarah Shrubb, for helping to put the words in the correct order and the commas in the correct places.

Foreword

BY PAT FARMER

GROWING UP IN THE Western suburbs of Sydney provided me with many happy memories — thoughts and pictures that would comfort me for the rest of my life, especially throughout the long arduous days of pounding the pavement around Australia.

As a kid, life was simple. It consisted of school, fishing in the local creek, playing football with all the other kids in the neighbourhood, and backyard cricket matches where everyone lived out their dream of playing for the Ashes.

The equipment was primitive, but adequate. Our bat was made from an old fence paling, skillfully carved into shape with Dad's handsaw and penknife, while a garbage bin acted as the stumps. (Sometimes the keeper would move the stumps left or right to suit my little brother's wild spin bowling.) The fluff of the tennis ball was ripped off to make it look more like a six-stitcher cricket ball. Our garbage bin stumps proved beneficial when the light faded fast on balmy summer Sunday afternoons — it may have been difficult to see the ball, but the 'crash' on the bin meant there was no argument as to whether or not you had been bowled out.

On January 2, 2000, I was invited by the Prime Minister, Mr John Howard, to run a lap around the Sydney Cricket Ground to commemorate the 'Centenary of Federation Run Around Australia'. Australia was playing India in the third Test and there wasn't a spare seat at the ground. I wondered if I would get the chance to meet my heroes. I had long been a fan of Steve Waugh, Justin Langer and, indeed, all the Aussie cricketers over the years … how great would it be to meet them?

Well, the lunch break came and I was summoned from the Prime Minister's box to go out onto the ground. I quickly changed out of my suit into my running gear, and went down the stairs. I had fears about whether or not I would be well received by the crowd, but as it turned out, the reception could not have been better. The crowd had been hyped up by the fine efforts of the Australian team and they erupted into jubilant cheers.

The greatest thrill for me, however, came soon after, when Steve Waugh asked me to address the players during the lunch break. Steve, like many true professional sporting captains, has recognised the need to develop a positive mental attitude within each team member. During my brief speech, I mentioned how important it was to attack any game one step at a time, to concentrate on one delivery at a time. By doing this, whether you are bowling, batting or fielding, you can ensure the best possible cumulative effort.

In that Test, Justin Langer, in particular, was able to dig deep and apply the method of concentrating on one delivery at a time. In doing so, he scored a double century for the first time in his professional career.

I also strongly suggested to the players that they should think back to when they were younger, when they were sitting in the grandstand watching their heroes perform, and remember how important it is to the supporters that they see their heroes win.

I firmly believe that if you want to do something, anything, with all your heart, you will find a way and if you don't you will find an excuse. These words rang true when Steve Waugh led his team to win that series. To realise that there is no force on earth greater than your own will is a moment that is truly unforgettable. Steve is renowned for his strong sense of will, which makes him a truly remarkable athlete. But I feel it is his ability to find something extra within himself, and to then share it with others, that makes him a truly remarkable person and athlete.

I wish him well.

Pat Farmer
September 2000

Introduction

BY GEOFF ARMSTRONG

DURING THE PAST EIGHT YEARS, I have been fortunate enough to be involved in the production of seven Steve Waugh tour diaries. Starting with the 1993 Ashes tour, I have followed (from, sadly, my editor's desk) Steve to South Africa, the West Indies, the World Cup, and then back to England. In 1998, we took a break, so Steve could showcase many of his finest, quirkiest and most interesting photographs in *Images of Waugh*. But then it was back on the cricket caravan, to follow the Australian team through 1998 and 1999 — to Malaysia, Pakistan, Bangladesh, Australia, the West Indies and England — an adventure that culminated in great triumph for the Australians in the World Cup final at Lord's.

That 1998–99 book, *No Regrets: A Captain's Diary*, was different from Steve's previous diaries, in that where his previous works had focused in detail on just one tour, *No Regrets* provided a more general overview of a sustained spell of cricket. *Never Satisfied: The diary of a record-breaking year* is built on a similar format, offering extended 'grabs' from the captain's log as his Test and one-day sides put together astonishingly successful records throughout the year of cricket that was 1999–2000.

In that time, August to August, Australia contested 13 Test matches (for 10 wins, two draws and one loss) and 30 one-day internationals (22 wins, six losses, one tie, one game abandoned). Off the field, Steve was involved, as Australian captain, on just about every single day, whether it was discussing games played or to be played, building game plans, training, travelling, treating injuries, calling room service, dealing with the media, being part of the media, responding to controversies, servicing sponsors (his own and Australian cricket's), and so on and so on and so on. And always learning, as a player, captain and adventurer. And, of course, writing page after page. Many of those written words appear in this book.

The demands on Steve's time during '99–00 were so consuming that sometimes in *Never Satisfied* three or four days, even an entire Test, are covered in a single diary entry. Steve has also opted to concentrate on the personalities involved in the cricket, issues that developed from the events on and off the field, and peculiar and amusing anecdotes and accidents that occurred, rather than simply summarise ball-by-ball plays, dismissal after dismissal, run after run. In particular, Steve focuses on the tactical battles and in-depth planning that are such a part of the modern game.

In doing so, the captain offers us a rare insight into how the Australian teams — Test and one-day — go about their business. Steve describes the influence of Geoff Marsh, coach until the conclusion of the Sri Lanka tour, and then John Buchanan, who began his tenure as Australian coach before the home Test season. As this book went to press, 10 months and nine Tests after his initial appointment, Buchanan is still to experience anything other than an Australian Test win. Steve also talks about the qualities and characteristics of the Test and one-day teams, and the men under his command. He has clearly taken great pleasure in the performances of the new breed of Australian cricketers, who have emerged to keep the team at the top of the world game despite the retirements in the past four years of great players such as David Boon, Craig McDermott, Mark Taylor and Ian Healy.

Sitting alongside Steve's diary entries in *Never Satisfied* are a number of features, including some of the notes he used for his pre-match addresses to the team. We are also given access to three instances of the 'feedback sheets' coach Buchanan gave Steve immediately after each Test of the summer was played (each player received a similar sheet from the coach, analysing his individual contribution), and also many of the poems and quotes team members created or found and then read to their mates before matches. To keep Steve's diary entries in context, throughout this book is a cricket 'timeline', which briefly chronicles all the events, issues and cricket relevant to the Australian team that were played out in 1999–2000. And further complementing Steve's paragraphs is a vast array of photographs, many taken by him, and a comprehensive statistics section that features complete scorecards and averages for all 13 Test matches, and abbreviated scores and averages for the one-day internationals.

From my perspective, it has been extremely interesting to watch Steve grow as an author and cricketer in the time that I have worked with him on his books. Unusually among sportspeople, he delights in writing his own copy; my job is not that of a ghost writer but an editor, photo researcher and project manager. To be involved has been a supremely interesting and rewarding publishing experience, one that has consistently emphasised for me what his cricket and now captaincy also clearly show — that he is among the game's most interesting, clever and dedicated people. I think his books have helped his cricket, too, by making him a keener observer of all around him and giving him a greater chance to dwell on and learn from sporting experiences that might otherwise have been forgotten. One revealing statistic is that his Test batting average has risen from just above 36 to just above 50 in the days since he began his writing career.

Steve is as loyal a man as you could meet. I am not surprised that the captain, when asked — in a pre-Sri Lankan tour questionnaire offered to all the players by team psychologist Sandy Gordon — what 'pressure situations' he found 'particularly mentally demanding', began his reply with, 'selection meetings — having to leave out players'. In the current Australia Test and one-day sides, this means being forced to omit men who have served him well and backed him (and themselves) unequivocally — little wonder that the scenario disturbs him. (The entire questionnaire, and Steve's response, is reproduced opposite the diary entry for August 14, 1999). Off the field, he is perhaps not as organised as when he is scoring Test centuries, but in the same way that he has worked out batting as well as any player in the past 30 years, he knows how to get things done and always delivers. He has recognised what his readers enjoy, and delights in giving them that and, with each book, a little bit more.

This book is due for its initial release in the first week of November 2000, around three weeks before the first Test of the 2000–01 Australian summer. Steve Waugh's team will be chasing their 11th straight Test victory, which would equal the record for most consecutive

Test-match wins currently held solo by the West Indies team of 1983–85. Although, these cricket days, it is far from politically correct to talk in such a way, I would be loathe to bet against Steve's men achieving this feat. Read *Never Satisfied* and you will learn how totally prepared, confident and focused the Australians will be going into that match and series. You'll learn, too, about their pride in the baggy green cap and how much they savour walking on the same cricket stage that the legends of the past strode on in years gone by. And you'll learn how much they enjoy it all.

That last attribute, I reckon, might be the key to what makes them so dominating. Steve and his players love the cricket and the camaraderie, and revel in each other's success as few, if any, have done before them. They are a happy and mighty team. The title of this book does not mean that they are hard to please, but simply that they are extremely ambitious. They want to keep winning, establish new records and constantly set themselves new standards of excellence. As Steve put it to the Australian squad during the New Zealand tour: it is not sufficient to merely be good when it is possible to try to be great.

The best, for team and captain, may yet be to come.

Geoff Armstrong
September 2000

STEVE WAUGH

PART ONE:

RAINY DAYS IN SRI LANKA

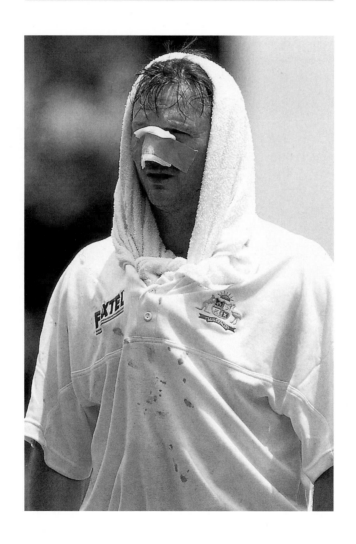

August 14 BRISBANE

IT'S BEEN THE BEST part of two months since the World Cup final, that glorious day, June 20, when I lived out one of my cricket dreams. Still vivid, too, are the fantastic matches against South Africa — the 'super six' match in which I played perhaps my best-ever one-day innings and the semi-final tie that (I've been told countless times since) kept half of Australia awake through most of the night back home.

Not surprisingly, I was more than a bit rusty today, when I picked up a bat for the first time since the Cup. Still, it was good to be back with my teammates, the men who'd climbed with me to the top of the cricket tree. At a press conference, many of the questions homed in on our hunger — having won the World Cup, could we remain focused for tournaments such as the one we were about to fly to Sri Lanka for? I don't see this as a problem, and said so, because I am confident that everyone in the squad has a strong desire to remain the No. 1 ranked team in the world. After the World Cup, I truly felt we

A few days before we departed for Sri Lanka I had the privilege of meeting Sir Donald Bradman at his home in Adelaide. This was one of the great highlights of my life. Interestingly, the portrait in the background of this photograph is just about the only cricket-related item I saw in the house.

I quickly realised that there is so much we can learn from Sir Donald. We talked about the players of his day, the wickets he scored his runs on and captaincy. I was surprised when he told me how much he enjoyed the one-day game.

I was astonished to discover that Sir Donald was never once hit on the hands during his 20-year Test career. 'How is that possible?' I asked. 'You only get hit on the hands if you miss the ball,' he replied.

The three captains in the 1999 Aiwa Cup in Sri Lanka – Sachin Tendulkar, me and Sanath Jayasuriya.

could say this about ourselves in regard to one-day cricket. My hope is that if we can achieve a run of success in the Test matches ahead of us, then we'll also be able to *clearly* claim top-dog status in the traditional form of the game.

In front of us is an imposing schedule. A limited-overs series in Sri Lanka, followed by three Tests. Then a one-off Test match in Zimbabwe, the first ever between the two countries, before three more one-day internationals. Back home for three Tests against Pakistan, then three against India. Then the World Series, featuring Pakistan and India. Then a six-week tour of New Zealand, for six one-dayers and three Tests. And finally to South Africa in April, for a three-match one-day tournament.

The possibility of a letdown is something we discussed at our first team meeting here in Brisbane. The World Cup had, after all, come at the end of a long campaign that had included Test and one-day series in Pakistan, Australia and the Caribbean. But that journey, I feel, is no excuse for us now; in this modern world of cricket we now live in, two months off is plenty of time to recharge the batteries. 'It's time to switch on again,' I told the lads, 'this is where the hard work begins for us.'

Staying on top will be a huge challenge. I can't recall a team being clearly the No. 1 in the world in both forms of the game since the famous West Indies sides of the early 1980s. If that's what we are now, then it is not by any big margin, and we know that there are many good sides eager for a chance to knock us off. Rising to this challenge will be fun and absorbing, and rebuffing our opponents and improving ourselves will be extremely satisfying.

It seems that every tour of Sri Lanka comes with a security risk, but after being briefed two days back about the current situation — four people were killed in a bomb blast in Colombo last Friday — I'm confident everything will go off without a hitch. Sure, it's a little intimidating going to a country where such things can happen, but unlike in 1996, when the government was advising Australians not to travel to Sri Lanka unless it was

The Australian one-day team left Sydney for Sri Lanka, to play in the Aiwa Cup, a one-day tournament that would also involve Sri Lanka and India.

Australia arrived in Colombo for the start of their tour of Sri Lanka. When asked by reporters whether his team saw the Aiwa Cup as merely a warm-up for the Tests to take place later in the tour, Steve Waugh responded, 'It's always the real thing. These games are as important as any other one-day game or Test match.' ... Waugh was also asked if he expected any problems on the field with former Sri Lankan captain Arjuna Ranatunga. 'Everyone mellows with age — he sent me a fax after the World Cup,' Waugh replied. 'I don't have a problem with the way Sri Lankans play the game. I don't think our players have any problems with your players. Maybe there were one or two incidents with Ranatunga, but other countries would probably say there were one or two with me and Ian Healy, and Mark Waugh and Glenn McGrath. So I don't see that as any big deal.'

completely necessary, now they are happy to advise even tourists to stick to their travel plans. So there'll be no problem for us. And anyway, conditions couldn't be any more 'suffocating' than they've been in the past. We're used to being shadowed by military types with submachine guns and walking through metal detectors at our hotels. This, unfortunately, is life as a touring cricketer in this part of the world.

What about the problems between ourselves and Sri Lanka? This was another common theme at the press conference. I have always felt that the 'acrimony' between the two teams has been vastly exaggerated. Sure, words are going to be exchanged in the middle — that happens

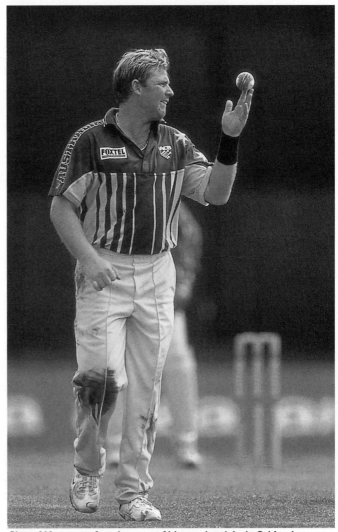

Shane Warne, performing one of his magic tricks in Sri Lanka.

BRISBANE PRE-SEASON TRAINING CAMP, AUGUST 1999
Mental Skills for Performance Management
— from Sandy Gordon, team psychologist

1. How can I best help you *the cricketer/performer*? Take some time to write down the pressure situations that you find particularly mentally demanding.

- *By being honest. Constructive help is always appreciated. Likewise, positive reinforcement is needed by all players — even the senior guys.*
- *Pressure situations: Selection meetings — having to leave out players; Having to maintain high standards, both personally and as a team — in particular, the hard work and commitment needed to achieve this.*

2. How can I best help you *the person*? It is very important to me that you are able to consider my assistance in your non-cricket performance roles (eg. as a partner, father, businessman, etc.).

- *Making sure cricket is not always my focal point on tour and the centre of talk all the time. It's important to branch off (eg. family issues, news of the day, world events, etc.).*
- *Positive reinforcement. Guidance as to how the team is functioning, and in particular how I'm performing.*

3. Write down your specific goals for 1999–2000.

A. Technical (eg. to improve the appropriate use of bottom hand in batting)
- *To keep working on soft hands for singles to rotate the strike.*
- *Make sure my front knee bends, for balance, when going forward.*
- *Get forward early on in my innings.*

B. Tactical (eg. to improve consistency in bowling the right length)
- *Keep on thinking one step ahead of the opposition. Make sure each loose ball is punished to the maximum.*
- *Back my gut instincts as a captain.*

C. Physical (eg. to improve my overall flexibility)
- *Core stability (gut work).*
- *Flexibility, stretching, massage, suppleness.*
- *Keep weight under control to stop joint soreness (knees).*

D. Mental (eg. to improve my self-talk/inner dialogue)
- *Stay hungry and be focused for each game.*
- *Get myself in that zone of intensity and desire that leads to success.*

4. What do you realistically wish to achieve within the Australian team(s) by the end of the New Zealand tour? (eg. to cement a spot in the top order) How will you set about achieving this/these goal(s)?

- *Be the team everyone looks up to.*
- *Be ruthless; win the games that are so-called 'dead rubbers'.*
- *One day team — play to the standard we achieved in the World Cup final.*
- *Test side — back to basics, get tougher, be more of a team, less individual.*

As a player — play each and every ball to the best of my ability by implementing the basics (ie. desire, pride, concentration and technical ability).

The Australians won a five-wicket victory over a Sri Lankan Board President's XI in Colombo. After winning the toss the locals reached 5-208 from their 50 overs (Glenn McGrath 2-17, Jason Gillespie 2-40). The Australians reached that target in the 46th over. Adam Gilchrist made 45, Ricky Ponting 60 (retired hurt) and Darren Lehmann 37.

Monsoon rains were threatening to prevent play in the opening matches of the Aiwa Cup. Overnight rain had saturated the town of Galle, where the first match, between Sri Lanka and Australia, is scheduled for August 22. Rain in Colombo had also forced the Indian team to cancel its scheduled outdoor practice session ... Sri Lanka's new skipper, Sanath Jayasuriya, told reporters that he had asked his players to forget the past and try to develop good relations with the Australians. Elsewhere, Indian captain Sachin Tendulkar revealed that he had fully recovered from a slight back injury and was ready to play.

In the opening game of the Aiwa Cup, Australia defeated Sri Lanka by 51 runs in Galle. Michael Bevan, with 44, top-scored in Australia's rain-shortened innings of 9-206. During the innings, Adam

between any two sides. Nowadays we have a match referee and two umpires to monitor the situation and make sure things never get out of hand. We'll continue to play it hard, but after the game we can still have a drink together and forget about on-field gamesmanship. As far as I am aware, there are no problems between players once we're off the field. It's often some sections of the media and constant television replays that exacerbate these things.

Another topic for conversation with the press guys was the battle for places, in particular the spinning spot. Our last Test match had been in the West Indies, in Antigua, when we'd made the controversial decision to go with Stuart MacGill ahead of Shane Warne. Since then, though, Warney had won the man-of-the-match awards in the World Cup semi-final and final, bowling as well as he'd ever done in the process.

'I like a team where everyone is playing for their Test spot,' I responded, 'and that's the way it should be.

'It keeps the guys hungry and focused — you never want to become complacent.'

AUSTRALIAN CRICKET TEAM — Team Rules

1. CURFEW and ALCOHOL:
a. Curfew is 12 midnight in the hotel.
b. No alcohol day before a Test match.
c. Alcohol up to and including dinner each day on tour.
d. Curfew and drinking rule is left flexible after a win (according to captain/coach).

2. CLOTHING:
a. Team shirt to all team meetings.
b. Team shirt and dress shorts or tracksuit pants on bus to and from all matches.
c. Correct training attire to be worn at all team training sessions.

3. PUNCTUALITY:
a. All players to be on bus prior to designated departure time.
b. All players to proceed immediately to recovery sessions after dropping gear in room upon arrival back at hotel.
c. All players to be at breakfast 20 minutes prior to designated time of departure for ALL matches.
d. All players to be at team meetings prior to designated time of meeting.

The torch lighting ceremony in Galle. Moments earlier, Indian captain Sachin Tendulkar had almost set me alight, as I climbed up onto the stage.

August 22 GALLE

'It is not the critic who counts; not the man who points out where the strong man stumbles or where the doer of deeds could have done them better. The credit belongs to the man who is actually in the arena, whose face is marred with dust and sweat and blood ... who, at the best, knows, in the end, the triumph of high achievement, and who, at the worst, if he fails, at least he fails while daring greatly, so that his place shall never be with those cold and timid souls who knew neither victory nor defeat.'

— **Theodore Roosevelt** *(presented by **Shane Warne**, one-day international v Sri Lanka, August 22)*

RELYING ON A SET-DOWN schedule in Sri Lanka or on the Indian Subcontinent is definitely not advisable, but even more naive is to expect that there won't be any late changes or even completely new arrangements introduced at the drop of a hat.

Just two days before the triangular tournament involving Sri Lanka, India and ourselves, we were told that a glorious opening gala ceremony was being proposed for the morning of our opening match. The affair, it was estimated, would go for around an hour and a half. How anyone could think that the players would gladly stand in the stifling heat for 90-plus minutes and then go out and contest a 100-over match was beyond belief. Eventually, thankfully, some commonsense prevailed and the ceremony was cut to 30 minutes, which meant, among other things, that the dignitaries and politicians would now have to turn up for the function on time.

My duty during the ceremony was to carry a lit torch and help ignite a cauldron. My

Team Meeting: The Captain's Notes

BEFORE ONE-DAY SERIES IN SRI LANKA

- The honeymoon is over. We've had a great time since the World Cup, but it's time to knuckle down. Sri Lanka have been training for past month.
- Everyone is now after us — it's great to get to the top — the challenge is to stay there. Let's set a 70 per cent winning target again, maybe even increase it.
- The standard was set at Lord's (discipline, passion, togetherness).
- We're facing different conditions here; need to score heavily in the first 15 overs.
- Sri Lanka will probably come out blazing.
- I want everyone to think about these conditions and how we should play (remember Jayasuriya and Kalu!).
- Our goal is to make the final — and win it.
- Upcoming practice game – get what you need out of it.

Gilchrist was controversially ruled run out by the video umpire even though replays showed that he was safe. In reply, the home team was bowled for 160 in the 38th over. Gillespie, with 3-26, was the best of the bowlers, while Shane Warne's second wicket was his 204th in one-day internationals, a new Australian record, breaking Craig McDermott's old mark. This was Australia's eighth consecutive win in one-day internationals.

August 23

Australia defeated India by eight wickets in their second match in the Aiwa Cup, in Galle, in a game interrupted by rain and reduced to 38 overs per side. Adam Gilchrist (68) and man of the match Andrew Symonds (68 not out off 68 balls) starred for Australia.

Early on our tour of Sri Lanka, Darren Lehmann sought some help on a minor shoulder ache from team physiotherapist Errol Alcott. In the background is our security officer, Reg Dickason, who followed us on this tour, wherever we went.

fellow captains, Sachin Tendulkar and Sanath Jayasuriya, had similar tasks. Part of the trick was to negotiate some steep stairs, which I happily did, though not, perhaps, as safely as I first imagined. When I rejoined my teammates, they told me with a laugh that Sachin had gone within a whisker of lighting me up as he climbed the first step. More farcical situations soon followed. It is always a moving moment when the Australian national anthem is played — you stand there, all in a line, chests strutting out and goosebumps on the arms, as *Advance Australia Fair* plays. Not surprisingly then, it was something of a downer when over the PA system the words 'Once a Jolly Swagman ...' reverberated around the ground. As much as I love *Waltzing Matilda*, it loses its impact in such circumstances.

The cricket itself was very encouraging — a five-wicket victory which featured some fine batting from Michael Bevan, Adam Gilchrist and Mark Waugh, and an excellent opening spell from Jason Gillespie. Dizzy finished with 3-26 from six overs, precipitating a Sri Lankan collapse that left the crowd silent and the home team reeling at 4-41 ...

August 23 GALLE

'Winning is a habit and it's become a habit with this team.
We endured the hard work, the doubts and the bagging before we achieved our dream.
We must play with an aura deserved of the World Champs tag,
But remember, each player must contribute to keep pulling wins out of the bag.
For we are now the benchmark every team's out to chase,
Don't forget the one percenters and to put the fundamentals in place.
Let's keep enjoying our cricket and savouring our achievements,
And continue playing like whirlwinds who don't know what defeat is.'
— **Dave Misson** *(read before one-day international v India, August 23)*

HAVING OPENED OUR CAMPAIGN with an encouraging win over Sri Lanka, today we delivered a highly professional performance to beat India by eight wickets in Galle. Perhaps the most exciting aspect of our display was the fact that we didn't have any bad moments in the whole game — when you play that consistently you always put a lot of pressure on the opposition. The way Jason Gillespie and Damien Fleming bowled in the game's opening overs set the tone for the rest of the day, and though the ordinary weather turned the game into a 38-overs-a-side affair our top-order had few problems reaching the 159-run victory target. Andrew Symonds, who I promoted to No. 3, was in magnificent form ...

August 25 COLOMBO

IT WAS DURING ONE of our regular chats on tour, not only as coach and captain but also as good mates, that Geoff Marsh told me he was calling it a day after this Sri Lanka tour. After 21 years as a player and coach, he'd decided to quit, and the news was made public yesterday.

Initially, I was somewhat shocked and saddened, because we have come to almost accept that certain people will always be there as part of what is virtually our second family away from home. 'Swampy' is everyone's mate within Australian cricket circles, but in his mind his 'blood' family had sacrificed enough and it was time to turn his attention to his

August 24

Australian cricket coach Geoff Marsh announced that he was resigning, effective at the end of the current tour of Sri Lanka. Marsh explained that family commitments and personal priorities had prompted his decision. The Australian Cricket Board said that an interim coach would accompany the team to Zimbabwe, where the Australian team will head immediately after the Sri Lankan tour.

August 25

Sri Lanka defeated India by seven wickets in their Aiwa Cup match in Colombo.

August 26

Australia defeated Sri Lanka by 27 runs in a day/night match in Colombo. Mark Waugh top-scored with 84 as Australia reached 9-241 from their 50 overs. Sri Lanka recovered from 4-48 in the 14th over to reach 214 all out, with McGrath and Warne both taking two wickets.

August 27

The Australian Test players left for Sri Lanka for their three-Test tour. Most media interest was in veteran wicketkeeper Ian Healy, who acknowledged that after a slightly disappointing tour of the West Indies earlier in the year, he could not afford another below-par performance. 'You won't last in the Australian

three much-loved children and his long-suffering, but always supportive wife.

The strain of non-stop touring, tearful goodbyes and long periods of time away from home, plus the fact that the summit had been reached and conquered by winning the World Cup told him the time was right to walk away and get some balance and reality back into his life. Perhaps the chief catalyst for Swampy's decision was the recent death of his long-time best mate, whom he had always treated as a brother, back in Perth.

The team will sorely miss him, for he is a character who doesn't come along every day, and quite often his strengths and values aren't easy to define from outside the team. His greatest asset was a genuine ability to make everyone feel comfortable and relaxed, which made the Australian dressing room a warm and friendly place to be. It enabled younger and less experienced players to feel at ease in what sometimes can be a daunting environment. He also had the ability to teach others about team spirit, team togetherness and how to make the most of your God-given talents.

To an experienced player like me, Swampy had the intuition to know when a word of encouragement or a positive comment was needed to boost a fragile state of mind. Quite often, it was as simple as 'well done' or 'your footwork looks good', but invariably his instinct to be supportive was spot on.

His loyalty to mates and to team spirit and togetherness is legendary, which is why you'll never hear a bad word

Geoff Marsh in Colombo, sharing a laugh with reporters after announcing his decision to retire as Australian coach.

Swamp and me at our hotel in Colombo, after he had announced he was calling it quits.

uttered in his direction. Keeping it simple was his philosophy as coach, with the basics such as consistency, discipline, patience and passion the key attributes he looked for in his players.

Occasionally, Swamp would motivate us all without even knowing it. In Pakistan last season, for example, we noticed our coach had added a bit of girth to his midriff and was regularly seen looking down and pinching himself in the hope it would magically disappear. Being a fitness fanatic and known as a man of rock-solid physique, this new look was a killer blow … and one, of course, that was mercilessly exploited by the lads, who would often fire questions at him such as: 'What bra size are you Swamp?' or 'Did you swallow one of your sheep?'

Enough, said Swamp, was enough. A $500 bet was agreed to between the coach and me, with a target of 90kg being set as the weight he needed to be by end of the World Cup. This was a big ask considering that was his old playing weight and when the wager was made Swamp was 12kg adrift.

This, I thought confidently, was money in the bank. But as the sun rose every morning on our tour of Pakistan, this maniacal figure dripping in sweat could be seen beating a path, Cliffy Young style, around the hotel's front garden. This inner strength and stomach for a fight not only ensured that Swamp did melt away to 91.5kg, but it also set an example to all the lads that anything is possible if you want it enough and are committed to the task. Feeling a mixture of admiration and empathy (much more the former than the latter), I called the bet off.

Our recent World Cup triumph in England was a career highlight for all involved. One lasting memory for me is that of the entire squad gathering on the Lord's wicket to sing our team song, arm in arm, after the match. Walking back to the pavilion afterwards, Swamp turned to me and said: 'Tugga, it doesn't get any better than this.'

As usual, he was spot on.

cricket team if you put two ordinary tours together. I've just got to get on with it and do my job,' Healy said.

August 28

Australia's fourth match in the Aiwa Cup, against India in Colombo, resulted in a 41-run victory, after Steve Waugh's team scored 252 from their 50 overs. Adam Gilchrist made 77 and Andrew Symonds 45. Jason Gillespie (4-26) inspired an early Indian collapse that left them 5-44, before Sadagopan Ramesh and Robin Singh instigated a fightback. The final wicket fell in the 49th over. This was Australia's 11th straight win in one-day international cricket, one short of the world record.

August 29

India defeated Sri Lanka by 23 runs in a rain-interrupted Aiwa Cup match in Colombo. Despite the Indians' win, Sri Lanka qualified to meet Australia in the final.

August 31

Sri Lanka won the Aiwa Cup when they defeated Australia by eight wickets in the final in Colombo. Although eight of the visitors' first nine batsmen reached double figures, only Steve Waugh (43) scored more than 32 in Australia's 202 all out. Romesh Kaluwitharana hit an unbeaten 95 off 117 balls as Sri Lanka reached their target with more than 10 overs to spare.

August 28 COLOMBO

WHEN YOU SEE AN opponent in Australian domestic cricket you can get a feel for their cricket skills, but it's not until you play alongside a guy that you can fully value his talents. Andrew Symonds is as dry as a lime burner's boot, as laid back as one can be, and always straightforward and honest in what he says.

Away from the pressure of playing in front of family and friends and the spotlight that is invariably generated by a home debut, 'Symmo' is making an instant impact in his full series offshore. Today, batting three, he hit a solid 45, five days after he smashed the Indians in Galle. He can bat anywhere from No. 3 to No. 8 and can bowl successfully at different times during a one-day innings, which are great attributes for an all-rounder to have. In his case, these skills come on top of his brilliant athleticism and an innate ability to 'read' a game when we're in the field. He's a guy with enormous talent who will excite the Aussie crowds for many years ...

Andrew Symonds, one of our best performers in the Aiwa Cup.

August 31 COLOMBO

'Twelve in a row? Let's give it a red-hot go.
We have confidence and momentum, let's use it to bury 'em.
Be the man today, the one who makes the difference,
So we can have a beer tonight and sing our first song since England.
Let's not forget it's Swampy's last one-day stand,
A bloke who's given us all some good advice,
A determined focus and a helping hand.
They'll come at us hard, these little Lankan whippets,
And when they want a friendly chat, we'll just snarl and tell 'em to zip it.
So, for the record, the Fox, Tugga's 273rd and our own self-pride and honour,
Let's make Premadasa a Sri Lankan bloodbath we can all enjoy and savour.'
— **Dave Misson** (read before Aiwa Cup final v Sri Lanka, August 31)

WE WENT INTO TODAY'S final very confident after playing so well in our four lead-up games, but our preparations on the morning of this crucial match took an unexpected turn when Tom Moody suffered an allergic reaction to some anti-inflammatory gel that had been administered the previous night, causing swelling and pain in his back joints. It was the start of a disastrous day that saw us fritter away an important toss with some timid batting against their spin-bowling quartet.

With the Poms' world record of 12 straight victories in one-day internationals up for grabs (our run of 11 wins in a row stretched back to the early games of the 1999 World Cup), we were strangled out for 202, including a first ball duck from our main man, Bevo. At least we managed to struggle on and post a reasonable score, but it felt as if it was at least 20 runs short of what we needed. Then, as Kaluwitharana very quickly pulverised our attack, we realised we were at least 50 runs short. Sadly, it was a match we never really got into — I guess we were due for a bad match. I just wished we hadn't timed our poor effort to coincide with a final. The result was a huge letdown, as we had set ourselves the goal of winning all five one-dayers on this tour.

As well, it would have been nice to win in front of the Test boys, who had arrived yesterday. It was great to have them train with us and be in and around the change rooms. However, there is a downside to the two teams being together — certain players would like to be in the other squad, and I have sensed an element of unneeded pressure being created by guys, who are fighting for places in the other's squads, being under the same roof. This crossover of the Test and one-day teams is something officials need to look at for future tours, when one-day tournaments and Test series follow straight after the other.

All in all, it has been a day we'd like to forget. All facets of our game were not up to standard, while the locals excelled and confounded the critics with a terrific all-round performance. Sometimes it just isn't meant to be, in the same way it wasn't meant to be for South Africa when we squeezed past them in the World Cup semi-final. Our batting today was impatient, but credit must be given to the Sri Lankan bowling, which was disciplined, and their agile, sharp outfielding, which enabled them to keep the pressure on and not allow us to gather any momentum.

Right: Jason Gillespie celebrates another wicket in Sri Lanka. Right at this moment, Dizzy was our form bowler, and seemed destined for an impressive summer.

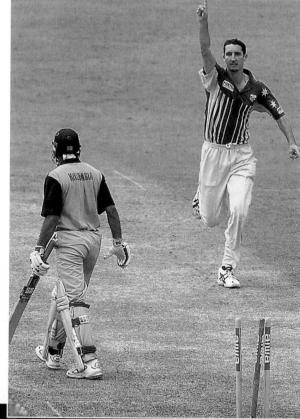

Below: The fact that we'd won our four preliminary matches comfortably counted for nothing when we were soundly beaten by the Sri Lankans in the final.

Under the guidance of fielding coach Trevor Chappell and team coach Dav Whatmore, the Sri Lankans look a strong, tight unit, in direct contrast to the outfit that disappointed in the World Cup. In comparison, our bowling and fielding weren't up to the recent, lofty standards we have set for ourselves — being realistic, such a display had to happen eventually because we have been absolutely outstanding in our previous 11 games.

Losing the final was a letdown, but we have gained many positive points from this series. The impressive entry of Andrew Symonds into international cricket was important and the sight of he and Ricky Ponting prowling the inner circle is worth paying the admission price for. Symonds' composure under pressure was evident, as was his sensible shot selection, and his bowling has potential.

Likewise, Adam Gilchrist was outstanding with bat and gloves. He continually got us away to an excellent start in our innings, further enhancing his claim to be the most destructive batsman in world one-day cricket. But perhaps the most exciting aspect came in the form of Jason Gillespie. He looked tremendous, causing all batsmen problems with his relentless pressure on top of his great focus and determination.

'Dizzy' is a class act and the pace and bounce he has generated on the slow, low wickets of Sri Lanka has been quite extraordinary. He and Glenn McGrath form a deadly pace duo on the field; off it they do a pretty good 'dumb and dumber' routine, with 'Pigeon' even copying Lloyd Christmas's haircut perfectly. I reckon the future for 'Dizzy' will be similar to the path Glenn is following towards greatness. Together they will form the most lethal opening pairing in world cricket for years to come.

Now the time has come to switch over to Test cricket, with the specialist one-day guys on the plane home while the Test boys settle into Colombo. With tours on a tight schedule these days we have only one lead-up game before the first Test in Kandy, making it a really tough decision as to who to leave out.

I expect this series to be tough, with Arjuna Ranatunga and Aravinda de Silva likely to return for Sri Lanka, adding experience and technique to their squad. The wickets no doubt will be low and slow, suiting their spin attack and batting, which can be inferior on bouncing wickets.

If the Test strips do turn, we are well equipped to cope, with Colin Miller, Stuart MacGill and Shane Warne all eager to contribute. If 'Funky' Miller does play, let's hope he does well so he can give us all five minutes' rest from his favourite pastime of recalling the day he hit Curtly Ambrose for two sixes in Antigua earlier this year!

September 1 COLOMBO

I'VE ONLY HAD THE task of being 12th man a few times during my career, but I've had the job enough to know that it can be an experience that brings you down to earth with a thud. To be at the players' beck and call is a true test of just how good a 'team' person you are, because the role forces you to make a full commitment without being able to reap the personal rewards on the field.

Damien Martyn has been put to this test on plenty of occasions in recent times and has always done a great job … until yesterday's last match of the one-day series, the final against Sri Lanka. During our stop-start-stumbling batting effort, I had managed to find

The Australians began their four-day match against a Sri Lankan Board XI at Colombo. Only 25.2 overs were possible on the day, and at stumps the Board XI was 2-69. Earlier, the toss had been decided on a 'best out of three' basis after Steve Waugh objected to the initial toss being conducted on the steps of the away dressing room. That first toss was won by Hashan Tillakaratne, the Board XI captain, Waugh won the second, which was made on the ground, but then the third toss went in Tillakaratne's favour.

The Australians trailed the Sri Lankan Board XI by 53 runs with just one first innings wicket still in hand at stumps on day two of the tour match in Colombo. Glenn McGrath took 4-52 and Ian Healy made five dismissals (three catches, two stumpings) in the Board XI's first innings of 228, while Steve Waugh (42) was the best of the Australian batsmen.

The Australians were 0-39, chasing 321 runs for victory in their match against the Sri Lankan Board XI. Colin Miller (6-57) and Shane Warne (3-74) had earlier combined to dismiss the locals for 271 in their second innings.

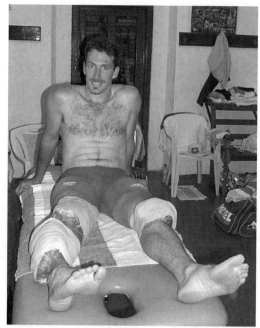

A typical end of day for an international pace bowler. Damien Fleming, complete with ice packs, after a day's play in Sri Lanka. Here, Flem clearly has a slight knee problem and a dose of shin soreness, but you can bet he'll be ready to back up again in the morning. I don't know how the fast bowlers keep doing it, year in year out, day after day, tour after tour, but having Errol Alcott — in my view the best physio in the business — around certainly helps.

some semblance of form and had reached around 30 not out. I was sweating quite profusely in the intense humidity and blazing hot conditions in which the game was played, and gave the customary signal for a fresh set of gloves to be sent out. I fully expected to see 'Marto' race out at the completion of the over, but instead all I could make out in the dressing room was a group of teammates running around like headless chooks and no Marto in sight.

I couldn't hold the game up, and batted through another over, after which Adam Dale rushed onto the ground with the much-needed replacements. Before he could escape, I reminded him that it was 'bloody important for the reserves to watch the game and stay awake'. I wasn't happy, and to make matters much worse, soon after I played a poor shot and lost my wicket.

I was still cursing when I came through the dressing-room door, to see Marto lying on the rubdown bench and talking earnestly to team physio Errol 'Hooter' Alcott. I was

Team Meeting: The Captain's Notes

FIRST TEST v SRI LANKA, AT KANDY

- 'Back to Basics' tour.
- Pressure and partnerships (both batting and bowling). Let pressure be on them more than us — the team under the greater pressure will lose the match.
- Whoever wins first session normally wins first day, wins first Test, wins series. Therefore, it's crucial we set the tone early.
- Let's be disciplined in everything we do! No short cuts.
- Bowlers: be prepared to be boring if it means the outcome will end up positive for us.
- Batsmen: know your game, back yourself, be patient!
- Fieldsmen: hunt in packs, make it happen, no quiet periods! Make it 11 versus two.
- Reserves: help each other, don't leave it to the 12th man to do all the work.
- As a team: let's make them feel uncomfortable; let's intimidate them; let's use our aura without being big-headed; let's have positive, aggressive body language; let's not be affected by the umpiring; let's play tough Test-match cricket (don't get distracted from your job); let's remember it's an honour and a privilege to play for Australia — don't take it for granted.
- Well done to Kat and Haydos — welcome to the team.
- Look around at this team. There isn't another one with as much talent. But this doesn't guarantee success. A great challenge.
- A lot of talk about these wickets, but we can play well in these conditions (eg. Bangalore and Rawalpindi in 1998).
- We must do our homework and plan well.
- Each player must have a plan.
- The main reason why we have lost in the past is that we've forgotten that Tests are won over five days – be patient!

Areas to improve

- Team spirit: I'd like to see more of an effort to be together. Has to be a genuine effort, not manufactured. It's no coincidence that together teams win close matches. Take, for example, Port Elizabeth in 1997 and the World Cup semi. Did we have that in the Windies, in Barbados?
- Discipline: We've set the team rules, let's respect them, because if you don't it shows lack of respect for your teammates and, in turn, can fragment the side.
- Enjoyment: Enjoy each other's success, and have fun on the field.

just about to point out that he should have been watching the game when I noticed an enormous ice pack on his ankle.

Hooter filled me in on the details. In frantically trying to do the right thing for his captain, Marto had scampered down the stairs that led on to the ground but had missed the last step and taken a major tumble, much to the amusement of all in the vicinity. He had even tried to soldier on after the fall, but after hobbling a few more paces gave up and had to be escorted, ego bruised and body battered, to the safety of the change rooms. His unsympathetic colleagues thought it was a laugh, and so, eventually, did I. This was, certainly in my experience, the first time a 12th man has ever been injured while performing his duties during a match.

September 6

The Australians won their tour match against the Sri Lankan Board XI by four wickets, courtesy of a much-improved second-innings batting display. Greg Blewett led the way with 148, Michael Slater made 51 and Justin Langer 52.

September 7

The ACB announced that Allan Border would temporarily take over as Australia's coach for the upcoming tour of Zimbabwe. Press reports suggested Border and Queensland coach John Buchanan were the leading contenders for the job on a permanent basis.

September 9 KANDY

ONE OF THE REASONS people love sport is its unpredictability and the twists and turns it can produce. One of the reasons why we have team meetings is to try and counteract this to a certain degree, and to at least control what *we* are trying to achieve. Going into this match, we had talked about the importance of asserting our authority early on, and being positive as well as trying to squash any thoughts of complacency that we might have been entertaining.

After winning the toss and electing to bat on a flat, dry wicket, we were intent on trying to establish a sizeable first innings score, to enable us to dominate the Sri Lankans thereafter. Unfortunately, our plans went badly astray and our lunch of chicken curry, lentils and dahl with naan bread tasted pretty ordinary, because we'd slumped to 7-61 by the break. It was an atrocious batting display, with nil application and dedication, and has set us up for a real thrashing unless we can find some massive improvement very quickly. Seeing us crash was like watching a highlights package, with loose shot after loose shot interspersed with the odd boundary and then another fall of wicket. If there is something we need to work on as a team, it is trying to stop the blood flow when the opposition are inflicting heavy

Michael Slater (left) and Colin Miller are pictured here in our warm-up match against a Sri Lankan Board XI.

wounds on us. We have talked about trying to win each session of play, but if that doesn't happen we need our opponents' advantage to be a slight one not a landslide. These 'landslide' sessions are what cause losses and here we started with a shocker …

September 12 COLOMBO

IT WAS A COUPLE of hours after the close of play on day two of the Kandy Test when I glanced across at my roommate and said: 'What are we doing here?' Jason Gillespie had a cast on his right leg from thigh to toe, I looked like the twin of Hannibal Lecter.

We were indeed a sorry pair in our Colombo hospital beds as we tried to piece together the events of that horrific collision …

Needing desperately to get a wicket to get back into the match, I had just moved myself from midwicket to a position to stop the sweep shot, at a 45-degree angle behind the wicket. Colin Miller enticed Mahela Jayawardene to play the shot the very next ball and as so often happens, got a top edge that flew high in the direction of square leg.

Unfortunately, just when I thought I had the catch under control, it disappeared into the sun for a split second, causing me to prop momentarily before having to adjust and dive in the hope of clinging on to what had become a difficult chance. It was in that desperate lunge that I felt I had run into a brick wall. The force of the impact in the middle of my face was intense, and the shock and realisation of what had happened were frightening.

My initial thought was: 'This isn't going to be too good … I know I've done some damage here.'

Hoping for the best, I reached for my nose and discovered it wasn't where it should be. Instead it was in line with my right eye, while a cool sensation engulfed the left side of my face. My real concern was my eyesight, and not being able to initially see out of my left eye had me panicking, but the lads at the scene assured me it was because it was covered in blood.

The cool and calm of team physiotherapist Errol Alcott in assessing the situation was vital and put me at ease. Being an integral member of the Australian squad since 1984, Errol has acquired an 'instinct' for injuries that is second to none, and a feel for what might happen on the field.

Word has it that as soon as the ball went high into the air Big Hoot stopped typing on his personal computer and grabbed his emergency medical kit, and within 60 seconds of the collision, he was peering down at my shattered nose, assuring me that I'd live. It wasn't until I was in the dressing room that I realised Dizzy had also been hurt. As I was getting a photo or two taken for the record, two of our squad carried in Jason, clutching his leg in obvious pain, and moaning as if his injury was serious.

The trip to Kandy hospital was almost comical had it not been so serious. The ambulance, or rather the battered old mini-van, had a shonky manual gearstick, which was being tortured by a driver who obviously harboured ambitions of a Formula One career.

By this stage Dizzy was in agony as we collected each bump in the road and I was on the verge of fainting due to a mixture of shock and confinement in the van. The blood continued to flow down onto my shirt and, internally, down my throat. Luckily the hospital

The first Test in the 1999 Sri Lanka–Australia series began in Kandy. After winning the toss, Australia collapsed to be 7-60 before lunch on the first day. An eight-wicket stand of 107 between Ricky Ponting and Jason Gillespie allowed the tourists to total 188 (Chaminda Vaas 3-43, Nuwan Zoysa 3-38, Muttiah Muralitharan 4-63), with Ponting last out for 96. Sri Lanka were 2-69 in reply at stumps.

The second day of the first Test was marred by a horrific collision at backward square leg between Steve Waugh and Jason Gillespie which left the Australian captain with a cruelly broken nose and Gillespie with a shattered right leg. Both were airlifted by helicopter to Colombo, and it was announced that neither would take any further part in the match. After Sri Lanka were bowled out for 234 (Aravinda de Silva 78, Colin Miller 4-62, Shane Warne 5-52), Australia slumped to 6-89 by stumps, a lead of 43.

Queensland pace bowler Scott Muller was named as Jason Gillespie's replacement for the remainder of the Australian cricket tour of Sri Lanka and Zimbabwe ... Sri Lanka won the first Test after Australia was dismissed in their second

wasn't far away, but it was here the chaos really started, with at least 50 people joining Errol, Jason and me in a hot, humid room where our injuries were assessed. Word must have got around, because everyone wanted a photograph or an autograph to add to their collection, even though we were not exactly at our mental or physical best.

An hour later it was confirmed we both required surgery, so arrangements were hastily made for our helicopter flight to Colombo.

It was here that Dizzy nearly had his worst nightmare realised when, after being slotted back in the ambulance, the rear door was on its down swing before our ever-alert physio screamed: 'Stop it!'

Thankfully they did, because Jason's injured leg was still protruding out the back of the van by a good six inches, with the door about to slam on to it.

Our next adventure was the helicopter trip, and it was here the pain really set in. Dizzy complained of a constant ache while my nose felt like a vice had been attached to it as a steady stream of blood ran down my nostrils and out of my mouth. However, the assessment by the specialists and the subsequent operations were excellent and handled no differently from what you would expect in Australia.

It was during the nights while recovering in hospital I found some humour in the whole situation. I've never seen a man more petrified of a needle than Dizzy, so when it became the only choice for pain relief, it provided me and the nurses who administered it with a good laugh. Needless to say Dizzy wasn't amused, wailing and screaming as if he had just taken a bullet.

Funny it was, but not even that rated with another occasion when the pain again became too intense for the big fast bowler. Tablets hadn't produced the desired effect so, after much debate and convincing, a suppository was called for to speed his pain relief. Having our beds less than a metre apart gave me a classic close-up of a face contorted the moment a pair of latex gloves were snapped on to the fingers of a male nurse. To Dizzy's distress, a rather large suppository didn't insert as it should have and a second attempt was needed to finish the job.

I just hope the whole ordeal makes Jason even hungrier to make it back and be even stronger and better than he is now. For Australian cricket's sake, let's hope so.

The fateful crash. I was running back from short fine leg as Jason Gillespie charged in from the deep backward square leg boundary. Both of us had eyes only for the ball. For a moment I lost the ball in the sun, which meant I had to make a dive at it. And as I dived, Dizzy kept charging. The result, as these photographs show, was a cruel collision, a broken nose, a broken leg and a broken wrist … and a missed chance.

Top: In the immediate aftermath of the collision most concern was for me, while Dizzy (sitting, in white hat) had only Heals to offer him sympathy.

Middle: This photograph was taken by Dave Misson minutes after we got back to the dressing room. I asked him to take the snap because I realised that wasn't going to make it hurt any more and I wanted a reminder of exactly what the collision did to my face. What I didn't count on was Misso's face going a few shades paler.

Bottom: This is how my nose looked around three hours after the crash. By this stage, we were in Colombo, being assessed by the city's top surgeons. The very ordinary looking moustache had come about because of a 'facial hair growing' competition that was being conducted by the team in the lead-up to the Kandy Test. It had been running for around two weeks, and was due to finish straight after the Test match. When I look at these photographs now, I cringe as much at the moustache as I do at the badly broken nose.

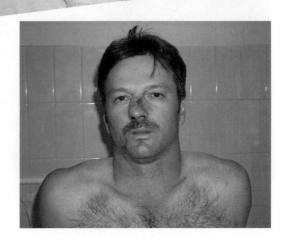

With Galle's imposing fort as a backdrop, Shane Warne attacks the Sri Lankans during the opening game of the Aiwa Cup tournament.

We travelled to Galle for the second Sri Lankan Test, to find, just outside our hotel, a beautiful beach, typical of much of the magnificent Sri Lankan coastline. On the beach I saw a local fisherman (above and below), who was using a rod made of bamboo and a makeshift, homemade hook. In the photograph above, Matthew Hayden is in the background. A little later on, Haydos left his sandals on the beach while he walked though the waves, about 15 metres out, to give his fly fishing rod a workout. When he came back, the sandals were gone, and you can guess who our No. 1 suspect was.

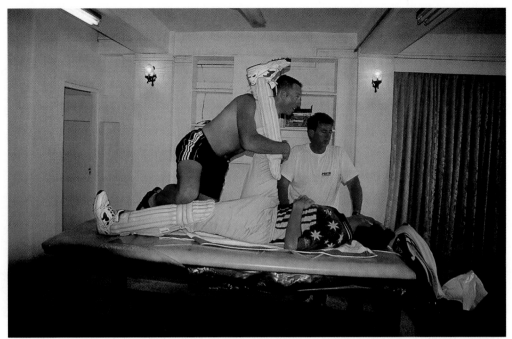

Above: Fitness advisor Dave Misson (left) and physio Errol Alcott stretch Adam Gilchrist before Gilly went out to bat in the Aiwa Cup final in Colombo.

Below: This was the view from my hotel room on the morning of the first Test match against Sri Lanka, in Kandy. The hotel is situated on top of a mountain, and it took about 10 minutes up a narrow, winding path to get to reception. The focus of this photo is a group of children, whose exercise in the schoolyard this morning was a form of martial arts that I am not familiar with.

Above: This was the view at sunset in Galle, looking out from my hotel balcony at the fantastic coastline. The locals up the top of the rocks were just some of the cricket fans who hung around the hotel, seeking a glimpse of the cricketers. This was one of the best hotels we've stayed at in India, Pakistan or Sri Lanka.

Below: Two angles of Damien Fleming's bowling action, which reveal the great stress he puts on his body every time he sends down a delivery.

Above: What you can see are the guys preparing for our Sri Lankan one-day tour team photo to be taken in the grounds of our hotel. What you can't see are the heavily-armed security guards who constantly patrolled the area while we were there.

Below: Another view of the ground at Galle, this one taken from inside the city's famous fort during the rain-ruined second Test.

While in Kandy in Sri Lanka, we visited the Temple of the Sacred Tooth, one of the most important of all Buddhist sites. We were given a special invitation to see the so-called 'Sacred Tooth' of Buddha, and encountered these two gentlemen (below), who were praying just outside the entrance to the shrine where the Tooth is encased. In the photograph above, Lang and I have just emerged from that shrine.

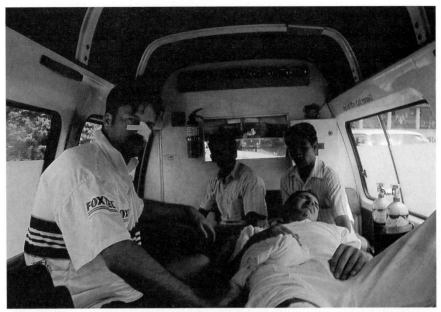

Above: The so-called ambulance, more like a mini-van, in which Dizzy and I were taken from the ground after our collision in Kandy. Dizzy is obviously distressed from the pain of his broken bones, while I'm not looking too flash either.

Below: Like the photo above, this shot was taken with my camera, by Errol Alcott or Dave Misson. It shows Dizzy and I being helped out of the ambulance and into the army helicopter that flew us back to Colombo. By this stage, I was feeling reasonable, but once I got on the flight it was a different story — I started to feel nauseous, with blood flowing constantly down my throat and out my nose. All up, it wasn't the most pleasant trip, as Dizzy was in agony throughout as well. Minutes after this photograph was taken, the chopper was flying back over the ground from where we'd come. The boys later told us that the sight of it gave them a bit of a lift, and they played pretty well that afternoon.

innings for 140 and the home team lost four wickets in reaching their target of 95. This was Sri Lanka's first victory in a Test match against Australia.

September 17

The Australians began their three-day tour match against a Sri Lankan Board XI in Colombo by making 226 after being sent in. At stumps the Board XI were 3-29, after Damien Fleming had taken two wickets and Scott Muller, with his first delivery after flying over to replace the injured Jason Gillespie, took the other.

September 18

The Australians took control of their match against the Sri Lankan Board XI by dismissing them for 185 and then reaching 3-225 by stumps. Michael Slater was the star with the bat, making 119.

September 21 GALLE

I've noticed a slight improvement every day since the nose operation. The first day out felt as if I had just been on my own buck's night, but each day afterwards the hangover became less and less intense. However, the feeling of being continually about to lose my balance stayed with me for at least a week.

In the days leading up to the second Test, which will begin tomorrow here in Galle, I've felt as if I had a 50-50 chance at best of playing. But being captain, I believed I had to play through most things — unless, quite obviously, I couldn't. My real fitness test came the day before the match, when I had a 40-minute net session against our coach, fitness adviser, local net bowlers and a former player, now journalist. The session was a struggle, with continuing headaches and bouts of nausea and light-headedness, but I talked myself into believing I was okay to play. I certainly wasn't 100 per cent, but then again I can't remember the last time I played in that sort of perfect nick.

My doctor here in Sri Lanka was against my playing, as he feared another knock would mean that the whole process of hospitalisation would need to be repeated. From my point of view, I couldn't see myself injuring my hooter twice in two weeks, when I'd only ever damaged it once in 30 years of competitive sport.

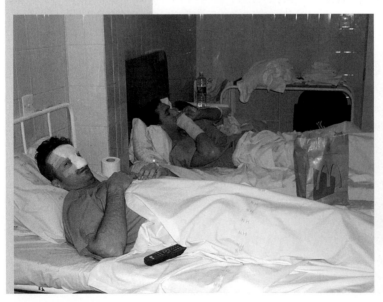

Dizzy came out of his operation about an hour and a half before me, so he was feeling okay well before I was. Errol Alcott, who had come with us to Colombo, went down the road to the local McDonald's to get something for Dizzy, which he's scoffing here. This was the highlight of his day, while all I could do was feel sorry for myself and wait the 90 minutes or so until I was allowed to eat anything after my surgery.

A Reality Cheque by Dave Mission

'Bad luck, Slater.'

'Yeah, thanks mate.'

'Ninety-six, four short of century.'

'Yeah.'

'Bad shot!'

No, this is not a conversation between our sports psychologist, Sandy Gordon, and Michael Slater. This honest assessment of Slats' misfortune in the first innings of the second Test, in Galle, was given by PD Nimal, our jack-of-all trades, baggage man, 'gofer' and room attendant for the Sri Lankan tour.

PD is 40 years old. He has been working at Sinhalese Sports Club, the premier social, sports and cricket club in Colombo, for the past 21 years. He is about 1.73m tall (5ft 8in), has thinning hair and his work rate is higher than rugby league's Gary Larson or the AFL's Paul Kelly. We had a guessing competition, winner take all, to estimate his 'skinfold' reading (level of body fat). The boys each put in 100 rupees and I was the official tester. His reading was 32.2mm, a level similar to that of an elite marathon runner. He has an amazing work ethic, and an even more amazing ability to intuitively understand the requirements of an idiosyncratic group of elite sportsman who are used to having their demands met.

Three days into the tour, he had mastered the often delicate art of mixing the players' Powerade drinks so they weren't too weak or too strong. By then, we had already taken for granted his hauling of our kitbags, two at a time, at the beginning and end of each match. Tell him once and it'll get done. Before the coach and support staff are changed and down on the ground ready for warm-ups, he has taken down the team kit, as well as an esky full of cold waters. Geoff Marsh and I have joked that we will invite him to take the players for warm-ups on the last day of the tour. His energy and enthusiasm are genuine. His attitude and manner has typified the Sri Lankan people since we have arrived. They have a spark about them. Look into the eyes of Pakistanis and you will often see a blank hopelessness. The Sri Lankans, in contrast, retain a magic, a zest for living. Grudgingly, our tour party has accepted Tony Greig's simplistic and generalised assessment that they are 'always smiling, always happy' as being pretty spot on.

Because of political unrest prior to the tour, our security has been extremely tight. Besides Reg Dickason, our own security manager, whom we also know as 'The Smiling Assassin', agents from the Presidential security force have accompanied us throughout the entire trip. These men are the most elite policemen in Sri Lanka, commissioned to guard and protect national and international political and religious leaders. They are absolute professionals, understated but forceful when required. They also have hard names to remember, so we gave them some nicknames: 'Saskwatch' the bus driver, so named because of the size of his feet; 'The Runner', a guy whose job, it seemed, was to run next to our bus in heavy traffic (he was actually a former Sri Lankan 5000m and 10,000m champion); 'Pushy' (short for his real last name of Pushpakamara), a stylish young bloke who had a definite eye for the ladies; and finally 'Elvis', the boss, a young man who always had a smile on his face,

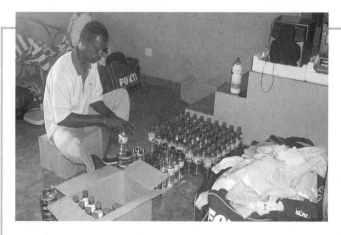

PD Nimal prepares the Powerade, a task he performed every morning during our tour. PD was a great help to everyone, a man who saw part of his role as baggage carrier as ensuring that no one else ever lifted a bag over his shoulder. He was a really nice fellow who didn't ask for anything in return, despite the fact that his normal wage was negligible by Australian standards.

who was always immaculately dressed, but had a ruthlessness that meant he never had to give orders twice.

When we first arrived in Sri Lanka, I was naturally keen to kick off my training program for the tour. The Taj Samudra, our hotel in Colombo, is across the road from a pretty beachscape, spoiled only by the raw sewerage that is being pumped into the water directly from an open outfall, and by half the city's rubbish that has been washed up onto the shore. The promenade looked like a great running track. I did the right thing and let the security guys know I was going running. They asked me to wait a couple of minutes. The shift captain then came back with his running gear on and six other guys in tow. He had on a pair of old tracksuit pants, a skintight polo shirt and his 1972 trainers. I was confident I could shake him in the first 200 metres. It was a great run, spoilt only by the heat and the pollution. I shook my man within five minutes, but he kept popping up at different places on my course, as did about four of his colleagues. It wasn't until I had been running for 20 minutes that I realised that two guards in a truck had been following me the whole way. I ran for about 30 minutes and then staggered into the Taj, joined by my six companions. I felt like a US President.

Capitalism and its given appendages have definitely arrived in Sri Lanka. While the Internet, DVDs and mobile phones are prevalent, the marketing of these products remains trapped in the late 1980s. B-grade actors, C-grade scripts and D-grade jingles dominate television and radio. Sri Lankan TV ads are a mixture of hard-edged realism, with incongruous happy endings. My favourite was a plug for cold sore cream. A bunch of hip teens are sitting around discussing their cold sores (what else!), when one decides to give the others a viewing. We get the tight close-up of this red, pussy cold sore. Fast forward to a week later and we have the same teens, the same discussion and our mate turns over the bottom lip, to reveal nothing but his shiny white teeth. Great to watch during a meal.

I suppose the advances associated with capitalism bring some downsides. Our intrepid outdoors man, Matthew Hayden, otherwise known as Rex Russell-Butler (a combination of Rex Hunt, Peter Russell-Clarke and Harry Butler), pulled out his ever-present rod and tackle bag during our stay in Galle. Our hotel was perched on a rock face that had our fishing fanatic salivating. He sprang out of bed at 5.30am one morning and perched himself on one of the rocks overlooking what he thought was a pretty encouraging fishing hole. Two thrown-back, undersized fish later, he returned to where he thought he had left his designer

Swiss thongs, only to find they had been flogged. We urged him to scour the markets and bazaars where there was no doubt the much-prized footwear would have fetched top dollar, but he concluded that if someone had got up at 5.30am to steal a pair of thongs, they could have them.

PD Nimal works six-and-and-half days a week. Between the hours of 8am and 3pm on weekdays, he basically runs administrative errands at SSC, depositing cheques, sending invoices and delivering documents. After 3pm, until 6pm, he attends cricket practice with the various SSC teams, organising drinks, cleaning equipment and ensuring practice runs smoothly for the respective coaches. On the weekends, he attends matches where SSC teams are involved. He is the room attendant for all home matches, but also ensures that drinks, food and equipment are properly arranged for those teams playing away from SSC. His half-day off occurs on Mondays, when he isn't required to attend cricket practice. I asked him what he does during his time off and he replies that he takes either his son or daughter for some extra cricket or netball practice. He is paid 14,000 rupees per month (about US$200).

Before we left, we had a whip around for PD and also for our liaison officer, Pemlal Fernando. At an informal presentation after the Third Test was abandoned, team manager Steve Bernard presented each man with an envelope containing about US$1000. Nimal accepted his graciously, thanked us very much and proceeded to hoist two more kit bags onto his shoulders and carry them to the bus. Later, he pulled me aside and said, 'Doctor [he called physio Errol Alcott Dr No. 1 and me Dr No. 2], no other touring team has done this for me. You have made me and my family very happy.'

We take for granted too often the difference between material happiness and true happiness. There wouldn't have been many other times in his life where PD Nimal would have gained happiness from material gain. He exuded a happiness of spirit that Westerners — and probably a cricket touring party living five-star lives — rarely see. Perspective often provides a great reality check.

Misso carries out 'fat tests' through-out our tours. Normally, a reading of 60 or less is a considered fair, but when PD Nimal was tested his score was 32.2, one of the lowest measure-ments ever recorded.

In the background, stuck to the wall, are two sheets. The right sheet contains the team's goals for the third Test, while on the left is a chart that records our efforts session by session. We've received a tick in the first and second sessions of day one, and a square in the third, which means it was fairly even. Day two's third session has a picture of a raincloud to signify it was washed out. These symbols remind us about how we are going and ensure that we never get too far ahead of ourselves.

The Australians won their tour match against the Sri Lankan Board XI by 247 runs, after bowling their opponents out for 90 in their second innings. Damien Fleming took three wickets, Muller and Ponting two. Muller also injured the webbing on his right hand while trying to take a return catch. Earlier, the Australians had declared their second innings at 5-296, with Mark Waugh out for 43 and Simon Katich unconquered on 36.

Australian captain Steve Waugh suggested he may need to field in a helmet if he is to take part in the second Test, due to start in two days time. 'I'm a better than even chance but it's by no means a certainty that I will play,' Waugh told AAP. 'It's a Test match, I'm captain of Australia, I am not going to walk away from it easily. The advice is not to play but doctors always look at the worst-case scenario.'

At stumps on the first day of the second Test, in Galle, Sri Lanka were 6-254. Aravinda de Silva made 64, Russel Arnold 50 and Mahela Jayawardene 46, while Shane Warne took three wickets.

September 22 GALLE

'The second Test is upon us and starts here today,
Sri Lanka lead 1-0, with two to play.
The first Test did not go well and we played poorly,
With Tugga and Dizzy out, we missed them sorely.
Now with Tugga back, his nose reasonably intact,
And Flem in for Diz, we'll pull together and make this pact:
"We'll beat anyone, anywhere, on any wicket,"
And show them why we're the world's best when it comes
  to Test cricket.
Let's crush them early and never let up,
Until they are broken and ready to give up.
Patience, discipline and pressure are part of our plan,
So let's outplay these blokes, man for man.
"Never give up", that's the Aussie way,
Let's not die wondering when the umps say, "Play".
So have faith in each other and belief in ourselves,
Because the victory drinks taste better,
When they come from the top shelves.
If we bat or bowl, just get out there and look busy,
And let's do it for each other and do it for Dizzy.'

— **Glenn McGrath** (read before day one,
  second Test v Sri Lanka, September 22)

THERE'S SOMETHING SPECIAL about the opening ball of a Test match, as the hush descends over the ground in eager anticipation of what is about to transpire.

This feeling is somewhat lost when there's only a couple of hundred watching from the boundary — as there was in this historic city, with the famous Galle fort looking down upon the ground.

But even without the atmosphere of a big crowd, for me the moment a quick bowler starts his run-up the adrenalin begins to flow, as it marks the beginning of a journey that at this stage no one can predict the outcome of. Normally, that opening delivery is an uneventful ball … unless you're watching Slats batting, because he often begins with a boundary.

On this occasion, Glenn McGrath landed the first ball of the Test on a dime, enticing the Sri Lankan captain Sanath Jayasuriya to lunge half-heartedly at the ball, to do no more than give Warney a regulation catch at first slip. One for none, you beauty!

Muttiah Muralitharan, Sri Lanka's prolific wicket-taker. Next to Warney, I would rate Murali the best spinner in the game at present – certainly, he's the most awkward slow bowler I've faced in recent times in international cricket.

September 23 GALLE

TO SUCCEED IN TEST-MATCH cricket, it is vital that the engine room (the top three in the batting order) runs smoothly. During our first innings, both Greg Blewett and Michael Slater played beautifully — and, I must say, differently — against Sri Lanka's dangerman Muttiah Muralitharan. Blewey used his pads to fend off the sharply turning offies, while watching with an eagle eye for Murali's desperately hard-to-read straight ball that often bounces prodigiously. Slats, on the other hand, went on the offensive, using his fleet-footedness to great advantage in a gem of a knock till he fell in the cursed 90s for the seventh time in Test cricket.

Luckily, our opening partnership was a sizeable one, because the rest of us managed to score less than 100 between us. The mysterious Murali, with his unique action, proved too tough an assignment. Still, it was great to see both Slats and Blewey do well, because theirs is an opening combination like no other. Openers must trust each other completely, learn to read each other's body language, protect each other in difficult situations, bleed for each other and get on well both on and off the field. Opening bats are the first barrier for the opposition to try to break down; if they stay strong, it gives the team a huge lift …

September 29 COLOMBO

AFTER ALL THESE YEARS of watching Shane Warne torment the opposition with a dazzling array of flight, guile, cunning, variation of angles and skill, we are suddenly on the receiving end. Muttiah Muralitharan is presently at the height of his powers, and it is fair to say he has been the difference between Sri Lanka and us as we head into the decisive third Test tomorrow. The outcome will depend on how well we can handle Murali's unique brand of bowling.

The second Test was evenly poised at stumps on day two, with Australia 5-188 in reply to Sri Lanka's 296. Shane Warne had finished the home team's innings with 3-29 off 25 overs, while Glenn McGrath also took three wickets. Michael Slater (96) and Greg Blewett (62) put on 138 for the first wicket — the first century opening partnership for Australia in a Test match since August 1997 — before four wickets fell for 28 runs in the final session. Steve Waugh was 2 not out at stumps, Ponting 0 not out.

Five hours' play was lost during the day and no cricket was possible before 4.30pm. Australia were all out for 228 (Muttiah Muralitharan 5-71, Rangana Herath 4-97), and Sri Lanka were 0-44 when play finally ended ... During the day, it was revealed that Simon Katich had contracted chicken pox.

No play was possible in the second Test, because of continuing rain.

The Test was abandoned at 10.50am, after rain stopped play at 10.18am. In the little time available, the Sri Lankans' second-innings opening partnership had extended to 55.

Australian fans might be a little shocked at this high appraisal of our nemesis, but his form and performances in Australia can't really be taken into account as he has been under a 'throwing' cloud on both tours to our shores. With the absence of this distraction here in Sri Lanka, he can relax in the knowledge that he won't be under such close scrutiny, and consequently he lets his talent loose.

Facing Murali is like being part of a David Copperfield show, with reality and optical illusions being so closely intertwined that it is hard to tell the difference. Playing him for the first time certainly takes some getting used to, because the ball seems to come out delayed from his hand, a split second later than you think it will. He has a high, front-on action, whereas most off-spinners tend to stay side-on and come across their bodies after the ball is released.

Murali bowls as if his wrist is double-jointed, and from 22 yards away, his subtlety in delivering seemingly similar balls that are in fact completely different presents the greatest of challenges. The key to being in charge of the situation revolves around surviving the first 20 minutes or so, when the adjustment period is being negotiated. The use of the front pad is crucial, as you can't be given out lbw if you get forward, because his extreme turn is always going to leave the umpire with an element of doubt.

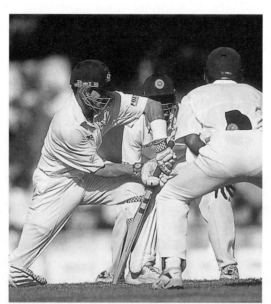

Greg Blewett on the defensive against Murali in Kandy. Note the bat tucked in behind the front pad, and the close-in fielders, preying on the slightest error.

When your confidence is high, you can use your feet like Michael Slater and Greg Blewett did in the Second Test, or alternatively sweep with the spin to cut down the risk factor. For a left-hander, the options are more limited, because you are faced with the problem of having to guess at times whether or not it is safe to leave the ball that pitches on the stumps and is supposed to turn.

Murali's most dangerous weapon is the one that bounces more than normal and goes straight on, which accounted for Slater and Mark Waugh in the first innings at Galle. We all know Murali is a quality bowler, but if we play him well and each player works out a game plan to deal with him, we should be on our way to levelling the series …

October 2 COLOMBO

'It's the team that makes the running,
That pulls off the victory that is stunning.
Let's not wait for them to crumble,
We must dictate terms in this final Test rumble.
Build pressure, take it to 'em,
Don't die wondering, believe we can do it.'

— **Dave Misson** *(read before day one, third Test v Sri Lanka, September 30)*

RICKY PONTING'S CENTURY WAS one that will, in all probability, not be fully recognised for its quality because it was scored on foreign soil and could only have been seen back home on pay TV. But to score runs against Murali on a turning wicket takes great skill and courage, for you must have an element of daring about your strokeplay. Inevitably, there'll be times when it seems that he holds all the aces and you've got all the dud cards, but in these circumstances you have to back yourself, which is what Punter did.

The reasons behind Punter's success are his quick feet, placement of his shots to loose deliveries and his much-improved technique at sweeping to anywhere on the legside. This

The third Test, in Colombo, began with Australia at the crease. At stumps the tourists were 4-203, after Greg Blewett had made 70, Michael Slater 59 and Justin Langer 32. Slater and Blewett added 126 runs for the first wicket.

Only 38 overs were possible during the day, as Australia took their first innings total to 7-318. Ricky Ponting went from 11 not out at the start of play to 90 not out when stumps were drawn.

Owing to rain, there was only time for Australia to be bowled out in their first innings for 342, with Ricky Ponting remaining undefeated on 105 and Damien Fleming making 32.

last feature was clear to see throughout this innings, and was also crucial because it made Murali alter his plans instead of settling into his usual rhythm. He also had to adjust his field placements, which are normally pretty much set for the entire innings. Without doubt, Punter's improvement on this tour has been the standout for us, and further proves that if you work hard enough at your game the results will follow ...

October 3 COLOMBO

WITH SO MUCH RAIN having fallen in and around Colombo lately, it was a miracle we played as much as we did here. It was a tribute to the groundstaff here, who have been up and working at 5am each morning to get the surface playable.

In these idle times, a cricketer sometimes wonders just how much of his life he's wasted hanging around dressing rooms. Luckily, cards rescues many of the players and a favourite one of the boys is the kids' game, UNO, which invariably turns into a slanging, sledging match. It's amazing that grown men can play this game for hours on end, but that's exactly what half the team did while the monsoon rains tumbled down. Other options available to kill the time are book reading, crosswords, perhaps a postcard, or worst case you could clean your gear or even partake in some fitness work ...

Below: Uno is a card game recommended for kids, 10 years and under, but as you can see the boys got great value out of it during the rain interruptions that plagued the latter stages of the Sri Lankan tour.

Right: Punter, not long after he scored a hundred in the third Test.

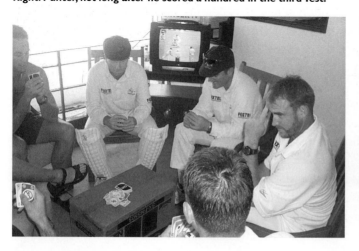

October 4 COLOMBO

THE TORTURE IS FINALLY OVER. Waiting around a cricket ground for five days with the result of the series dependent on Mother Nature is at best frustrating, at worst stressful. Unfortunately for us, the monsoon season arrived at precisely the wrong time, with 20 inches (50cm) of rain falling in the past week, putting a halt to our aspirations of squaring the series and thus avoiding our first ever series loss against Sri Lanka.

To be fair to our hosts, they probably had the better of the series and deserved the accolades that have been flowing their way.

The defining moment or session was the very first of the series, when in our first two hours of play in Kandy we collapsed to 7-61 at lunch on a flat wicket. As I've written earlier, it's bitterly disappointing when something like that happens, but doubly so when we pride ourselves on setting the tone of the match from ball one, recognising that the first session of any series is crucial.

Our pre-game talk then had centred around this theme, with the theory that whoever wins the first session normally goes on to win the first day and consequently the first Test. On most occasions, that means they win the series as well.

How prophetic these words were to become.

Yet tasting defeat can be positive, if we use it in the right way. Losing can sometimes be good for the team and the individuals in it. It makes you look for the reasons why and once they are identified a plan to rectify the situation can be put into place.

For us, we must make sure we definitely are hungry from ball one and not just imagining we are. Sometimes it's a fine line, but once you are in that so-called 'zone' where you are focused, the difference is immeasurable. The hard part is to recognise this as individuals, but I believe we have all learned a lot from this tour, for our attitude was much stronger and committed in the last Test when we had the feel of a team that knew it was going to win.

Ricky Ponting was the standout for us. His maturity is not only obvious as a cricketer on the field, but off it as well, with ideas on opposition players, increased intensity at training and a giving of his all to improve in all areas. At the top of the order, Greg Blewett and Michael Slater played very impressively in the last two Tests. Shane Warne looked impressive whenever he got the ball and his duels with India's Sachin Tendulkar will be a highlight in Australia this season.

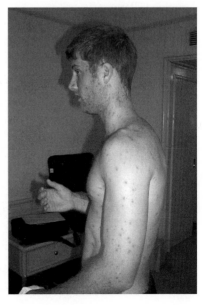

Simon Katich shows off the physical effects of his chicken-pox, which ruled him out of the second Test at a time when it seemed he might well be playing because of my broken nose. Kat was basically bedridden for a couple of weeks, quarantined from the rest of the squad, which is not the sort of thing you want to happen on your first tour with the Australian team.

Again, the inclement weather dominated the day, with Sri Lanka struggling to 4-61 off 21.5 overs. Damien Fleming took three of the four wickets, for 14 runs. For the second Test in a row, Sri Lankan captain Sanath Jayasuriya was caught in the slips off the first ball of the innings. Glenn McGrath was the bowler on both occasions.

Western Australian fast bowler Matthew Nicholson was named to replace injured paceman Scott Muller for Australia's cricket tour of Zimbabwe ... The final day of the third Test was completely washed out, giving the series to the Sri Lankans 1-0, their first series victory over Australia. Sri Lankan captain Sanath Jayasuriya called the series win 'the greatest achievement of my life'. Steve Waugh commented, 'The next time we play here, we'd like to have a full series, but the people here have been great. The hospitality has been fantastic. I think the grounds are excellent, but the weather we can't do anything about.' Ricky Ponting was named man of the series.

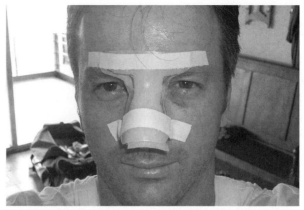

One last look back at Sri Lanka. This was a prototype of a protective nose-guard that Errol Alcott built out of moulded plastic, in response to the doctors' request that if did I try to play in the second Test I should wear some kind of shield to protect my still-healing nose. I only wore it during one practice session. Unfortunately, that was as far as the experiment went — it was uncomfortable, impeded my line of vision, and I reckoned it wasn't really going to protect me if I got belted again anyway. In the Test, I made do with a normal batting helmet and grill.

The rest of us had the odd positive moments, but all probably felt like leaded cars using unleaded petrol.

We have a chance to redeem ourselves on our mini trip to Zimbabwe, with new stand-in coach Allan Border taking over the reins from Geoff Marsh. Also joining us is Matthew Nicholson, in the cursed fast bowler's spot previously held by Jason Gillespie and Scott Muller, before both suffered injuries and had to go home.

'Nico' looks the goods to me, having made a very noteworthy debut last Boxing Day at the MCG against the Poms. His statistics weren't startling, but I'd rate his performance higher than the Glenn McGrath and Gillespie debuts of years gone by and look what has happened for those guys.

Sometimes a player can be too harshly dealt with after a debut. It is an intimidating environment with much at stake, not to mention the huge adjustment to one's life after they don the baggy green. It is why I believe Nicholson might be a special talent, because he looked so at ease and comfortable in the surroundings.

It would be great to come back to Australia in a winning frame of mind before we lock horns with Pakistan and India. We have just three weeks and one Test in Zimbabwe to make sure we do.

PART TWO:

A LONG TRAIN TO HARARE

October 12 VICTORIA FALLS

A 'TEAM BONDING' EXERCISE that will stay with me forever is the Bulawayo to Victoria Falls railway journey many of us have just completed. Rarely on tour these days do we get a couple of days off and even less often do we get an opportunity to travel the country via this particular mode of transport. An Ashes tour is always a great one, because we spend so many hours hurtling down those motorways together on the team bus, watching videos, playing cards, reviving old memories and just plain old getting to know each other.

On this occasion, we had just completed a comprehensive win against a Zimbabwe Board XI and were given a choice of three ways to get to Harare in time for the Test match. A chartered plane, a hired coach or by rail to the Victoria Falls and then a plane trip. Being an avid 'Tommy Tourist' and inquisitive by nature, I joined fellow squad members Ponting, Blewett, McGrath, Langer, Nicholson, Hayden, Katich, MacGill and Misson to experience African rail travel and to see one of the natural wonders of the world.

In preparation for the trip, our unofficial tour leader, Stuey MacGill, went shopping, and the quality and quantity of food and more importantly beverages he garnered was excellent. With our music box to keep us company, we had the time of our lives — it was like being on that school excursion where you let your hair down and experience life. Stories were exchanged, drinks were downed, even cigars

Just prior to this photo being taken, at around 6.30am, I stuck my head out the window and my hat and sunglasses blew off. Now, I'm sure, there's a local strolling around wearing a near-new pair of Polaroid sunglasses and an Australian cricket hat.

Victoria Falls is one of the most awe-inspiring sights I've ever seen. At the time of year we were there, only about a third of the Falls is actually covered in water, but that still made it around a kilometre wide.

were lit, as we meandered through the African scrub under skies full of stars that really did sparkle like diamonds. The trek was a 15-hour marathon, with 36 stops, but to us all time was standing still and we couldn't get enough of it. The music of The Eagles — which was played again and again as we chugged along — will stay with me always, as a reminder of the night. In the years ahead I'm sure we will all rewind our memory tapes to reminisce again about every aspect of the adventure.

I will also never forget the ridiculous hats which we all had to buy from a local during the trip then wear for the remainder, or the loss of my hat and sunnies when I stuck my hungovered head out the window to take a snap of some leaping gazelles as a glorious sunrise lit up the cloudless horizon.

During this rail adventure, I began to write a newspaper column, which was supposed to appear under my by-line but took an unexpected turn. Yes, the first paragraph was penned by me, but then the page was passed around, the story being built upon until its conclusion by Stuart MacGill. It is a collection of spur-of-the-moment thoughts that may not completely make sense, but therein lies the fun of the exercise. It is simply the random ideas of a group of guys who have been together for a while and needed to blow off some steam before the serious business of another Test match. And — Oh! I almost forgot — there may be an influence from a couple of Red Bull and Vodkas in among the words as well ...

SIMON KATICH:

No matter what age you are, experiences like this are ones that will never be forgotten because they are shared. When you have the chance to share something like this with your mates it will burn in your memory due to the camaraderie and the simple fact you're sharing it together. We may never get the chance to do this again, to sit on a train riding through Africa all night, and you just live the moment for what it is.

MATTHEW NICHOLSON:

That's right. You have to enjoy it for what it is. Some of us won't reach our individual goals but to contribute to a team success is the ultimate reward. Your country and everyone in it is the beneficiary of the Australian team's success, particularly us.

It's good for us to remember we could be sitting behind a desk for a living instead of representing our country and seeing the world in the process. Soak up every experience, good and bad, learn from them all and prosper.

Having seen the Falls in full flow in the past, I reckon this might have been the best time to see it, because there was less spray and mist (though still plenty) and we were able to take in its full beauty.

MATTHEW HAYDEN:

For now the clickety-clack is the only thing bringing the air of expectation and the event that will follow. Victoria Falls, one of the seven natural wonders of the world, is as yet unseen. But it will certainly be forged into the minds of myself and my 10 colleagues who dared to board this train and embark on our adventure.

STEVE WAUGH:

We've eaten cheese balls, drunk Zambezi lager, shared tales of our youth and listened to tunes ranging from *You're So Vain* to *Tequila Sunrise*. We've grown closer to each other simply by being in each other's company. You know you've had a good time when the inconvenience of stopping every 15 minutes to let the oncoming train pass by as you pull into the waiting bay doesn't cause you to lose patience.

Neither does the jerky rollicking motion of a well-worn track disturb your enjoyment or the regular interruptions of a compartment neighbour from Malawi who requested Creedence Clearwater Revival because his dad used to listen to them in his youth.

STUART MacGILL:

Looking back then. A day spent in the nets or an experience with teammates who all claim they want to die for one another. How can you possibly make a statement to this effect without even knowing the people touring with you?

'Know yourself' is the one tip that should be given to any new member of the Australian cricket community, to ensure their guaranteed acceptance and to provide a solid foundation for success.

The outstanding feature of our 11-hour train journey to Victoria Falls was the way all the tourists became aware of, then ridiculed and finally came to accept the different personalities involved.

This may simply have manifested itself in the music being played, but however cliched it might seem, it was somehow a symbol of what subtleties are involved in forging a successful team. In these 11 hours, Australian cricket may well have returned to the days when it was okay to behave as an individual within the team environment.

As long as preparation remains the key, evenings such as these will always be crucial if

Some of the contenders in the team's facial hair contest. Anti-clockwise from above right: Geoff Marsh, Dave Misson (top right), Greg Blewett, Glenn McGrath. What you can't see in Misso's photos are the black socks and sandals that complemented his appearance. At left are the top three, as judged by Reg Dickason, a man with a moustache to rival Newk or Big Merv: Justin Langer (left), Misso (the champion, centre) and Michael Slater.

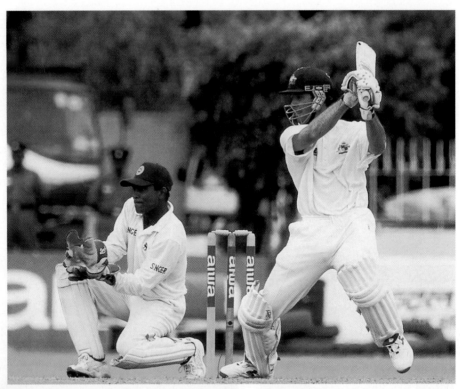

Above and left: Ricky Ponting's century in the third Test, in Colombo, was one of the best Test-match hundreds I've seen made away from Australia. He scored his runs in difficult conditions, on a turning wicket against probably the most difficult spin bowler I've ever had to face — Muttiah Muralitharan. Punter was the only Australian player who really came to grips with Murali's bowling during the tour. A year earlier, he had been a batsman who didn't sweep much, but he decided that the shot was one he needed to perfect if he was going to succeed against the spinners at the top level. It certainly helped him score many runs throughout this tour.

One of the highlights of our Zimbabwe tour was the train adventure we took to get to Victoria Falls. We all bought hats, of varying quality and appeal, off the locals. Top: Dave Misson and Simon Katich; middle: Justin Langer and Stuart MacGill; bottom: a self-portrait, complete with a cigar that never got out of its wrapper.

Lang reckoned his hat was the best he'd ever bought, an excellent purchase at around the equivalent of five Australian dollars. Magilla was also pretty keen on his purchase (which cost about the same), but for the life of me I couldn't see why.

In the top shot, Misso is actually wearing the hat I bought, while Kat has on what we decided was the worst piece of headgear collected during the journey.

Above: An intrepid group of Australian cricket tourists pose for a group shot after disembarking from the Bulawayo to Victoria Falls train. The trip took 15 hours, included 36 stops, and was fantastic!

Below: Not only does this photograph capture something of the beauty of Victoria Falls in Zimbabwe, it also shows one of the locals taking a bath in one of the small pools situated right next to the precipice of the Falls.

Right: On the outskirts of Bulawayo in Zimbabwe is a wildlife orphanage Park, where I was lucky enough to get this close-up look at this rhinoceros.

Left: The animal Glenn McGrath is introducing himself to is a serval, a relative of the leopard.

Below: This giraffe was among a number of animals we spotted during a drive through a wildlife sanctuary outside Harare. Funky Miller is the observer in the foreground.

Above: Misso, Haydos and Blewey took a particular liking to this leopard. The animals in this sanctuary were either orphans or had been born with a deformity that left them unable to fend for themselves in the wild.

Left: During our match against a President's XI, which preceded the Test against Zimbabwe in Harare, we saw and were impressed by the style and enthusiasm of some of the young kids who joined us at the nets before play.

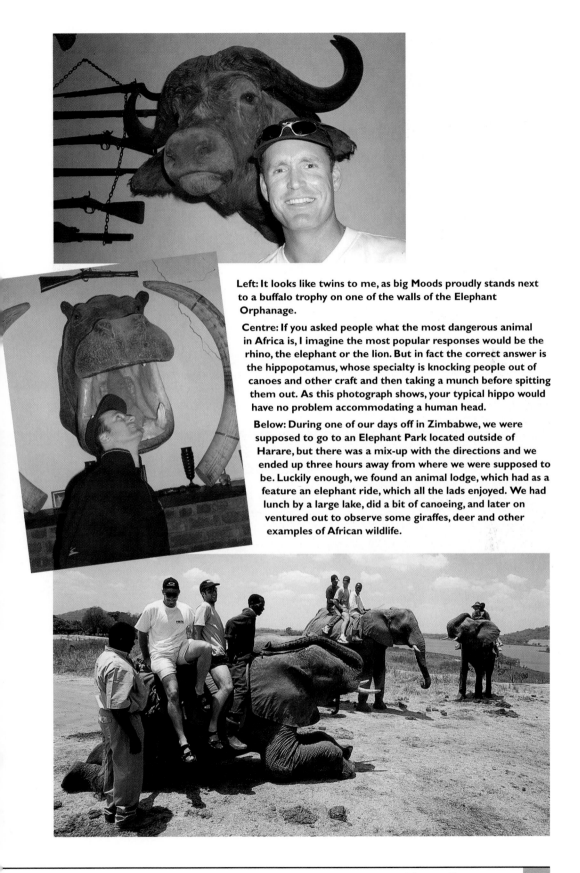

Left: It looks like twins to me, as big Moods proudly stands next to a buffalo trophy on one of the walls of the Elephant Orphanage.

Centre: If you asked people what the most dangerous animal in Africa is, I imagine the most popular responses would be the rhino, the elephant or the lion. But in fact the correct answer is the hippopotamus, whose specialty is knocking people out of canoes and other craft and then taking a munch before spitting them out. As this photograph shows, your typical hippo would have no problem accommodating a human head.

Below: During one of our days off in Zimbabwe, we were supposed to go to an Elephant Park located outside of Harare, but there was a mix-up with the directions and we ended up three hours away from where we were supposed to be. Luckily enough, we found an animal lodge, which had as a feature an elephant ride, which all the lads enjoyed. We had lunch by a large lake, did a bit of canoeing, and later on ventured out to observe some giraffes, deer and other examples of African wildlife.

Above: Damien Fleming, Matthew Nicholson, Ricky Ponting and Simon Katich enjoy some of the product of one of our sponsors in the dressing room after our Test win over Zimbabwe in Harare.

Below: To liven things up near the near the end of the one-day series, I set this unconventional one-day field for Flem's bowling.

Australian cricket is going to base its successes on the concept of a team. We have a great team spirit and as long as the feelings generated in the Geoff Marsh years continue, I'm sure the enjoyment we've had tonight and the success that goes with it on the field will continue long after I'm gone.

October 13 HARARE

ONE OF THE GREAT pleasures of playing cricket and touring the world is having the opportunity to visit places, observe different cultures and see things you would otherwise never have experienced. Today, 24 hours before the inaugural Australia–Zimbabwe Test match, we were invited to an animal orphanage situated just outside of Harare. This is an institution specialising in saving rhinos, but it also accommodates lions, tigers, snakes and a wide assortment of other animals.

My day was going along very peacefully, as I took in the beauty and majesty of these great wonders of nature … until I reached the lions' cage. The trainer of these cats was putting on a nice little act, getting the king of the jungle to perform for us, until suddenly it turned away as if it wanted no more of the show. Naturally enough, we thought the entertainment had finished, so we turned away and were about to stroll off to the next exhibit. That was until someone yelled, 'Look out!' Of course, our natural reaction was to spin around, which proved to be a fatal mistake, particularly for yours truly, because I was confronted with the sight of the backside of a lion with its tail high up in the air. Before I could take cover, I was sprayed from head to waist with a golden shower, while Lang copped the remnants on his shirtfront. As bad as my acute embarrassment was, the stench of big cat urine was far worse to cop — a putrid, reeking odour that burnt the nasal hairs and lingered in the air. More good news came from the owner, who chuckled, 'By the way, you'll never get rid of that smell.'

Moments after this photo was taken I became the fortunate or unfortunate one to be urinated on by the lion. As things turned out, it proved to be good luck, as I went on to score 151 not out in the Test match a couple of days later, but at the time it wasn't a very pleasant experience.

October 14

The first-ever Australia v Zimbabwe Test match began in Harare. Zimbabwe captain Alistair Campbell won the toss and batted, and at stumps Australia was 0-6 in their first innings, after bowling the Zimbabweans out for 194. Glenn McGrath and Shane Warne each took three wickets.

October 15

Australia moved on to 5-275, a lead of 81, in their first innings of the inaugural Test against Zimbabwe. From 2-7, Mark Waugh (who made 90), Justin Langer (44) and Steve Waugh (90 not out) led the Australian recovery.

October 16

Zimbabwe reached 1-80 in their second innings after bowling Australia out for 422 on the third day of this one-off Test match. Steve Waugh went on to 151 not out, his 20th Test century, and Damien Fleming hit 65, their eighth-wicket partnership being worth 104. Heath Streak took 5-93 for the Zimbabweans ... In Pakistan, Malik Mohammad Qayyum, the judge heading a commission enquiring into allegations of bribery and match-fixing, submitted his report to the Pakistani Sports Ministry. He commented that the report contained evidence of wrongdoing by a number of players.

I learned later that this was, in fact, the orphanage's party trick, and that the accuracy of the lion was legendary. So at least I wasn't the only one who'd acted as a human dartboard at some point in the lion's lifetime. Trying to find some good news in the whole affair, I talked myself into believing that the fact that the lion had selected me was a good luck omen. This may sound weird, but cricketers have some crazy superstitions. Some blokes reckon that if a seagull poops on you while you're fielding, it means good things will happen for you. I was a disbeliever until I saw Heals cop a rather large blob on his glove during an Adelaide Test one year, and then snare a simple caught behind off the very next delivery.

October 14 HARARE

'We've got one Test to play and our best is yet to come,
We've been threatening for a couple of matches, so let's
    put these guys under the gun.
We must back ourselves and play with some shit,
And at the end of this historic Test, let 'em know they've
    been hit.
Don't wait for someone else, be the man today
And show these Zimbots how the boys in the baggy green
    can play.'

— **Dave Misson** (read before day one, Zimbabwe Test, October 14)

TO MANY, THE DECISION to send Matthew Hayden and Stuart MacGill back to Australia in time for a Shield game was a commonsense one. From the moment we, as selectors, decided that neither would be in the final XII for the Test, and with no other cricket to be played on tour, we felt that they would be better off getting into some form through match practice back in Australia, rather than sitting around and not playing here. This is a new policy, but I believe it is a wise one. In the past, some players have gone away on long tours in good form but through lack of opportunities have returned home out of nick and with in-form players challenging for their positions, or even having jumped ahead of them in the queue. To me, Haydos and Magilla deserve the opportunity to have the best chance of forcing their way into the Test team in the near future, and this was a decision that I feel rewards them with this chance ...

Stuart MacGill (left) and Matthew Hayden bid farewell to Glenn McGrath before their mid-Test departure back to Australia. There was some comment about that Magilla and Haydos were being treated badly, but I thought things were handled correctly.

October 15 HARARE

CRICKETERS THESE DAYS are surrounded by information and statistics about their careers, so upcoming milestones and significant cricket facts are pretty well known. This said, I'm not sure if Mark Waugh knew that if he scored a century against Zimbabwe then he would create history by becoming the first player to score a hundred against each Test-playing country.

As things turned out, he failed in this quest by 10 runs, but it was the manner in which he was dismissed that will probably cause him a few nightmares in the future. To be caught and bowled by the part-time, 'pie-chucking', left-arm orthodox spinner, Grant Flower, was a real catastrophe, but if it was any consolation, his twin had a slice of luck in the 90s. I am already the current world record-holder for the most Test-match 90s, and wasn't keen to build on that and create a tally that won't be broken, so I certainly feel an extra bit of tension whenever I move past 89.

Over the years, I've had a string of unfortunate incidents that have left me just short of the magical three figures. There are two not outs, including an unbeaten 99 when Mark (as my substitute running partner!), got run out by an inch at the non-striker's end. Once at Rawalpindi in Pakistan, I was out for 98, when a Waqar Younis thunderball ripped into my ribcage, cannoned off my elbow to my hip, down to the back of my heel, before finally dislodging a solitary bail. My first Test 90 came one ball before the umpires took the teams off for bad light, and another happened when I pulled out the hook in England only to see Tim Curtis take a freak one-handed overhead catch. South Africa's Daryll Cullinan did much the same at the MCG one year to cut me off four short of my century. This time in Harare, however, the gods finally smiled upon me, when I was given a life courtesy of a

Australia completed a 10-wicket victory on the fourth afternoon of the Test against Zimbabwe, to win the Southern Cross Trophy. Glenn McGrath, Damien Fleming and Shane Warne each took three wickets in the home team's second innings of 232. Zimbabwe were 2-200 before Gavin Rennie was dismissed, the start of a collapse that saw eight wickets fall for 32. No. 3 batsman Murray Goodwin was last out in the Zimbabwe second innings, for 91.

sitter that Grant Flower put down at point. The instant I hit the ball I began cursing myself for stuffing up yet again, and when it hit the deck I couldn't believe my good fortune.

It was special to be the first Aussie to score a ton against Zimbabwe, as it's a landmark — no one else can be the first — that can't be taken from me. It wasn't my best Test hundred, but it was important for me in that the innings was built around good concentration, a part of my batting I haven't been happy with lately.

October 17 HARARE

COMING INTO THIS HISTORIC Test, the first between the two countries, we weren't exactly setting the cricket world ablaze. From my point of view as captain, I felt we were missing a couple of key ingredients: enjoyment and hunger. But I wasn't exactly sure what the problem was. When a team isn't going as well as everyone wants or expects, it can be hard to pinpoint the problem, and for me this was a source

Funky Miller poses for a team photo all of his own in Harare.

of frustration. Our tour to Sri Lanka was an enormously trying one, with constant rain, poor practice facilities, lack of options away from the game, the announcement that Geoff Marsh was retiring, injuries and ill-discipline off the field — all these things, but not one in particular led to a 1-0 loss over the three Tests.

Personally, Sri Lanka was the toughest tour I've ever been on, both physically and mentally. The severe injury I suffered in Kandy was extremely painful, of course, and the time away from the team while recovering left me feeling helpless about and distant from what was going on. I could see not only my strength as a leader fading through my absence, but also a team that was losing focus and direction.

The laid-back atmosphere of Zimbabwe has offered a much-needed tonic for the Aussie team. Our enjoyment seems to have resurfaced. Stopgap coach Allan Border has been the perfect man for the job during this mini-tour, with an approach that is in many ways old-fashioned, but it livened us up and got us going. Our training sessions have featured good old hard work. Social activities such as having a beer together after the tour games have been encouraged and suddenly our hunger has begun to return.

As a result, the much-anticipated clash between the two teams in Harare proved to be an enjoyable and successful encounter — especially for us, as it got us back on the rails and gave us confidence for the testing times that lie ahead.

Looking back on the Test, I believed that winning the toss would be important to us as the wicket was nicely covered in grass, and as such would assist our pacemen, Glenn McGrath, Damien Fleming and to a lesser extent Colin Miller. Amazingly, the local captain, Alistair Campbell, called correctly and decided to bat first, obviously more worried about the prospect of batting last against Warney, but he'd clearly forgotten about what might happen on day one to his now-exposed batsmen.

Bowling Zimbabwe out for 194 was, to me as a captain, definitely a positive result. Even better, our bowling kept improving the longer the innings went. The wickets were shared equally, except for Miller, whose 19 overs for 36 runs went unrewarded — but only in terms of wickets to him. From a team point of view he did a great job, as his miserly spells allowed me as a captain to attack from the other end while the Zimbabweans searched desperately for a way to break the shackles imposed upon them.

Our reply was just what we had talked about. To have a lead of over 200 was the game plan, as that kind of total would leave Zimbabwe in an almost impossible situation to squeeze even a draw out of. Our final total of 422 was helped by the 'photographers' delight' Damien Fleming, whose flourishing blade carved an exquisite 65 while we all watched in awe.

We had to work very hard in the early part of Zimbabwe's second innings, but got the rewards later on when the last eight wickets fell for 32 runs. This left Slats and Blewey needing to score just five runs for the victory.

One of the most encouraging signs was the way we kept on believing during Zimbabwe's second innings, when the total reached 2-200 and they were looking to set us a reasonably big score to win. Never once did our heads drop and our work ethic was great all the way through. If we can keep working on these aspects, I reckon nothing can stop us from achieving what we want to.

The two sides enjoying each other's company after the one-off Test match in Harare. These days, this sort of socialising between teams doesn't happen that often, unfortunately, so we really enjoyed ourselves as we talked with our recent opponents. The Zimbabweans are very similar to Australians in many ways — they love the outdoor life, they love their sport, they love their barbecues and they really enjoy mixing after a game of cricket.

October 18 HARARE

MY LASTING MEMORY of the Zimbabwe Test will be the fact it was played in great spirit. It was a genuine pleasure to play a team that wasn't interested in slowing the game down with time-wasting tactics. Instead, they were always ready to play. The bowler invariably was waiting at the top of his mark before even his own fielders were in their places. It may sound trivial, but in fact it was a reflection of the overall respect each team had for the other.

Normally after a Test match, you might find a few teams having a quick drink together, exchanging a bit of small talk before going their separate ways. Not so in Harare. Both teams and their administrators revelled in each other's company for a good three or four hours. For us, it was a chance to relax and appreciate what it is like to play Test cricket against semi-professionals and the difficulties the Zimbabwe players have. It really made us realise how fortunate we are in Australia and how much we have.

In Zimbabwe they have a very limited first-class competition, with only four teams from which to pick a national side. The facilities are very basic compared to ours, with a lack of quality wickets and indoor venues making it very tough on the up-and-coming youngsters. A huge dilemma facing most of their players is the fact they have to sacrifice their income to play for their country, with their jobs paying more than they get from international cricket.

A huge challenge for the bowlers is the lack of knowledgeable coaches with enough experience to effectively teach the team players. For example Heath Streak, who is a world-class bowler, has no one to turn to if he has troubles with his technique or confidence. He can only look within for solutions. It was certainly a two-way street in the change rooms, with all the Zimbabwe players saddling up next to an Aussie, while they picked each other's brains. Clearly our experience as Test cricketers was invaluable to them, particularly the younger players.

So keen were a couple of their guys to soak up the winning atmosphere of our room that they even wanted to stay for the singing of our team song, but our hospitality couldn't quite extend that far!

The Test itself was very competitive until the last session on day four. Rest assured, we had to play very well to win. If not for some sloppy fielding by Zimbabwe, the match would have been a lot closer than the end result, but I guess that's what happens when you are not used to playing tough cricket day-in, day-out.

In the Test, four separate incidents occurred the like of which I'd never seen in Test cricket. The first came during our first-innings bowling effort, when Ian Healy fielded at first slip for two deliveries of my four-over spell in his full keeping kit while Shane Warne assumed the position of wicketkeeper. The reason for this bizarre piece of cricket was to try to effect a stumping by throwing down the stumps from a distance. Their tailender, Bryan Strang, was continually charging down the pitch like a headless chook in a bid to slog me over the infield. The plan was for the ball to get past his bat and into Warney's hands, who would then throw down the stumps with Strang still short of his ground. Good in theory, but it never happened.

Incident No. 2 involved Colin Miller, our versatile multi-purpose bowler. During one of his spells, he ended up bowling to well-set left-hander Neil Johnson and debutant opener Trevor Gripper. Nothing unusual about that except that 'Funky' trundled down his medium-pacers to Gripper and then mid-over, reverted to off-spin for Johnson.

Bizarre incident No. 3 came in the form of Zimbabwe opening bowler Bryan Strang starting the innings without a fine-leg.

A final new experience for me was winning the Test match

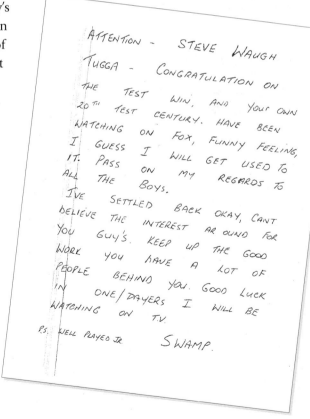

ATTENTION - STEVE WAUGH

TUGGA - CONGRATULATION ON THE TEST WIN, AND YOUR OWN 20TH TEST CENTURY. HAVE BEEN WATCHING ON FOX, FUNNY FEELING, I GUESS I WILL GET USED TO IT. PASS ON MY REGARDS TO ALL THE BOYS.

I'VE SETTLED BACK OKAY, CANT BELIEVE THE INTEREST AROUND FOR YOU GUY'S. KEEP UP THE GOOD WORK YOU HAVE A LOT OF PEOPLE BEHIND YOU. GOOD LUCK IN ONE/DAYERS I WILL BE WATCHING ON TV.

P.S. WELL PLAYED JR.   SWAMP.

The first one-day international of the Australians' tour of Zimbabwe was played in Bulawayo, with Australia winning by 83 runs. Mark Waugh made 106 from 97 balls, Ricky Ponting 67, and Damien Martyn 57 not out from 38 balls, as Australia hit 303 from their 50 overs. Neil Johnson scored 110 for the home team, while Damien Fleming and Andrew Symonds each took three wickets.

The Australians were back in Harare to take a 2-0 lead in the one-day series. Steve Waugh sent the home team in and his bowlers shared the wickets as Zimbabwe were dismissed for just 116, from 37.3 overs. Man of the match Damien Fleming took 3-14 from his 10 overs. Australia reached their victory target in 28.3 overs for the loss of just one wicket, with Mark Waugh making 54 not out.

Australia completed a 3-0 clean sweep of the one-day series with a second successive nine-wicket win in Harare. Zimbabwe made 9-200 from their 50 overs, with Andy Flower scoring 99 not out. In reply, Australia made 1-201 in 39 overs, with Ricky Ponting (87 not out) and Michael Bevan (77 not out) adding an undefeated 157 for the second wicket.

on a wide. It was a different Test, to be sure, one in which I was particularly pleased to make a big score because it was a historic occasion and for us a chance to set the standard for future Australian teams to emulate.

October 28 SYDNEY

'I'M JUST THE DRUMMER IN THE BAND' was always one of Ian Healy's favourite lines and in a way it was spot on. He was an integral part of the team, always doing the hard yards, putting in the effort away from the spotlight, igniting the side with energy and character and holding it all together for the rest to follow suit. His was the heartbeat and inspiration of the Australian cricket team for more than a decade, as he set the standard for quality by which all wicketkeepers in the future will be judged. Quite simply, Heals is now the benchmark for other keepers to aspire to.

To have played 119 Tests and 168 one-day internationals is a remarkable achievement in itself, but it is even more impressive when you consider the impact squatting 600 times a day in Tests and 300 times during each one-dayer must have on your body. And don't forget that this constant physical test comes on top of the many, many hours training that one has to do to remain at the elite level. Fortunately for Heals, he seemed to enjoy the physical aspect of training, especially the running and endurance work, and the evidence of this is borne out by his bulging calf muscles and solid quads and hamstrings. From the waist up, however, it's a different story — Heals with his shirt off might well be a candidate for a 'Mr Puniverse' title ... well, maybe not quite, but he's no Arnie Schwarzenegger. Then again, neither are many of the current crop of players in their 30s.

Heals' work ethic is legendary and was largely responsible for his cricket always improving through his career, instead of going the other way, as many players' games do with age. Getting up at 6.30am and descending to the depths of the hotel basement or to an adjacent car park became the norm rather than the occasional for Heals. There he practised his technique by throwing a golf ball against the wall, making sure his hands and feet were aligned in the proper place so that when it came to a game situation his automatic pilot would take over.

To remain at the top of any profession requires not only skill, but also the ability to be honest in your assessment of

Team Meeting: The Captain's Notes

FIRST ONE-DAYER v ZIMBABWE, AT BULAWAYO

- Boof 12th man, Chippen 13th.
- Let's make sure we have respect for Zimbabwe.
- Low key so far, but that changes from now.
- Jet lag. Get enough rest.
- Remember that we are the world champions: let's keep our own high standards, same as Lord's —— discipline, passion, aggression, hustle.
- These three games are important because: 1. We want to keep our reputation; 2. Players have sacrificed Shield games; 3. We want to keep on a roll — we've won 11 from 12, and winning is a habit; 4. We should show everyone how professional we are and that every game counts to us.
- Our goal is to win all three games.
- Zimbabwe – they're a good honest team with no superstars.
- Let's put pressure on their bowlers. They need to settle into a routine — let's make sure they don't get into one.
- Bowlers: be disciplined, create pressure by relentless line and length. First 10 overs are important — they like to try to dominate.
- Fielders: hunt in packs, no quiet times, put your hand up! Take and make half chances.
- Enjoy the experience.
- 7.50 departure tomorrow morning.

your own game. Heals was always looking to improve. Very early in his career, he was smart enough to change his training routine in regard to how many catches he would take — and the difficulty of those catches — during team practice sessions. In his eagerness to impress he was overdoing the number of catches that were being hit to him, and too many were all but unreachable as well. He was diving full length to either side, leaping skywards, straining every muscle and generally overworking himself. But after receiving advice from the great Rod Marsh, Heals decided that the 'near-impossible chances' workout was to be drastically reduced and replaced by quality sessions based on watching the ball into the gloves and focusing on correct movements and glovework. This change enabled Heals to be fresher and sharper for matches, and enhanced his confidence in his wicketkeeping technique.

Heals was a keeper who rarely made a mistake. He must have been doing a great job, because we almost took it for granted that whenever a chance came his way, it was going to be accepted. Generally, if you notice a keeper too much it's for the wrong reasons: either he's missing chances or letting byes go through. Heals rarely did either of these things. Such was our respect for and confidence in Heals that even his most brilliant catches were often underrated, simply because we didn't expect him to miss them.

His true greatness will be even more appreciated later, because we became so spoilt and desensitised that we accepted his technical genius when we should have been applauding it. His handling of Shane Warne was inspirational. It appeared he was never flustered by balls that turned at unimaginable angles out of the rough or leapt off cracks in the wicket. But when you think about it, it was quite a feat for Heals to rarely, if ever, not pick Warney

As Colin Miller (in the foreground) calls for quiet, Heals prepares for what would turn out to be his final rendition of *Under the Southern Cross.*

October 26

The ACB Chairman's XI defeated the Pakistanis by seven wickets in the visitors' first match of their Australian tour, a 50-over game at Lilac Hill. The legendary Dennis Lillee took 3-8 from eight overs, including Ghulam Ali, caught by Lillee's son, Adam.

October 27

The Pakistanis lost to Western Australia by three runs in a 50-over match at the WACA.

October 28

Long-serving Australian wicketkeeper Ian Healy announced his retirement from first-class cricket, after a career that featured 119 Tests and 168 one-day internationals. Healy left the game with more Test

— batsmen got it wrong regularly and while they were doing so they were blocking the wicketkeeper's view. Invariably, he was there to secure a delivery that looked to have bamboozled everyone else.

His innate feel for the job put him in the right position at precisely the right time. An example of this came during the Manchester Test of 1997, when part-time Chinaman bowler Michael Bevan delivered a quickish full ball down the legside to the left-handed opener, Mark Butcher, at a time when the Poms were working their way back into the match. Despite being blinded by the batsman's body, Heals swooped into the line of vision behind the batsman's legs, collected the difficult half volley and in the same movement swiped the bails off at exactly the instant Butcher was transferring his weight and was momentarily out of his crease. It was a moment of pure wicketkeeping brilliance that swung the momentum our way, as Heals so often did.

'Seizing the moment' is the phrase that best describes Ian Healy's cricket. It wasn't so much his enormous contributions but when he made them. Such efforts usually came when the team was backpedalling or up against it; it seemed that this was when he was at his most comfortable, bristling with competitiveness and bursting with positive vibes.

His batting was underestimated and undervalued, for he won many matches with his telling contributions and positive initiatives. However, his quest to get on with the game was both his strength and weakness. One lasting memory was a dismissal against the great Pakistani leg-spinner, Abdul Qadir, in a Test match in Lahore during Heals' first Australian tour, in 1988. The team had been made well aware of Qadir's genius at a team meeting — careful attention was to be the order of the day against his lethal wrong 'un. But Heals was a 'cutaholic' at the best of times and especially so when naturally edgy at the start of his innings, when he would invariably try to get one to the point boundary anyway he could, even if it meant cutting a Curtly Ambrose or Courtney Walsh yorker. On this occasion, I was at the other end when he came out to face Qadir, and gave him my 'two bob's worth' before he scratched centre. 'Have a good look at him,' I said, 'There's a bit of turn in the wicket.' First ball, Heals tried to smash a wide long hop to the point boundary but, unfortunately for our new keeper, it was the much acclaimed wrong 'un. Heals missed the ball by half a metre, and it thumped into his pads, plumb in front.

There can be a fine line between foolishness and bravery, but when he was batting Heals always took the opposition's attack on and confronted them, drawing them into a battle they didn't always want. This was the beauty of his batting. Such was the impact of his rapid-fire approach that bowlers always fancied getting him out with a loose shot and regularly threw away their game plan in the hope of a quick wicket. Most often, the opposite happened. Heals pounced and put the loose balls away and by the time the opposition woke up to the 'sting' he had his eye in and the tempo of the game had changed dramatically. It was like snaring flies in a cobweb the way he enticed unsuspecting victims.

Four Test-match hundreds are testimony to his batting prowess; ironically, it was his batting that also signalled for Heals that the end was near. During the series against the West Indies in early 1999, and then in Sri Lanka, his customary confidence and composure

Left to right: Junior, Heals, Hooter, me and Slats in the dressing room after we'd beaten Zimbabwe.

dismissals (395) than any other wicketkeeper …
Immediately following Healy's press conference, the ACB revealed that Queensland's John Buchanan would take over as the new Australian coach. 'I've never called myself an expert and I never will,' Buchanan remarked after his appointment was made public. 'But what I do offer is some expertise and, to me, that revolves around building a good environment in the team and utilising all available resources, internally and externally.'

October 31

Back in Australia, Steve Waugh claimed his team was not worried about having to face Shoaib Akhtar, reputedly the fastest bowler in the world. 'We're not worried about him,' he said. 'He is quick, but we've faced quick bowlers before — Ambrose, Walsh, Wasim Akram, Donald. We might get hit a few times, but that's Test match cricket. That won't affect our decision whether we bat or bowl, we'll play to our strengths.'

seemed to be missing, and he became frustrated by his high expectations that were not being met. His body language wasn't as intimidating or confronting as it always had been, but still we all hoped that he would regain his form. Everyone has their down times during a long career. Some niggling injuries to the calves and back in the West Indies had also seen his enjoyment of the game diminish, but I believed it was nothing a good couple of months off wouldn't fix.

Before the Zimbabwe Test, however, Heals met me in my hotel room to inform me that this was to be his last overseas Test match. Provided he received confirmation from the selectors, and approval from the people in the team that he respected, he was going to call it a day after the first Test of the upcoming Australian summer, at his beloved home ground, the Gabba in Brisbane. Having this type of discussion with a great friend and long-time teammate wasn't easy, but I respected his wishes and personally could see no reason why he couldn't end his career in front of his home crowd. Unfortunately, this wasn't to be, but Cinderella stories in sport are few and far between. The selectors have opted to let Adam Gilchrist start forging his destiny, so Heals today announced his retirement from all cricket, at a press conference in Melbourne.

Thankfully, back in Harare, Heals had ended his career atop a dressing-room bench leading us into the team song with his typical passion and fervour. I will always link winning a Test match with Heals' veins bulging from his neck, baggy green perched on his head and beer in hand, yelling at the top of his voice as if he was the luckiest man alive. Maybe he was. Anyone who was touched by him during his career was enhanced by his spirit and character, and that's a great legacy to leave behind.

PART THREE:

CAPS OFF TO A NEW MILLENNIUM

Australian selectors gave debut Test caps to Queensland paceman Scott Muller and Western Australian wicketkeeper Adam Gilchrist. Despite having played 76 one-day internationals, Gilchrist admitted he was nervous about his Test debut. 'I can't imagine what Heals must have been going through when he was playing his first Test after six Shield games,' Gilchrist said.

The Pakistanis' four-day tour match against Queensland at the Allan Border Field in Brisbane concluded with a 112-run win for the home team.

The great West Indian fast bowler of the 1980s and early '90s, Malcolm Marshall, died in Barbados. He was 41. 'It's a tragedy for cricket, especially for West Indian cricket,' said Australian captain Steve Waugh. 'It's scary that someone of my era in the game has gone. He had so much to offer, he was a great professional and a great guy as well.' ... Pakistani paceman Shoaib Akhtar knocked back requests for interviews in the lead-up to the first Test, in Brisbane. 'I've been told not to talk all tour,' Shoaib told waiting journalists. In the lead-up to the Test, the ACB had ruled that a videotape of Shoaib's action, submitted by umpires

November 4 BRISBANE

EVERYONE CONNECTED WITH the Australian team is aware that Pakistan will represent a major challenge in the upcoming three-Test series. In their own words, they are out to prove they are the best team in the world, and will also have the memory of their loss in the World Cup final six months ago to fire them up. Looking beyond Pakistan, we face another three-game series, against India, who beat us the last time we faced them in Test cricket, back in the first half of 1998. These six Tests, against tough opposition, will be a measuring stick for us, to see whether or not we are falling behind, stagnating or on the improve as a unit.

There is no doubt, whenever we approach a home series and a home season, that the planning undertaken beforehand plays a crucial role in how the team performs. A new element in this season's preparations will be the involvement of a new permanent coach, John Buchanan, the former Sheffield Shield-winning coach from Queensland. Having a new coach is, inevitably, a major change, especially when most of the guys had only met 'Buck' a couple of times before his appointment, and is especially potentially awkward this time because he only linked up with the team for the first time two days ago. This was certainly less than ideal for me, as before Buck arrived I had to contend on my own with a huge press contingent wanting interviews and thoughts about this game and the season, and at the same time make sure my own house was in order.

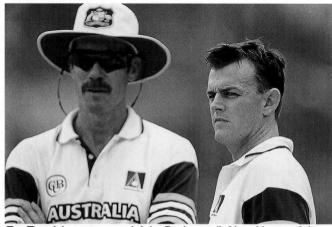

Two Test debutants – coach John Buchanan (left) and keeper Adam Gilchrist.

Team Meeting: The Captain's Notes

FIRST TEST v PAKISTAN, BRISBANE

- Funky 12th man.
- Congrats to Gilly, Scott Muller, Buck, Patty. Well done!
- Great challenge lies ahead. I believe we are good enough to win or draw every Test this year — I don't expect us to lose!
- We must believe this, but we also must put the work in — training, fitness, diet.
- Last Test in Sri Lanka and one-off Test in Zimbabwe: we had commitment, desire, pride, togetherness, will to win and the stomach for a fight – we had fire in the belly.
- I want everyone to motivate himself. Take responsibility. Never go quiet in the field. Be the person to alter the course of the match.
- As a team, we must seize the moment. Recognise the time to up the tempo and also to stem the flow if necessary. Play in sessions — the end result will come.
- The Three Ps — Patience, Pressure, Partnerships.
- Pakistan — we'll beat them with patience, consistency, discipline, game plans. They are individually talented, but are not strong in a long, sustained fight.
- Put pressure on their fielders. Be relentless with their batsman and be mentally aggressive with our batting.
- Be disciplined. No arguing with umpires.
- Everyone: do your job — do it for yourself, and let's look after each other.

However, by the time our first team meeting with Buck was completed, on his first day with the side, we all knew we had the right man on board. Buck backed up his initial talk to the team with notes written on butcher's paper, in the process addressing what he thought were our concerns about our games, and most impressively explaining what we are going to get from him and what he expects from us. The overwhelming message that came through was that we have a coach who is going to give his all to make sure we fulfil our potential as individuals and as a team. He is going to do this by being honest, fair, loyal, hardworking, committed and dedicated to the team. Crucially, he wants to get to know us as human beings as well as cricketers, and has stated his desire to make everyone more responsible for their own actions and to try to grow as people.

I came away from that meeting feeling very confident about the future, because many of his ideas and goals are similar to mine. As captain, I must give the players a clear picture of what I want and the things I expect to happen, as well as a guide as to how we should be playing our cricket. When I looked around the room at the talent in our squad and the potential the team has, I quickly came to the conclusion that it makes sense for us to be aggressive and positive in our outlook, and for each player to back himself and have faith in his ability. With the skill and enthusiasm in this side, engendering such a positive approach, I believe, will be a key factor in whether we succeed this summer. Everyone who plays cricket at the top level has talent, it's just a matter of whether or not they can reproduce their skills often enough to be winners. Players feel pressure and people doubting them. I believe it's my responsibility as skipper to make my charges feel wanted, relaxed and confident of their chances of success. Also critical is that everyone is able to put the

Terry Prue and Ross Emerson after the Pakistanis' tour match against Western Australia was not admissible because the match in question was not sanctioned by the International Cricket Council and consequently did not have an official ICC referee adjudicating. Shoaib's captain, Wasim Akram, was more forthcoming when pressed by reporters. 'He [Shoaib] is the best bowler in the world and he's going to show it in the Test match,' Wasim said. 'We don't have to say much about him because he's going to perform and we will talk about his performance,' Wasim said. 'He'll be quite fun to watch tomorrow, I can assure you of that.'

The first Test of the Australia v Pakistan series in Australia began in Brisbane. At stumps, Pakistan were 6-280, after reaching 3-265. Saeed Anwar made 61, Inzamam-ul-Haq 88, Yousuf Youhana 95, while Damien Fleming took four wickets. 'There wasn't as much in the wicket as I had expected,' Steve Waugh commented after play. 'But the first session tomorrow could well decide the game.' During the tea interval, recently retired wicketkeeper Ian Healy was given a lap of honour around the Gabba.

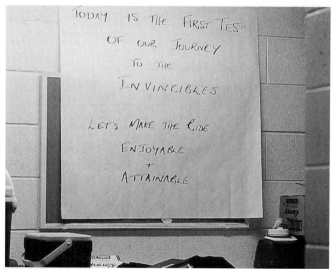

When John Buchanan hung this banner on our dressing room wall in Brisbane, my immediate reaction was that he'd set his sights too high – after all, there will always only be one team of Invincibles.

team first, ahead of self, which is a trademark of the players in all great teams.

After going through the Pakistani team at that meeting, player by player, assessing their strengths and weaknesses, I had listed what I thought to be our dangers for the season ahead. The quality and thoroughness of our preparation, or more to the point lack of quality and thoroughness, has sometimes caused us problems on home soil, and here in Brisbane this was my main worry. It has felt as if our time has been rushed, with too many functions, a new coach and the enormous media attention that focused on new wicketkeeper Adam Gilchrist, who was replacing the great Ian Healy on Heals' home turf. Complacency has sometimes caused us problems, too, and I wanted to make it clear that this was not going to be tolerated. Thirdly, I wasn't going to allow anyone's ego to cause any problems, because this will inevitably lead to divisions and cliques appearing, which is certainly not what we're about.

To be honest, I don't see these three potential problems appearing here, but I still felt it was better to let everyone know what to expect. To finish off my thoughts, I told the lads that in my view a drawn Test is no good to anyone in our camp, unless it results from a 'back to the wall' fightback that averts what seemed to be a likely defeat. We are, I argued, good enough to try to win all six home Tests and this should be our goal.

November 5 BRISBANE

REINFORCING MY MESSAGE to the team that we have the ability to go through the summer undefeated, Buck proceeded to start his reign as coach by saying to the lads this morning: 'Today is the first Test of our journey to the "Invincibles" — let's make the ride enjoyable and attainable.' And he reinforced that message by placing a banner on the dressing room wall carrying those words. I must admit when I first saw that banner, I thought Buck's ambition for us was tempting fate a little, because there was and only ever will be one Invincibles — Sir Donald Bradman's great 1948 side. But at least our new coach is setting his sights high, which in itself I've never felt was a bad thing.

Without doubt, the most crucial part of today's play occurred in the last half an hour. Having inserted Pakistan on the first morning — much to the surprise of many of the cricketing experts and media — until those last 30 minutes, we were having an indifferent day. Our reasons for bowling first were many and varied. Firstly, Pakistan hadn't played a Test match in the previous six months, which of course meant they would be a little scratchy in their batsmanship skills as well as being mentally unaccustomed to the constant demands of Test batting, patience and technique. Secondly, their tour match form leading up to Brisbane was ordinary, particularly their batting, and coming into the match many of

November 6

Australian openers Michael Slater (134 not out) and Greg Blewett (77 not out) led a stirring fightback which left the home side at 0-233 in reply to Pakistan's 367 after day two of the first Test. Earlier Pakistani keeper Moin Khan had smashed 61 from 68 balls.

November 7

The Australians batted through the day to be 9-515 at stumps on day three of the first Test, after Michael Slater went on to 169, Greg Blewett to 89, Mark Waugh scored an even 100, his 17th Test century, and Adam Gilchrist hit 81 from 88 balls in his debut Test innings. Slater and

their top players had spent precious little time in the middle. In this situation, it's always nice to feel your way into a match by fielding first to get some confidence and comfort. I didn't want to give them that luxury. The fact that Pakistan notoriously struggle on bouncy wickets with sideways movement also influenced my decision, as I believed Brisbane would accommodate our quicks in this regard. The final factor for me was the saturation of one-day games that Pakistan have played in the months leading up to this tour. If one isn't careful, some lazy habits can develop from playing the shortened version of the game.

Well, at 3-265 my somewhat controversial decision wasn't looking too flash and tomorrow's headlines were beginning to float across my imagination.

'Waugh Blunders at the Toss' …

'Australia Toss the Advantage to Pakistan!'

Thankfully, we kept on pursuing the Pakistani batsmen — as we had done all day without things falling into place for us. Now the game is evenly poised at 6-280. In fact, we probably had our noses in front psychologically because Pakistan would have felt the day was theirs until right at the very end. Conversely, we finished strongly and took plenty of heart from our battling day, not to mention the fact that

Slats' battle with Wasim Akram and Shoaib Akhtar in Brisbane was one of the highlights of summer. Shoaib hurled everything at him, bowling at close to 100 miles an hour, but Slats responded by playing some of the most breathtaking shots you'd ever want to see.

now we have a new batsman to bowl at in the morning with a newish ball and only the tail to come.

To many observers, I imagine this period of play may have seemed important but not crucial. For us, it was the latter, because it rewarded us for all our hard but previously unfulfilled work and lifted our expectations for a successful day two. Day one is seen as a day that can often set up the result in the first Test, which will more than often lead into a series win, particularly if it is only a three-match series. Knowing we could hang tough was a sign that we have a good team thing happening; this could prove to be a vital moment in our season.

November 10 SYDNEY

'Well here we are boys, at the start of Day Four,
The runs are on the board but I sense Warney wants more.
Scotty got his first run and went wild punching the air,
The fresh new emotions of Test cricket, there for all to bare.
Slats and Junior a ton, Blewey stiff not to join them,
Let's hold this momentum and really sink the slipper in.
The match is up for grabs but we have time on our side,
Let's show patience, discipline, pressure and that great Aussie pride.'

— **Adam Gilchrist** (read before day four, first Test v Pakistan, November 7)

OUR GENERAL PLAN for this Pakistan side in the first Test revolved around us being consistent, persistent, relentless and positive. We see them as a team full of individual stars, all of whom are capable at separate times of having their moments, but as a team they lack that crucial cohesiveness that means they often struggle to battle through the tough periods. This means that, provided we are consistent and patient against them, we'll eventually get chances to gain the ascendancy. This approach fits in nicely with the three 'Ps' we trust in — Patience, Pressure and Partnerships.

As I thought, the last hour on day one proved to be a telling phase of the Test, as we dominated proceedings from there on with some brilliant, uninhibited strokeplay from our batsmen. The quality of Michael Slater, Greg Blewett, Mark Waugh and Adam Gilchrist at the crease was a joy to watch and the scoreboard was ticking over at four runs per over. Batting was never made to be that easy, or to look so fluent. To cap it off, Warney bludgeoned a career-best knock to really unsettle the Pakistani line-up and distract them from the task ahead. Our total of 575 was scored at more than four runs an over, something that was especially pleasing because as players we want people to be entertained when they come to watch us play.

To win the Test required patience, above all else, particularly when things didn't fall into place on day one with the ball. We all knew that if we kept on doing the little things right, like being supportive in the field, bowling to our plans and not losing our patience, the chances would be created. And so it proved. The importance of our excellent comeback on day one was further shown through our continuing improvement in their second innings, which set us up for a great 10-wicket win. For the first time in a Test match, Ricky Ponting was able get up on the table to lead us into our winning team song.

Blewett's opening stand was 269, their third consecutive century partnership and the third highest ever by an Australian opening pair in Test cricket. Pakistani quick Shoaib Akhtar took four wickets.

November 8

After the final session of day four of the first Test was washed out, Pakistan were 4-223 in their second innings. Earlier, Australia were all out for 575. Shane Warne scored 86 from 90 balls for the home team, and added 86 for the last wicket with Test debutant Scott Muller. For Pakistan, Yousuf Youhana made 75 and opener Saeed Anwar was 118 not out at stumps.

Above: Michael Slater looking pretty pleased with himself after his hundred against Pakistan at the Gabba. When Slats makes runs, we invariably win the Test — he scores so quickly he gets us in a position where we can force a result because we've got plenty of time to bowl the opposition out twice.

Below: Adam Gilchrist during his exciting debut Test innings of 81 from 88 deliveries.

When Bob Simpson was Aussie coach, he didn't like to see anyone taking a nap in the dressing room, but John Buchanan and I believe that if it gets a player nice and relaxed and in the right frame of mind, then there's nothing wrong with grabbing a brief sleep at the appropriate time during a match. This photograph of Buck (right) and Dave Misson was taken during a rain delay in the Gabba Test.

Winning a Test is always sweet, but when you have three guys making their debut it's just that extra bit satisfying.

Gilly slotted into the team like he'd always been there, exuding poise, class and an ability to sense when to turn the match in our favour. His legside stumping of Mahmood off Shane Warne was pure class and one Ian Healy would have been proud of. Making six dismissals and scoring an excellent, important 81 is up there as one of the great debuts in Australia's Test history.

Local boy Scott Muller also had a fine first appearance, claiming three crucial wickets, putting on 86 for the last wicket with Warney and taking a great catch on the final day. This was a gutsy effort because I haven't seen too many more nervous lads in the baggy green; to overcome this and play well showed plenty of character from the muscle-bound Gold Coast boy who could easily slide into a lifeguard role on *Baywatch*.

New coach John Buchanan, who someone mentioned looks like Ned Flanders from *The Simpsons*, was tremendous in his debut, making his presence felt in his uncomplicated, unassuming way. Analysing the previous day's play and plotting what we needed to do in order to improve for the next day seems easy enough, but in reality it takes a keen eye and a feel for the game to make it worthwhile. 'Buck' certainly crossed our 't's and dotted our 'i's for us and it made all the lads feel at ease and comfortable in the knowledge that we were heading in the right direction.

November 11 SYDNEY

I DON'T RECALL EVER playing in a Test that was any more exciting or enjoyable for the fans to watch than the one just played in Brisbane. It was like playing five back-to-back one-day games in a row, with boundaries replacing the normally plentiful singles and barely a maiden over to be found.

One memory that will stay with me from the game was what happened on the first ball of the final day, a day that began with Pakistan 15 runs in front and with six wickets in hand. For our opponents, the objective would have been to try to bat through the day, or at least score enough runs so that we wouldn't have enough time to achieve a successful run chase. We had discussed our tactics for the day before the start of play, and decided that we would focus on trying to tie down Saeed Anwar, who was undefeated on 118 and his quick scoring by not giving him any width and bowling a fraction shorter in length. For Abdur Razzaq, we hoped to get him facing Warney as much as possible, because on the previous evening he had looked very suspect against the turning ball. At first glance, this may sound surprising for a cricketer from the Indian Subcontinent, but I have found that Pakistani batsmen — Salim Malik excluded — seem to struggle with the leg-spinners, and try to smash the off-spinners. This is certainly not the case with batsmen from India and also to a lesser degree from Sri Lanka, who are usually brilliant players of the turning ball. These guys have no fear about either hitting over the top or against the spin, which takes courage and a high degree of skill.

One of cricket's great strengths is its unpredictability, and the first ball of today's play highlighted this fact. Having carefully set a very aggressive field for Warney, complete with two close-in catchers, I stood back to watch the world's

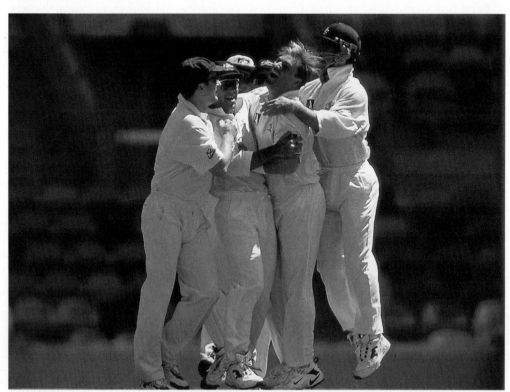

A brilliant way to start the final day. Ricky Ponting has just taken an outstanding catch off Shane Warne's bowling, to dismiss the dangerous Abdur Razzaq.

most accurate spin bowler work his magic. Instead, what we got first up was a shout of 'Oh, no!' from our star bowler, which immediately had one of our short legs, Justin Langer, backpeddling. But his comrade in close, Ricky Ponting, was oblivious to the danger and stood his ground. What Warney had delivered was a waist-high full toss, which caught Abdur Razzaq by surprise. Instead of smashing it into the outer as he might have done, Razzaq played a half-hearted push straight into Punter's lap, to give us the perfect start and set us up for a winning day ...

Another thing I will always recall fondly is having Ian Healy join us in the dressing sheds after the match. To be honest, the Gabba rooms are more like dungeons in that they are situated underground and lack any fresh air. However, they do have more space than any other in Australia, which gives the notoriously disheveled far corner of the room, where you'll invariably find Fleming, Warne and S. Waugh, a little more space to toss our gear around and make ourselves at home.

Because of the way his retirement was handled, we never really had the chance as a team to say goodbye to our great wicketkeeper in the way we all would have liked. So it was fantastic to have Heals present when the official handing over of the team song took place, with Punter taking the position on top of the table. In many ways, it was sad to see Heals with us but not really a part of it, but life goes on; Ian has had a great career and his legacy will live on much longer than most other players' will.

For me, the post-match celebrations were curtailed by the news that my very pregnant wife Lynette had just begun to experience contractions. It seemed our second child, already 10 days overdue, was on the way. I had been on the phone constantly as we knocked off the winning runs, and by the time the victory was confirmed I was as anxious as I'd ever been. I was on the first possible flight south, but actually made it with time to spare, as it had been another false alarm. Thankfully, everything ended up perfectly, and Austin Philip Waugh finally came into this world on the 11th of the 11th, 1999, a couple of days after the Brisbane win.

Team Meeting: The Captain's Notes

SECOND TEST v PAKISTAN, HOBART

- Well done in Brisbane — played excellent cricket for five days. We kept the pressure on them and they finally cracked.
- Over-rate: 16-plus. Shows we're looking to win.
- Let's not waste Brisbane. Forget the hype, we can take them down big time here.
- Stick to our basics: running between wickets, pressure on their fielders, don't allow their bowlers to settle into a rhythm.
- No mercy — let's keep our standards high, as we did in Zimbabwe and Brisbane.
- No quiet times – intensity, activity, energy.
- Patience.
- Pressure.
- Partnerships.
- Be ruthless — make them feel unwanted.
- Test goes for five days — hang tough.

November 18 HOBART

THE CHOICE OF 12TH man can be the toughest decision a captain has to make in a Test match. Of course I'm not alone in making this decision, but more often than not either Warney, Buck or a representative from the selection panel will ask, 'Well, who do you want in the side?'

Here in Hobart, it came down to a choice between Colin Miller and Scott Muller. There were many factors that needed to be considered. From Colin Miller's point of view this was his home ground in domestic cricket, meaning that he knew the conditions and would feel comfortable in the surroundings. He also wanted to prove himself against a team such as Pakistan, and was desperate to play in a home Test, which he was still to do. The mail from the locals suggested that the wicket may take some turn from perhaps as early as late on day two, so all of this added up to a fairly compelling case for 'Funky'. But Scott Muller also had a strong case for inclusion, having made his Test debut

The two leaders of the Pakistani bowling attack – Saqlain Mushtaq (left) and Wasim Akram.

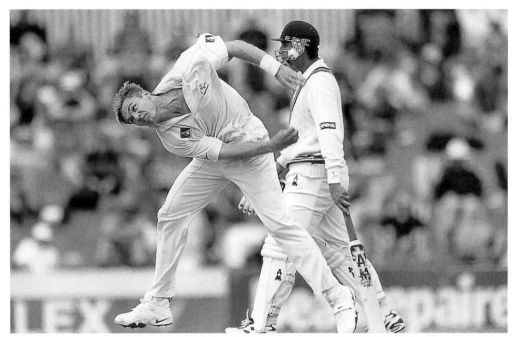

Scott Muller puts everything into his delivery during the second Pakistan Test, in Hobart.

in Brisbane as part of a winning outfit. Scott had taken some important wickets in that game without excelling, but nerves and expectations are always on edge when the eyes are upon you, and I thought he'd handled his first appearance pretty well. Also in Scott's favour was the fact that we never like to drop anyone after just one Test; we wanted to show faith in him by giving him another shot at it in slightly more relaxed circumstances, away from the Gabba. In such an environment, we believed, his ability and skill would come to the fore.

In the end, the key question was, 'What are we going to do if I win the toss?' If the answer was 'bat first', then Colin Miller would play, as his spinners would hopefully play an important part on a turning pitch in the last innings of the game. But if the answer was 'bowl first', I would opt for Scott Muller, as that would give us three quicks to exploit the favourable conditions early on.

I inspected the pitch an hour and a half before the scheduled start, and after consulting with Buck and Warney my mind was made up. The pitch looked a little more moist and damp than usual, and I believed our best option was to send the Pakistanis in. I expected that the bowlers from whichever team bowled first would get plenty of sideways movement. Thus the inclusion of Muller ahead of Miller ...

November 19 HOBART

ANOTHER GREAT THING about Test cricket is the way a game can be turned on its head by a brilliant piece of individual skill, and today we were on the receiving end. After having done some excellent work to remove Pakistan for 222 on day one, we raced to 1-191 in reply. But then the relaxed and contented ambience of our viewing area was shattered

The ACB announced that its premier domestic competition, the Sheffield Shield, would immediately become the Pura Milk Cup, following a major four-year multi-million dollar sponsorship deal with Australia's largest listed dairy company, National Foods Limited.

At stumps on day one of the second Australia–Pakistan Test, in Hobart, the locals were 0-29, having bowled out Pakistan for 222. Mohammad Wasim scored 91 for Pakistan, while the wickets were shared among the four leading Australian bowlers, Glenn McGrath (2), Damien Fleming (2), Scott Muller (3) and Shane Warne (3). McGrath's second wicket, Ijaz Ahmed, was his 250th in Test cricket.

Pakistan fought back on day two of the second Test, bowling out Australia for 246, after the home team had reached 1-191 (Blewett 35, Slater 97). Saqlain Mushtaq took 6-46. Slater's 97 was the seventh time he has been dismissed in the 90s in Test matches. At stumps, Pakistan were 1-61, and had a lead of 37.

The great Bill Brown gets a close-up look at Warney's spinning hand during the second Test. Bill was one of four Invincibles who came to Hobart, shared in our team dinner, and were always welcome visitors in our dressing room.

when Slats mishit a full toss and was out for 97. Sometimes, after a long partnership, you worry that the new batsman at the crease might not be 'switched' on and a little too relaxed, but in this case that problem seemed to apply to the entire remainder of the batting order. Within a session, we'd been bowled out for a paltry 246 and let our now excited opposition back into the game.

It was an inept and undisciplined batting performance by us, brought about by faulty shot selection and unacceptably poor concentration. The main destroyer was Saqlain Mushtaq, who bamboozled our lower order with his 'mystery' ball, a delivery that spins the opposite way from what you expect it to. Fair enough, this is a special ball delivered with the skill of an illusionist, but it's also one we have talked about in detail and always have a plan to. We believe that Saqlain hardly ever turns his off-break, and that his stock ball is the mystery delivery that turns like a leg-break. To counter him, we believe that early on, until you got accustomed to the difference in flight and bounce of this ball, you should play him as a leg-spinner and use your pads to neutralise the occasional off-break. However, for some reason we completely forget this strategy and paid the price, losing wicket after wicket to his 'freakish' skill. For us to win this match now, we not only need to adapt to the conditions and improvise where necessary, we also must remember to adhere to the basics — such as following our game plan …

November 21 HOBART

THEY SAY THAT 'catches win matches' and while I don't know if that's always true, I do know that a great catch can turn a game on its head. If ever there was a perfect example of such a catch changing the flow of the game, then it happened early in today's play, the fourth day of the second Test. Through one moment of brilliance from Mark Waugh, the momentum has shifted away from Pakistan, and given us a chance of victory.

Pakistan started the day at 7-351, a lead of 327, so we desperately needed some early wickets if we were going to get ourselves in a position where we'd be chasing a realistic victory target tomorrow. To do this, we really needed to quickly dispose of the imposing frame of Inzamam-ul-Haq, who had played quite brilliantly on day three to be 118 not out overnight. And we did, thanks to Australia's best 'gripper' (slip fielder) of the past 20 years.

Not only does fielding in the slips require enormous concentration, especially late in the day when, though you mightn't have touched a ball all day, you're still expected to be mistake free when needed. You need to be able to 'sniff out' a chance or 'feel' the moment a catch is about to come your way. This equation gets even tougher when a spinner is operating, you're close to the batsman, the delivery is a short one outside the off-stump, and the batsman is preparing to smash it through the offside field. At this point, you need to move quickly and take cover, because a top edge to that wild slash may result in a speeding ball heading straight for your eyes.

That's what happened here. But not only did Junior make the necessary movements after Warney dropped short and wide outside off-stump, he also managed to keep his eye on the ball as Inzamam came down on the delivery at blinding pace. It looked for all money to be a boundary off the bat, but Junior reacted instantaneously with a full-stretch dive to the right, gathering in the 'Kookaburra' by the ears a good metre to a metre-and-a-half behind his body. It was a catch that lifted everybody and changed the whole tempo of the game. From 8-357, Pakistan was all out for 392, leaving us needing 369 to win the Test ...

November 22 HOBART

'With our backs to the wall,
Let's throw the wall at the Pakis.
Embrace the challenge and enjoy the fight,
We must *all* believe that victory is in our sight.
Concentrate hard but stay positive out there,
So at the end of the day, a great victory we can share.'

— **Dave Misson** (read before day five, second Test v Pakistan, November 22)

RARELY IN LIFE and perhaps less frequently in sport do all the pieces of the puzzle come together as one to allow dreams to turn into reality. But it happened today in Hobart, when an epic masterpiece was forged by the contrasting styles, temperaments and techniques of Adam Gilchrist and Justin Langer.

This was a truly great win, one the whole team was proud to be part of. For me, it rates alongside the toppling of the West Indies dynasty in Jamaica back in 1995 and the courageous fightback against the South Africans at Port Elizabeth in 1997.

Pakistan appeared in control of the second Test, after batting through the third day to be 7-351 at stumps. Saeed Anwar made 78, Ijaz Ahmed 82 and Inzamam-ul-Haq was 116 not out. Shane Warne took three wickets for the Australians.

Australia restricted Pakistan to 392 in their second innings (Shane Warne 5-110), but then lost five wickets for 126 before recovering slightly to 5-188 at stumps, on day four of the second Test. In Australia's innings, Ricky Ponting made his third Test duck of the season, in three straight innings, having never previously been dismissed for 0 in a Test match. Justin Langer (52 not out) and Adam Gilchrist (45 not out) were at the crease at stumps.

A thrilling sixth-wicket partnership of 238 between Adam Gilchrist (149 not out from 163 balls) and Justin Langer (127 from 295 balls) steered Australia to a remarkable win in the second Test. Australia's total of 6-369 was the third highest successful fourth-innings chase in Test history, and the stand between Gilchrist and Langer was the highest ever made for the sixth wicket against Pakistan. Before the Test, there had been much press

Justin Langer during the fifth-day lunch break, when we still needed 92 more runs to win. You can see Lang has remains focused on the job at hand, though I could sense that he realised he was on the edge of creating something special.

To achieve victory is always sweet, but to rise above the nemesis of every sportsperson — self-doubt and uncertainty — requires something special. Not that we were doubting ourselves, but history suggested we had very little hope of chasing what was to become the third largest winning fourth-innings total in Test cricket against an attack littered with superstars who collectively have claimed over 800 Test victims.

On our side of the ledger, we had a clear vision, strength of team togetherness, pride in our performance and, crucially, a desire to smash some stereotypes that seem to strangle the life out of teams not willing to answer the questions that confront them.

From the outset of our innings, we were continually reminded that the task ahead was all but impossible, with figures continually being shown that making 300 in a run chase was only for the immortal teams of the past. In this scenario the answer for us was simple: don't look at how many we need but rather look only to the next ball and play

Celebrations during a special day in Hobart. Above: Gilly acknowledges the cheers from our dressing room, soon after the winning run had been scored. Right: Lang goes ballistic after reaching his hundred. He had gone into the Test with his place in the side under some media scrutiny, but this fantastic innings changed things.

that as best you can. If you repeat this process for long enough, the outcome will take care of itself.

It sounds easy, but the hard part is blocking out how many you need to win, how long you might have to bat for, the pressure of knowing if you get out it could cost you the match and endless other equations the mind may conjure up. At the start of the final day we needed 181 runs, with five wickets in hand, an equation most agreed favoured Pakistan.

A brief but to-the-point discussion by coach John Buchanan before play, with input from many of the players, made us all aware that the task ahead was very achievable if we kept to our basic plan of playing straight, keeping a short backswing to the quick bowlers to counteract their reverse-swing capabilities, running aggressively between wickets and having positive body language.

speculation about Langer's future in the side, but he earned the man-of-the-match award with his first-innings 57 and this century. 'The only support I needed was from the captain,' Langer commented at the post-match press conference. 'He said to me before the Test that it didn't matter what the press was writing — he wanted me in the side and so did the selectors. But it was still almost like being on death row for the week leading up to it.' During the day, the Australian selectors announced that Scott Muller and Colin Miller had been dropped for the final Test, starting in Perth in four days' time, with fast bowlers Brett Lee and Michael Kasprowicz being added to the 12-man squad.

The first hour of play was watched in the viewing area by a team full of nervous energy. Most appeared relaxed on the outside, but we were churning up inside. Each run was applauded with guarded enthusiasm, but we all had an eye on the scoreboard as the runs required were slowly added.

The second new ball came and went, coinciding with an increased steeliness to Langer's resolve and a blossoming of Gilly's instinctively natural strokeplay. We could all feel the tempo and mood of the game swinging in our favour. Meanwhile, the boys had become more assured and confident in the viewing area, buoyed not only by the body language of their on-field players but also by their management and reserves who sat directly behind us in the glass-enclosed section.

By the time the calamari, chicken wings and spring rolls had graced the players' dining room tables at lunch, we had whittled the equation down to 92.

It was during this break that the boys from the west faced their greatest hurdle: not thinking about winning, but instead focusing on the next ball they had to face. Another quick team discussion before the resumption cleared everyone's thoughts and reinforced the plans for the remaining batsmen.

The viewing area was now a place where the only

Gilly in the Aussie dressing room, straight after his epic hundred, reflecting on what he's just achieved.

movement allowed was a toilet break at the drinks interval. On the bottom row of seating, Greg Blewett and Ricky Ponting sat next to each other, reading magazines such as *Ralph* and signing unfinished autograph sheets. Two seats away, Funky Miller scribbled his way through 100 or so signatures while perusing the available newspapers. A couple of seats further along, Flem was plugged in to some inevitably obscure heavy metal band and to his right sat the spread-eagled Scotty Muller, with feet up on the window, trying to look relaxed.

In the middle row on the far left sat Slats, full of nervous energy, chatting away but not really focused on any one thing for too long. Junior occupied a seat three away and was continually tossing an orange Kookaburra cricket ball to and fro, up and down and all around, to disperse his nervous energy.

Warney was next along, padded up and very much feeling the pressure. Pigeon McGrath was two further down, looking like a condemned man as he contemplated his possible involvement at a later stage. At the end of the row sat a very edgy captain, amazingly tossing up an identical ball to Mark's. Maybe the twin thing was happening as I also tried to cope with nerves. Allan Border used to do the same thing in tight situations — his Kookaburra was known as his 'worry ball'.

In the back row sat our management team, each passing the time in his own way — maybe watching the small TV screen, or reading books and papers in between demolishing copious amounts of chewing gum.

It was a surreal atmosphere, particularly as it was like being in a time capsule, in our own room with no outside noise or fresh air coming in. The only sense we had available to us was sight, and it was all good as the target kept tumbling at an increasing rate.

Gilly reached a remarkable initial Test century with a typically thunderous off-drive, while Lang swept his way to a spine-tingling hundred that saw him leap for joy as if gravity had momentarily disappeared. We were in the home stretch now, and each run scored from 50 to go received a collective roar from the boys. It was goose bump material.

The script was starting to unravel quickly now and it seemed as if everything had slipped into fast forward, with runs flowing freely, bowling changes every over and fieldsmen scattering to all parts.

The fairytale ending didn't quite eventuate, with Lang falling at the last hurdle, only five runs from victory. But seeing him embrace his father Colin at the gate symbolised what this moment meant to all of us. It was a triumph for self-belief, faith and planning and further proof to anyone that if you want something badly enough, you can achieve it.

November 23 PERTH

THE NOW-FAMOUS PARTNERSHIP between Justin Langer and Adam Gilchrist will rightly go down as one of Test cricket's great stands. Statistically, it was extraordinary, but for us their most substantial achievement was to give us all tangible proof that *anything* is possible and that the game is never lost if you don't want it to be. When the going gets tough, we players always talk about coming from behind, but until you achieve this you're really not sure if you can or can't do it.

I can't stop talking about the two guys' effort. To see the pair put on 238 and we as a team

When asked how he would rate a 3-0 series over Pakistan, Steve Waugh replied, 'It would be great, because this Pakistan side is a very fine team. They're as good as anyone else in the world, definitely in the top three with South Africa.'

It was revealed that during the second Test on-field microphones had picked up a negative comment by an Australian player about recently dropped teammate Scott Muller. It was later confirmed that the remark had actually come from a Channel Nine cameraman.

Above: Gilly and Lang do a live cross to Channel Nine's *A Current Affair* after their record-breaking partnership. Of course, they needed to be on their best behaviour for this interview, and play things down a little, but after the media responsibilities ended our party began.

Right: With Bill Brown, toasting our victory.

reach the third highest winning fourth-innings total in Test match history to win — against an attack that includes Wasim Akram, Waqar Younis, Shoaib Akhtar and Saqlain Mushtaq — was indeed inspirational. Going into day five, we all thought we could win, but if we had lost an early wicket the pendulum certainly would have been leaning well in Pakistan's favour. In our corner, though, we could see our boys were focused and ready for the battle ahead. A feeling of total solidarity and belief began to engulf the side, and being among the boys in the change rooms as our run target diminished will always be a career highlight.

The sheer joy and excitement was overwhelming when Gilly smashed the winning runs, to complete a showcase hundred that demonstrated that he is a player of rare class and skill.

And a final tale. As well as some extraordinary cricket, the day also provided an outstanding entry in the 'best sledge of the season' competition …

'You wouldn't make our second XI.'

This was fired at Justin Langer by a Pakistani bowler, early in Lang's innings here in Hobart. I wonder what that unhappy tourist is thinking now?

November 25 PERTH

IF THERE IS ONE CRICKET pitch that is unique in world cricket, then it's the WACA strip in Perth. Nothing else in the game comes close to its marble-like hardness and trampoline bounce. These conditions are in stark contrast to those encountered by our foes on their home soil.

Much of the pre-match build-up to the first Test against Pakistan centred on the 'Rawalpindi Express' Shoaib Akhtar (left). Although he produced a whole-hearted and at times explosive display, our batsmen — including centurion Mark Waugh (seen above dodging a bouncer) — handled him well.

Left: While the big video screen at the Gabba captures Michael Slater celebrating his century in the first Test against Pakistan, a local worker is busy making sure the patrons are getting a crystal clear view.

Below: With hail threatening, the Pakistanis leave the field at the Gabba.

Left: This is one of my favourite photos of all time. Lang and Gilly are obviously very excited about what they've achieved and are having no problems smiling for the press photographers. I managed to get a shot standing behind the professional snappers. Why do I love the photograph so much? Because you can so clearly see the joy and the great thrill that the two guys got out of putting together their fantastic partnership.

Right: With the match won and Gilly and Lang the focus of the media's attention, Shane Warne settles back in his corner of the dressing room to have a quiet word with Australian selector Allan Border.

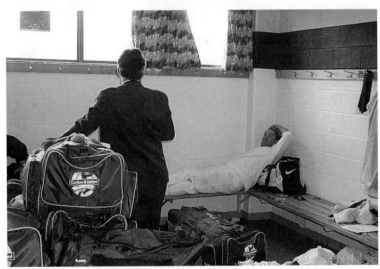

Lang and Warney at one of Hobart's McDonald's after our win in the second Test. Unfortunately, it appears that more of the sundae has ended up on Lang's nose than in his mouth. You'll notice, too, that he's still wearing his baggy green — as far as I'm aware this much-loved cap never left his scalp throughout our long celebration.

Scenes from our Test victory over Pakistan in Perth. Above: Damien Fleming celebrates the dismissal of Moin Khan, caught and bowled on the first day. Below: Justin Langer and Ricky Ponting dash between the wickets during their long and decisive partnership.

The Adelaide Oval has long been one of my favourite grounds, and I took great pleasure in making my first Test hundred against India there.

Above: Glenn McGrath bounces VVS Laxman during India's first innings. Note how low the batsman has to go to avoid the delivery.

Below: Sachin Tendulkar is controversially lbw in the second innings, trapped by a short ball that in my view didn't even bounce bail high.

Above: Greg Blewett runs among the seagulls at his home ground, the Adelaide Oval.

Below: Seagull trouble of a different kind for Mark Waugh in Melbourne, during the second Test against India.

This, to me, is a classic cricket shot. My feet, right back near the stumps, are in the correct position, my head is still, and I can sense that, for this moment at least, I'm in control.

In order for batsman and bowlers to compete at the top level in new or unusual conditions, they must either give themselves extra time in the middle, or head down to the nets and get used to this new environment. For a batsman, playing at the WACA represents a great challenge that can bring huge rewards if your preparation is spot on. Batting here, with so many balls bouncing above your waist, is such an exhilarating experience, but early on it can seem so tough that it is impossible to survive, let alone prosper. However, once you get in and become used to the extra pace and bounce, the pitch is the best in the world to bat on because it is so true and predictable. The key is to give yourself a chance.

PLAYER FEEDBACK SHEET

PLAYER: *S. Waugh*
MATCH: *Second Test v Pakistan, Hobart, 18–22 November 1999*

Items	First Innings	Second Innings
Match Results	Batting: 24 from 45 balls Bowling: — Fielding: —	Batting: 28 from 69 balls Bowling: 4-1-19-0 Partnerships: — Fielding: One catch
Match Statistics	BATTING % ones: 9% % fours: 4% % scoring shots: 24% Partnerships: —	BATTING % ones: 13% % fours: — % scoring shots: 26% Partnerships: -
Feedback	Batting: Make sure you're doing all the little things right (eg. throw-downs, nets, use of front pad to get foot/leg/weight correct). Be patient with yourself, which will give you every chance to notch big scores. Bowling: Know you are capable of doing the job that you are asking yourself to do. Fielding: Maintain your high standard of catching. Work on throwing — balance and techniques. Captaincy: I thought field placings, rotation of bowlers (although sometimes too reliant on Pidg and Warney), thinking/approach to game were very good. Do we overattack (ie. maintain attacking field positions) too long on occasions, rather than using defence as a means of attack?	
What key points will I work on?	Making time to clearly work out (not necessarily to the last detail) WHAT you are wanting to achieve and HOW you will do that. Possibly for the period up until the end of India series; but importantly for this Test, then your next match and so on. At end of India series MAKE TIME to set yourself for one-day series — again WHAT, but importantly HOW.	

This is a recreation of a player feedback sheet, which John Buchanan compiled for each player after a Test, and then handed to them in the lead-up to the next encounter.

Pakistan were bowled out for 155 on the first day of the third Test, in Perth. Glenn McGrath and Damien Fleming each took three wickets, and Michael Kasprowicz took four. By stumps, Australia already had a first-innings lead of 16, for the loss of four wickets, with Justin Langer unbeaten on 63 and Ricky Ponting on 62. The pair had mounted a recovery after Australia had collapsed to 4-54.

Australia appeared to be in an impregnable position after day two of the third Test, after Justin Langer (144) and Ricky Ponting (197) steered the home team to a first-innings lead of 296. The pair added 327 for the fifth wicket, the highest partnership by Australians against Pakistan in Test cricket and the sixth highest ever by an Australian pair. At stumps, Pakistan were 2-40 in their second innings.

Australia completed a 3-0 series clean sweep over Pakistan, by winning the third Test by an innings and 20 runs. Again the spoils were shared between the Australian pacemen (Warne taking just one wicket during in the match), with Michael Kasprowicz finishing with seven scalps on his return to Test cricket. Ijaz Ahmed scored

From the moment I heard that Pakistan wasn't going to practise before the game (instead, they decided to relax and take a break), I knew we had an enormous advantage. This decision was made even weirder by the fact that not only had their young inexperienced players not played here, even Wasim Akram had never previously played a Test match at the ground.

Once I knew about their sparse preparation, and recognised, too, the strong desire in our ranks to bury the 'dead rubber Tests' theory, I felt we had a huge opportunity to complete a 3-0 series victory ...

November 27 PERTH

COMING OFF A DUCK in Test cricket is not an easy thing, because these past setbacks invariably create doubt and promote anxiousness the next time around. So you can imagine what bagging three ducks in a row must do to your confidence. Mentally, you might be shot to pieces, downcast and miserable.

To see the way Ricky Ponting embraced this challenge was inspirational. He put in the extra hours at the nets to turn things around, and his positive attitude in team discussions was the sign of a future leader.

Punter not only got himself off the mark in Perth, he went on to smash a scintillating 197, scoring many of his runs during a fantastic partnership with the 'born again' Justin Langer. It was a contribution that enabled us to get out of a tight situation, after Pakistan had worked their way back into the match.

After Pakistan was bowled out for just 155, Wasim Akram trapped Slats lbw immediately, and then we struggled to 4-54. Another wicket and the match might even have been going their way. Instead, Lang and Punter took control, first steadying our ship and then building a partnership so that by stumps we were still only four wickets down and even had a narrow first-innings lead.

The greatest aspect of Ricky's innings was the way his self-belief shone through. As I've said many times, if there is one attitude we want to promote throughout this Australian side it is 'back yourself'. Here was an example of that philosophy bringing in the rewards for not only the individual but the team as well ...

Three photos taken during the match-winning partnership between Justin Langer and Ricky Ponting at the WACA. Above left: During a break in play, Lang heads off to his left to the Australian dressing room, while Pakistan's Saeed Anwar walks to the Pakistan dressing room, which is about 20 metres down to the right. Above right: Punter treads a similar path moments earlier. Left: While Mark Waugh (second from right) gives Lang a congratulatory pat on the back, 12th man Brett Lee has organised a drink for Punter.

November 28 PERTH

THE STRENGTH OF A TEAM can often be judged by the quality of its reserves, and we have indeed been fortunate in that regard in recent times. Not only are we talking about the impressive skills and techniques that these guys possess, but also attributes such as honesty, commitment, sacrifice, support and dedication to the team. Michael Kasprowicz has all of these in abundance and has never given less than 100 per cent support to those who have been given more opportunities than he over the past few years.

Even in times when many thought he was hard done by, Kasper never whinged or wavered in his belief that one day he'd be back. So it was with great satisfaction that he returned to the side and claimed seven wickets in this match — four in the first innings as our pacemen sliced through the Pakistani batting line-up and three more in their second dig as they failed by 20 runs to make us bat again. I reckon everyone in the team enjoyed seeing a guy who has experienced hardships and made sacrifices in the past do so well here.

November 29

Queensland defeated the Indians by 10 wickets at the Gabba, in the opening match of the Indians' tour of Australia.

November 30

Press reports indicated that Pakistan's fast bowler Shoaib Akhtar had been reported to the ICC for having a possibly suspect action. Videotape containing footage of him bowling in the three Tests against Australia was to be sent to the ICC, along with an official request that Shoaib's action be reviewed.

December 5

The Indians defeated NSW by 93 runs in their tour match at the SCG. The match featured on-field clashes between the Indians and the local umpires on days three and four.

November 29 PERTH

SO OUR SERIES AGAINST Pakistan has ended very well from our point of view, with a 3-0 victory, but in reality the series was keenly contested and evenly balanced for most of the time. It seems to me that the one distinguishing feature or attribute that has enabled us to succeed was our ability to recognise the crucial moments and then win these battles during the course of matches.

Going into the third Test of this series, we knew we'd been given a chance to brush aside a tag that had been hanging around our necks — that we were a team that performed poorly in so-called 'dead rubber' Tests. I concede that this label was partly justified, given some of our performances in the 1990s, but as captain I was very determined to make sure it wasn't a fair accusation nowadays.

Being 2-0 up in a best-of-three series was as good a place as any to start, and the boys responded in magnificent fashion. During the pre-match team meeting, we did something we have often done in the past — refer to a match or series by a motto that we have decided is appropriate for the task at hand. On this occasion, we had one word that we wanted to adhere to for the whole match and it came from Flemo …

'CLINICAL'.

After our great win in Hobart, it seems everyone was expecting us to win here. But we didn't want complacency to rear its ugly head, so whenever we needed to remember our obligations and ambitions, that word 'Clinical' came to the fore. And a victory in under three days reflected exactly the ruthless, professional attitude we were all searching for, and was achieved through following game plans, focusing on our jobs and, very importantly, enjoying ourselves.

December 8 ADELAIDE

WE FIND OURSELVES on the verge of a new Test series, a fact we have stressed at our team meetings this week — that this is a NEW contest, a fresh challenge. We can't dwell on the fact that we won the first three Tests of our summer because that part of the season is over.

Another recurring theme at our meetings has been the

A 3-0 series clean sweep over a side as powerful as Pakistan was certainly worth a smile or two.

opportunity we have to even the score after our last series against India, back in early 1998. We were outplayed then, two Tests to one, but we'd like to think it will be a different story this time, on our home turf.

To be frank, I feel that if we can dominate early then they might fall apart, particularly if we can get to Sachin Tendulkar. I see him as a reluctant leader in charge of a mentally fragile team that possesses a disastrous record away from home. On the other hand, I know that they are a dangerous foe, because they are very good frontrunners and have a batting line-up that includes four players with a Test average of over 50.

From a personal point of view, I'm looking forward to this series immensely. I haven't scored a Test century against India; in fact, I haven't played too many Tests against India. So I see this as a big challenge, for me and the team. If we want to stay on top of world cricket we have to keep winning series against all opposition. And if we want to win this series, we can't afford to slip up here. The first Test is always a crucial one in a three-match rubber. Few sides that lose the opening encounter come back to win a series.

Steve Waugh reacted angrily to claims that his team had been guilty of unnecessary sledging in the recent Test series against Pakistan. 'Let's get on and play cricket,' he said. 'I'm sick of all these headlines that have got nothing to do with the game. The last Test was the quietest we have had for a long time. I just can't believe what has been made out of that match.' ... A Prime Minister's XI defeated the touring Indians by 164 runs in a 50-over match in

I love playing in Adelaide. It's a beautiful ground, with a great wicket and the best outfield in the world. Throw in the cathedral in the background, the old wooden scoreboard and the grandstands that blend so well into the ground and you have an environment with a really nice feel to it, and a true sense of character and history about it ...

December 9 ADELAIDE

THE CONCEPT OF A pure 'batsmen's meeting' is a concept that Geoff Marsh introduced during his time as Australian coach, and we invariably gained huge benefits from these get-togethers. The key is to time these meetings so that everyone gains something from what is discussed.

Our batting efforts against Pakistan had been spasmodic, with some magnificent performances camouflaging to some degree a number of much smaller scores. John Buchanan,

PLAYER FEEDBACK SHEET

PLAYER: *S. Waugh*

MATCH: *Third Test v Pakistan, Perth, 26–30 November 1999*

Items	First Innings	Second Innings
Match Results	Batting: 5 from 8 balls Fielding: two catches Captained Test win (Series 3–0)	
Match Statistics	BATTING No. of balls: 8 % ones: 13% % fours: 13% Partnerships: —	
Feedback	Not certain your overall preparation for this Test was what you wanted; ie: possibly hoping it will come right in the centre the longer you are there (which, of course, it will). Need to give yourself the best opportunity of being there for a long period. Let me know if you need additional, modified or different preparation. Again, your captaincy was very good — setting your expectations of the team, spending time with players (especially bowlers), ensuring they are 'on target', utilising others, eg. Gilly, to assist, keeping the mood, focus of everyone buoyant but not overconfident, plus good use of four bowlers.	
What key points will I work on?	Busy few days leading into this Test — make sure you have YOUR time.	

Indian paceman Javagal Srinath had something to celebrate on the first morning of the Adelaide Test. But Ricky Ponting and I were able to turn things around.

a man who I had learned very quickly leaves nothing to chance, felt it was time for the batsmen to get together and work more as a group, which he felt would boost our collective confidence. Each batsman (the top six plus Gilly) was honest about his own form, what his expectations were, how he saw the Indian attack and what his goals were for the remainder of the home season. From my viewpoint, we all got plenty from the meeting, including an appreciation of each other's needs and ambitions, the importance of each of us supporting and backing up each other, and a reinforcement of the belief we have in each other. I think, too, that we'll be more on the lookout for any signs that one of our mates is struggling. We left each other with a first commitment that no one would wait for someone else to lead the way, and a strong reminder of the value of partnerships and that we had to try to set up the game for our bowlers, rather than wait for them to win the Tests themselves. It was only a 30-minute meeting, but one that made us all more relaxed within ourselves.

December 10 ADELAIDE

WE DECIDED TO BAT after I won the toss today. The wicket appears to be pretty flat, resembling a mosaic with tiny cracks already visible underneath a fine layer of grass. In my view this pitch could be difficult to bat on late in the match. I had heard a whisper that India were thinking of sending us in — which, given that they are a strong batting side and their main strike bowler is a spinner, would have been a strange, negative move.

This was the second example in 24 hours of the visitors' conservatism. Yesterday, at the normal pre-Test meeting called by the match referee, India's coach, Kapil Dev, and their

Canberra. David Fitzgerald and Andrew Symonds scored centuries in the PM's XI total of 5-334. Young NSW speedster Brett Lee then took 4-25, including Sachin Tendulkar, caught behind for 2.

December 9

Indian captain Sachin Tendulkar reacted to media questions about alleged Australian sledging by commenting that his team would not back down if the Australians were aggressive. 'One should expect that at this level,' he said. 'You are playing Test cricket, not club cricket, so it's bound to happen. But I feel there will be more pressure on the Australians to live up to their expectations.' Steve Waugh responded by saying, 'We'll be out there playing tough Test match cricket as we always do. I'm quite happy to be favourite and for people to expect us to win because I do as well.'

December 10

The opening day of the first Test of the first Australia–India Test played in Australia since early February 1992 ended with Australia 5-298. Before lunch at the Adelaide Oval, the home team had been 4-52, but Steve Waugh and Ricky Ponting combined in a 239-run stand that only ended when Ponting was run out for 125 just before stumps. Waugh was undefeated on 117 at the

management knocked back the idea of using the Adelaide Oval floodlights to counter any gloomy conditions that might occur during the match. They argued that they weren't used to the lights and wanted to experience them in conditions similar to a Test match before agreeing to them being used in Test cricket. But surely playing a Test under lights is no different from playing under lights in a one-day international? And anyway, I've only ever played one Shield game in my life under lights, but that didn't stop me arguing for the use of the lights here. Further, the Indians also argued that if it was necessary to play an extra hour on later days if time is earlier in the game, then they wanted the hour to be added to the end of the day, rather than play starting 30 minutes early and then extending 30 minutes after the normal scheduled close.

I could only conclude that their decision to reject the floodlights and try to shift that extra hour were negative plays built on the hope that any time permanently lost would increase the likelihood of the match ending in a draw. Which, to me, is crazy. Going into any match, you should always try to give yourself the best chance and most time to win.

I wonder what the Indians were thinking when we went into lunch on day one precariously placed at 4-52. We knew that a big first-innings score was essential if we were to win, so Punter and I, the not out batsmen, ate the Adelaide Oval's famous chicken and plum sauce amid an air of apprehension and anxiousness. Five minutes before we were due to go back out, I was visualising what I was about to encounter. I'm sure Ricky was doing the same. It was reasonably certain that we would be facing a rampaging Javagal Srinath, their pace spearhead, and the clever, probing consistency of Anil Kumble. But what we came across instead was the gentle medium pace of Sourav Ganguly, a bowler who relies heavily on his positive body language to faze his opposition, and Venkatesh Prasad, a steady bowler more adept at containing rather than dismantling. With this attack, the Indians seemed to be relying on us to suffer an immediate lapse in concentration or play a rash stroke if they were going to get a further breakthrough.

I would have thought this was an ideal time to seize the moment, but instead their negative attitude came through. They were hoping we'd make a mistake rather than making something happen themselves, as all good sides do. Ricky and I settled into a nice rhythm, getting a feel for the pace and bounce of the pitch without being in constant danger of losing our wickets to a dangerous delivery. By the time Srinath and Kumble came back, we were both well and truly set, and intent on a big partnership that eventually realised 239 runs.

This was a perfect example of a captain not following his instincts, but being persuaded by others to play safe. The end result for India was a fitting one, given their tactics.

December 11 ADELAIDE

THIS AFTERNOON PROVIDED one of the most intense pieces of Test cricket I've ever seen. Two of the game's finest batsmen, Sachin Tendulkar (the best of all, in my view) and Rahul Dravid, were confronted by two of cricket's most outstanding bowlers, Shane Warne (perhaps the greatest spinner of them all) and the magnificent Glenn McGrath.

In our team meetings leading up to the series we'd often spoken of such battles. Here on Adelaide, on such a good batting wicket, our strategy was to give them nothing. And for us, it was set up perfectly, with Shane already bowling superbly from one end and Glenn just one ball into his second spell when Sachin arrived at the crease. From the start, our great paceman was bang on line, constantly on or just outside the righthanders' off-stump. In all, his eight-over spell would cost just a single, as the runs dried up completely and these two distinguished batsmen did their best to simply survive.

This battle culminated in Dravid being snared at short leg by Justin Langer off Shane.

India's Devang Gandhi jumps for his life as I get a delivery to the cover boundary during my century in the first Test.

December 11

The second day of the first Test saw Australia reach 441, and India reply with 4-123. For the Australians, Steve Waugh continued on to 150, while Shane Warne hit his second innings of 86 for the summer, this one off exactly 100 balls. Indian captain Sachin Tendulkar was 12 not out at the close.

December 12

Australia went to stumps on day three of the first Test at 2-71, with an overall lead of 227. Earlier, India had been bowled out for 285, with Tendulkar making 61 and Ganguly 60. Most observers thought Tendulkar unlucky to be given out, caught at short leg by Justin Langer off Shane Warne.

December 13

The home team had moved to the verge of a fourth straight win for the Australian season by reducing India to 5-76 at stumps on day four of the first Test, after Steve Waugh had declared their second innings closed at 8-239 (Greg Blewett 88, Adam Gilchrist 43). The key Indian wicket, again, was Tendulkar, who was lbw to McGrath for 0 after ducking a

Our jubilation was obvious, at taking such a vital wicket and seeing our game plan rewarded. Shane turned straight to Glenn — we all did — this was an occasion when the scorebook should have recorded Dravid's wicket as being 'caught Langer, bowled Warne/McGrath'. The pressure they built and then sustained was phenomenal. Rarely have two bowlers combined so well.

The contrast to our last series against India, on the subcontinent in early 1998, when Sachin dominated Shane for most of the series and Glenn was absent, injured, was stark. Now we were on top, trying to turn a hard-won advantage into a decisive edge.

Even with Ricky's run out late yesterday, our aim this morning was still to reach 400. That's what we thought the wicket was worth. But then Adam Gilchrist was dismissed by the first ball of the day — which made things interesting at 6-298 — only for Shane Warne to come out and play his best-ever Test innings. By the time he was finished, having smashed an important 86, we'd reached 441. That great position was accentuated when we reduced India to 2-9. Dravid and VVS Laxman mounted a fightback, but then McGrath came back to get Laxman with the first ball of his second spell, which brought Tendulkar to the crease.

These last two days have been immensely rewarding. As captain, I gained great satisfaction from the manner in which we fought back after our top-order collapse on day one, and from the superb way we stuck rigidly to our bowling plan this afternoon. And batting-wise, I enjoyed the fact that I played, technically, one of my best innings, and also that I became the first player to score a century against all eight opposing Test countries and in the process passed the 8000 Test runs milestone.

At stumps tonight, India still needed a further 119 to avoid the follow on, although whether we'd enforce it is debatable at this point. The weather could still be a factor, and I think this wicket will get harder to bat on the longer the Test match goes. Already, there have been some signs of deliveries keeping unusually low. Still, we're very happy with our position, but fully aware that there is still much work to be done. After all, we were 4-52 at one point, much worse than where India's batting finds itself at stumps.

Clearly, much depends on the Indian captain now. The first session tomorrow is going to be crucial.

December 14 ADELAIDE

FOR THE BEST PART of four days, this was a tight, intriguing, enthralling and entertaining Test match, in which no quarter was asked or given. Played on a wicket that offered something to all the fine players on both sides, it was also often one of the mentally toughest I've played in. The Adelaide pitch was quick to penalise any player who lost his concentration or intensity, and asked us all to be at our very best if we were to succeed. In the end, the scoreboard suggested that we had won comfortably, but we knew that while our victory was decisive, there had been many times when we had been far from comfortable.

Fortunately, our great bowlers, Shane Warne and Glenn McGrath, coped outstandingly well with the challenge the Adelaide pitch set them. I have already written about our great bowlers' superb effort on the second afternoon. Two days later, they were at it again, smashing through the top of the Indian batting order as we reduced India to 5-76 by stumps. From that point, we knew that only the weather could prevent us going one-up in the series, and extending our Test-match winning streak to five.

On the third morning, Sachin Tendulkar had been magnificent until Warne dismissed him for 61. This was a reminder of just how dangerous an opponent the Indian captain is,

Adam Gilchrist takes a blinder to dismiss Sourav Ganguly as India crashes to defeat in the first Test.

bouncer that did not rise nearly as high as he anticipated, and struck him on the shoulder as he crouched.

Australia duly won the first Test of its home series against India, by wrapping up the Indians' second innings for 110. Damien Fleming finished with five wickets, and was unlucky to miss out on a Test hat-trick when first slip Shane Warne dropped a chance offered first ball by Javagal Srinath. Fleming would have become only the fourth man in Test history to grab two hat-tricks, his first having come in Rawalpindi in 1994. Steve Waugh was named man of the match ... Press speculation about Mark Waugh's place in the Australian side mounted following the Test, in which he scored just 5 and 8. 'I'm not a selector but if I was a selector, I'd be picking him because he's a match winner and a proven Test match player,' was Australian captain Steve Waugh's comment about his brother's future. The Adelaide Test was the 98th of Mark Waugh's career.

but after he and Ganguly were dismissed either side of lunch, our bowlers toiled hard to break down the bottom half of their batting order. Then, after Justin Langer batted superbly on the third afternoon, we headed into day four with hopes of some quick scoring, followed by a declaration that would give us plenty of time to bowl India out once more. But led by Anil Kumble, our opponents fought back magnificently, forcing us to bat into the final session and in the process confusing us as to just when was the right time to declare.

This was the first important declaration of my Test captaincy career, so I wanted to get it right. The pitch was slow, keeping a bit low, and getting slower and lower. In Dravid, Ganguly and especially the great Tendulkar, India have three batsmen capable of rising to any challenge. In Glenn McGrath and Shane Warne, we have two of the game's finest bowlers, plus Damien Fleming, our form bowler of the summer. We remembered our victory in Hobart against Pakistan, when we managed to reach 369 on the fifth day, despite losing 5-126. The last thing we wanted to do was lose the match, after working so hard to get an advantage. The other last thing we wanted to do was be too cautious, wait too long, and waste the advantage we'd worked so hard to get.

Eventually, we opted for a target of 396, leaving ourselves a little less than four full sessions to force a victory. I was ready for a long battle of attrition over the game's last four sessions, but I hadn't counted on just how well our guys would come out and bowl. Glenn McGrath started the procession in the very first over by having Gandhi caught behind, Damien Fleming followed up by getting a beauty through the defence of Laxman and then Shane Warne came on to get the key scalp of Dravid.

Enter Tendulkar. After watching the Indian captain cruise to a half-century in India's first innings, we decided to make things more difficult for him the second time around. We had our man where we wanted him, exposed to the new ball and under enormous pressure to make a big innings. Glenn McGrath executed our new strategy perfectly, as only a truly great bowler can, peppering the maestro with an assortment of short-pitched deliveries intermingled with impeccable line and length 'corridor' bowling. This gave Tendulkar no chance to score, let alone dominate.

Damien Fleming
misses out on his
second Test hat-
trick when Shane
Warne at first slip
puts down a chance
from Javagal Srinath
on the final day in
Adelaide. For most
of the Australian
summer, Flem was
our most prolific
wicket-taker.

It was like two boxing heavyweights going toe to toe in the ring. McGrath jabbing continuously, looking for a weakness, while Tendulkar weaved and ducked, searching for a counterattack. Then, out of the blue, came the Muhammad Ali-like knockout — an attempted bumper than cannoned off one of the widening cracks and consequently didn't bounce anywhere near as high as Tendulkar expected. Instead, he was struck on the body as he crouched low, waiting for the ball to fly. From my side-on view in the gully, I was certain the ball would have hit the stumps high up, close to the bails, but for it striking Tendulkar. Thankfully for us, umpire Daryl Harper agreed, but what he probably didn't bank on was the uproar his decision created in the media, particularly in India.

We couldn't be concerned with that. From our point of view, the dismissal was a reward for clever team planning and perhaps a pointer for the rest of the series. Could the Indian batsmen counter the bounce in the Australian wickets, which is more pronounced than what they are used to back home?

With India in huge trouble at 4-27, many critics, I imagine, were pondering why I'd delayed my declaration. To me, though, the Indians' struggles merely showed just how well some of our batsmen, especially Greg Blewett, had battled in our second innings.

On the fifth morning the consistent Damien Fleming ripped through the rest of the

Greg Blewett gets a ball to the point boundary during his gritty, crucial knock in our second innings of the first Test against India.

Indian order, to give us victory by 285 runs. This Test, then, became something of a mirror of the first Test of our recent series against Pakistan. That match we won by 10 wickets, a margin that failed to reflect the closeness of the game. Here, too, I think the sides were closer than the final winning margin suggests. In the end, I think we prevailed because our great players were simply magnificent, and every Australian player was patient and persistent, and stuck rigidly to the game plan.

December 15 ADELAIDE

ONE INTERESTING ASPECT that we discussed before the first Test was how the Indians use extremely heavy bats. These are great on low, slow wickets such as the ones they often see at home, where batsmen generally play vertical bat shots, hitting through the line. However, on fast bouncy wickets where the need for horizontal bat shots is far greater, that extra weight in their bats may cause a problem with their timing and technique. With this in mind, our quicks employed a fair bit of short stuff at them, which definitely unsettled their top-order players. Even so, Tendulkar inevitably stood out, and without doubt his two dismissals proved to be the turning points of the game.

Winning this match comfortably has given us the impetus we need to continue in our pursuit of something no other Aussie team has done — victory in all six home Tests. The boys feel good about themselves and the unit continues to grow closer and tougher by the minute. Nothing seems too big an ask or issue to stop us.

It's certainly been a pleasure captaining the Australian side this summer — we have matured greatly as a unit and as individuals to a point where our aims and objectives are all being funnelled in the same direction. Our goal for the season is to win or at least draw every Test, but importantly to also not get too far ahead of ourselves. To achieve this we have team meetings where there is input from all the players on how we are going to approach the match. This involves pinpointing the strengths and weaknesses of opposition players, looking at our own game and seeing what we can improve on, and what things we can continue to do well. An overall strategy is put into place and with the commitment of all the players it will guarantee that we are going to be very tough to beat.

This latest Test victory in Adelaide was further confirmation of our self-belief and faith in each other. To be 4-52 on a flat pitch may have led to an element of panic, but in all honesty there was an air of calmness and assuredness about where we were heading and what needed to be done. This feeling is something that comes through trust, hard work and camaraderie.

One innings played during the Adelaide Test didn't receive a lot of kudos, but *was* very important. Greg Blewett's second-innings 88 from 262 balls was vital to our team, but much more than that, it showed that you can play ugly and still get runs. This may sound strange, but to a guy who is normally fluent and aesthetically pleasing to the spectators, it goes against the grain to struggle and look awkward. For him to not only survive a period like this and to then go on and make runs is a major breakthrough for it shows his game is maturing and evolving.

This is what we want everyone to aspire to, and what the team needs to do in order to stay at the top and one step ahead of everyone else.

December 25 MELBOURNE

MY FIRST TEST WAS a Boxing Day Test, back in 1985 … against India! Apart from a nervous first Test innings, this also represented my first Christmas in Melbourne, away from the usual backyard festivities, instead celebrating with my new teammates in a Melbourne hotel. Now, here I am, enjoying another Christmas Day in Melbourne with my family, the members of the Australian squad and the families of my comrades. The only party of this kind I've missed in all those years was in 1991, when I was out of the Test XI. That season Australia was playing … India!

We go into this Boxing Day Test on a roll, aiming for our sixth consecutive Test victory. However, we are aware that the heavy weight of cricket history suggests that this will be

PLAYER FEEDBACK SHEET		
PLAYER: S. Waugh		
MATCH: First Test v India, Adelaide, 10–14 December 1999		
Items	**First Innings**	**Second Innings**
Match Results	Batting: 150 from 323 balls Bowling: - Fielding: two catches	Batting: 5 from 23 balls Bowling: - Fielding: one catch
Match Statistics	BATTING No. of balls: 323 % ones: 15% % fours: 5% % scoring shots: 25% Partnerships: 1x200, 1x100 FIELDING: No. of touches: 38 % misfield: 3% No. of throws: 19 % good throws: 100%	BATTING No. of balls: 23 % ones: 9% % fours: — % scoring shots: 13% Partnerships: — FIELDING: No. of touches: 17 % misfield: — No. of throws: 1 % good throws: 100%
Feedback	Batting: Obviously, your innings here, then followed by the Shield 100 in Perth, places you in great shape for this Test. Fielding: Because you occupy key catching and throwing positions on the field, you need to maintain high skill levels (balanced with physical constraints). Would like to see you do more ring (approximately 20 to 30 metres in) work. Captaincy: Again, use of bowlers, field placings and approach excellent. May need to look at rotating the part-timers in to relieve frontliners (eg. Blewey, Junior, self).	
What key points will I work on?	Provided your preparation is good, then — as you say — the difference between 'great' and 'good' is concentration. That is your test this game.	

Mark Waugh (closest to camera) in the nets in Melbourne, searching for a return to his finest form.

extremely difficult. While there have been a number of occasions in the past when the Australian team has won five Tests straight, only once in the long history of the game has that run been extended to six. That happened back in 1920–21 when Warwick Armstrong's team went on to win eight in a row, all against England.

The Boxing Day Test match is a highlight of the cricket year for any Australian player lucky enough to be involved. Playing in front of a full house at the MCG is a great experience, and this year there are many drawcards, not least the prospect of Shane Warne breaking the great Dennis Lillee's Australian Test wicket-taking record on his home track. Against Sachin Tendulkar, too. The Victorian crowd will definitely spur him on, and I'd love to see him do it in front of his keenest supporters.

Much has been made of how bouncy the MCG pitch might be, and how much it is helping the pace bowlers these days. However, having inspected the Test wicket, I think there will be some turn. Warney and Anil Kumble could have key roles to play.

That we'll be in for some exciting cricket is a certainty. This is a Test match full of potentially thrilling confrontations, including the possibility that our new fast-bowling prospect, Brett Lee, will be making his Test debut. As I write, we haven't yet settled on our final XI. Letting the new boy loose on the Indian batting line-up is tempting — Brett is very quick, as quick as any paceman I have ever seen — but to do so would mean Michael Kasprowicz being extremely unlucky to be left out. As captain, I'm just grateful to have such talent available.

From a personal point of view, I'm eagerly looking forward to the days ahead. I made a hundred in NSW's second innings of our just-completed Pura Milk Cup game against Western Australia in Perth, and am striking the ball very sweetly in the nets. My brother, in

Sachin Tendulkar denied that the Indian camp had complained about the Australian umpires. The Indian press had been scathing about the officiating, especially the decisions that cost Tendulkar his wicket in each innings in Adelaide. Indian newspapers had also carried reports questioning the legitimacy of the bowling action of Australia's latest fast bowling sensation Brett Lee.

Australian captain Steve Waugh marked his first appearance for NSW in 1999–2000 with an innings of 128 against Western Australia in Perth.

The four-day tour match between the Indians and Tasmania in Hobart ended in a draw.

The Australian selectors retained Mark Waugh and recalled Brett Lee for the second Test against India, at the MCG, beginning on Boxing Day.

Another Christmas Day in Melbourne, my 14th in 15 summers. I hope I'll see many more!

contrast, is under a bit of pressure, but every time an Australian batsman has been under scrutiny this summer he has responded with a big innings. So it wouldn't surprise me at all if Mark responds with a magic hundred. Then he can go on to play his 100th Test match in Sydney, an event the entire Waugh clan is looking forward to.

December 26   MELBOURNE

'Boxing Day Test, let's punch these guys senseless.
The scars are there to be opened but only WE can decide their
   usefulness.
Let's be focused on the process before we get carried away
   with the outcome,
Concentrate on specific plans and the runs and wickets will
   come.
Enjoy the occasion, only 12 Aussies do it every year,
Put festivities out of our mind and remember why we're here.
As Albert Camus, a great philosopher was heard to say,
"Do not wait for the final judgement, It takes place every day." '

— **Dave Misson** (read before day one, second Test v India, December 26)

ONE OF THE MOST awkward situations a batsman can find himself in is the one where, because of inclement weather, you're continually on and off the field. Not only do you have to start over again each time, by switching on and getting a feel for the conditions, but every time you go back on the bowlers are fresh, and your opponents have regrouped and been able to assess and revise their tactics.

As well, the light is inevitably poor, and the wicket has been 'juiced' up by the moisture in the air and on the wicket.

Thus, you can see why we were ecstatic to lose only three wickets on the first day of the second Test, thanks largely to the efforts of Michael Slater and Mark Waugh. The first session was abandoned because of the rain, before it was finally decided play would start at 2pm. From there, for the rest of the day, it seemed play might be about to stop. Adding merit to the performance of our two batsmen was the fact that Mark was under pressure because of the media speculation that his spot in the side is in danger, and that Slats' natural instincts are to attack rather than defend. It was a real tough scrap out there, particularly in the last session. That these guys survived represents a real triumph for the team, and I know India are aware that they have let a huge opportunity slip by. Now, with the prospect of a bright sunny day tomorrow and with only three wickets down, we have a feeling we have definitely won the first battle of this Test match.

December 27 MELBOURNE

THE DELUGE THAT ENDED PLAY this afternoon, was something I have never seen in Melbourne before. Brisbane maybe, or perhaps Colombo or Kandy, but not here. For a while, it was almost impossible to see across to the other side of the ground, such was the intensity of the storm.

Even with the batting of Slater, Gilchrist and Ponting and the bowling of Prasad, the weather has been just about the major story of the Test match so far. We can only hope that the meteorologists' forecasts for more rain are misguided. With better weather and the memory of last season's thrilling Test match, when England won by 12 runs late on day

Michael Slater gets one down to fine leg on the rain-interrupted first day of the second Test. He may not look in total control here, but this innings was actually one of his most important of the season.

Australia finished the first day of the second Test against India, at the MCG, at 3-138 after play did not begin because of rain until 2pm and was then curtailed by bad light at 5.46pm. Michael Slater was unbeaten on 64, Steve Waugh on 5. Mark Waugh, whose place in the Australian XI was questioned before the match, made 41.

In a day restricted to 45 overs, Australia's first innings moved on to 5-332. Michael Slater was out for 91, Steve Waugh for 32, Ricky Ponting was undefeated on 59, Adam Gilchrist on 77. After play, Indian bowler Venkatesh Prasad was fined 35 per cent of his match fee and given a suspended suspension for an over-exuberant celebration after dismissing Slater.

Australia went on to 405 on the third day of the second Test. Gilchrist was out for 78, Ponting for 67, but Damien Fleming made 31 not out and Brett Lee hit 27 in his debut Test innings. Lee then made an immediate impact with the ball, taking five wickets (including Sadagopan Ramesh with his fourth delivery in Test cricket) as India fell to 9-212 before reaching 9-235 by stumps. Sachin Tendulkar, with a stirring 118, was their one significant run-scorer.

The scene outside our dressing room after rain had flooded the MCG during the second Test. Beyond the puddles you can see fitness advisor Dave Misson on his way back to our rooms, and you can also see, on the wall behind the fans who are trying to keep their feet dry, posters featuring the captains of the six Australian state teams. My poster, as captain of New South Wales, is second from right, to the right of Tasmania's Jamie Cox.

four after the first day was lost completely, still strong, we remain confident that we can force a historic sixth straight Test win.

There is no doubt that batting was easier first thing this morning than it had been in the last half hour on day one. Thus, both Michael Slater and I were disappointed we didn't capitalise as a long innings was there to be enjoyed. Fortunately, Ricky Ponting and Adam Gilchrist stepped up, scoring rapidly and putting us in a position where we can definitely still win, despite the first two days' rain.

December 29 MELBOURNE

WHILE ONE-DAY CRICKET readily accepts and even expects batting orders to be flexible, and one-day captains are expected to be proactive rather than reactive, tradition dictates that in most cases Test matches should be allowed to run their course. It has always intrigued me as to why this is so, but it was nevertheless with some trepidation that I promoted the in-form Adam Gilchrist to No. 4 in our second innings. The logic was simple enough: we needed quick runs so we could declare and attempt to bowl India out in this match that had been shortened by rain, and as Gilly has demonstrated in the one-day game time and again, when it comes to scoring rapidly he's as good as it gets. I knew deep down that this was the right move, but such is the high regard we all hold Test cricket in that I nearly changed my mind for fear of reprisals later if the move backfired. However, my mind drifted back to our team goals and plans — to play positively and to back ourselves at all times. It then became a simple decision and proved to be a successful one, as Gilly hit 55 off just 73 balls.

Despite Tendulkar's superb century yesterday, we still won a first-innings lead of 167, which thanks to Gilly's efforts (and Mark Waugh, who made 51 not out) today we were able to turn into a lead of 376 before I declared in the final session. By stumps, India had crawled to 1-40. With a full day's play, and Warney on song, I think we will win.

December 30 MELBOURNE

I'LL TAKE TWO IMAGES of their battles here in Melbourne away with me. First, there was the astonishing six over 'straightish' long-off that Sachin hit in the first innings, during his superb hundred, which came after a long spell in which Shane has kept him pinned down, watchful and defensive. And then there was the brilliant top-spinner Shane produced from his bag of tricks today. It dipped in towards the stumps, Sachin misread the line and was gone, lbw. From the moment the umpire's finger went up, we were going to win the Test. The last six Indian wickets, of which Tendulkar was the first, fell for 62 runs in 27.3 overs.

When two great champions clash it's pure sporting nirvana for all involved — teammates, opponents, spectators, media, everyone. In India's second innings, Sachin was looking very ominous, as he settled into a groove, playing conservatively while punishing anything slightly off line or too short or too full. At the same time, Shane was desperate to take his

Glenn McGrath attacks Sachin Tendulkar during the Indian maestro's impressive century at the MCG. The clash between Tendulkar and our star-studded bowling attack was one of the standout features of the first two Tests.

India added only three runs to its overnight total (Lee 5-47), to which Australia responded with 5 (declared) for 208, of which Adam Gilchrist, promoted to No. 4, made 55 and Mark Waugh managed 51 not out. At the close, India, needing an improbable 376 to win, were 1-40 after 21 overs.

Australia won the second Test by 180 runs soon after tea on the fifth day, despite a defiant 52 by Sachin Tendulkar, which lasted nearly three hours until Shane Warne trapped him lbw. Tendulkar was later named man of the match. Strangely, the only Australian bowler not to take a wicket was the usual spearhead, Glenn McGrath, while 'part-timers' Greg Blewett and Mark Waugh took three wickets between them for just 29 runs.

Pakistani pace bowler Shoaib Akhtar was banned from international cricket by the ICC over his bowling action, but has vowed to return. The decision has ruled Shoaib out of the upcoming World Series. 'They've just told me to re-model my action, but I can't say anything more because I'll be in trouble,' the fast bowler told reporters in Perth, not long after the Pakistan team arrived back in Australia for the one-day tournament.

wicket. Though Shane had dismissed Tendulkar once in Adelaide, he still believes there is more to be done to counter the ledger, which was balanced in the Indian captain's favour after our 1998 tour to India. It was a watchful Tendulkar facing Warne, a strategy similar to the one he'd been employing against Glenn McGrath.

Tendulkar was clearly intent on attacking our other bowlers and taking as few risks as possible against our two champions. To dismiss him, we needed something special and Shane produced it, as he so often does.

It's only very rarely that you get to see or play with a guy who bursts on the scene and grabs all the attention, as Shane did when he first emerged on the cricket scene. Just like Shane Warne, Brett Lee is much more than just a passing fad. He's a once-in-a-generation player, enormously gifted, with class and flair, the ability to ignite the imagination of all spectators, and such an impact player that he'll quickly be changing the way kids want to play the game. Warney turned leg-spinning into a highly fashionable art, with potential young champions taking it up in their thousands. I reckon 'Binger' will do the same for pace bowling. They both have an aura and presence about them, we in Australian cricket are so lucky to see them both play at the same time.

Brett has lightning speed, an athletic build and a good cricket brain, but he's also down-to-earth, has a hunger for success and what all great bowlers need – a ruthless streak. The only two things that can stop him are one, injury, and two, if he's unable to keep his feet firmly on the ground. That second danger won't be easy to repel, because he could, in time, turn into his own industry, but so long as he surrounds himself with good people and retains the humility and level head he has now, he'll be fine.

It was no surprise at all for me to see him tear into the Indians, claiming seven wickets for the match, including a 5-47 in his first innings as a Test bowler, on a day when the great Tendulkar was in magnificent form. Some people said Brett was being pushed forward before his time because he was from NSW, but my answer to that is you only judge people on what you see and not where they come from. As soon as I saw him in our recent Shield game in Perth — the first time I'd played with him — I knew he was special. The WACA boys not only looked out of their depth facing him, they seemed genuinely fearful for their safety.

Above and below: Tendulkar is lbw, not offering a shot to a Shane Warne top-spinner, on the final day of the Melbourne Test.

Two images of Brett Lee from the Melbourne Test. Left: In the dressing room after his debut Test, with a piece of the centre wicket, a stump and the ball with which he took that maiden five-for. In the background is Adam Gilchrist, icing his knees after another day of constant squatting behind the stumps.

Below: His press conference after taking five wickets on his Test debut. This is the normal occurrence after each day's play — the captains appear on most days, definitely after the first and final days and sometimes in between, while notable performers are also asked to step forward. This conference was held in the players' dining room. Usually, you'll face around 20 to 30 print journalists, as well as four or five TV cameras, and the process will take around 20 minutes to half an hour.

Pakistan team manager Brigadier Mohammad Nasir suggested that Shoaib would be allowed to stay in Australia for a few days. 'We want to see him at practice,' he said. 'As I understand the objections that have been raised, they are not serious. He has to remove these minor things. He'll be alright.'

December 31 SYDNEY

AS CAPTAIN, I'M FINDING myself on a constant learning curve. But if there is one piece of advice I'll be passing on to the 41st captain of Australia it will be to listen to those around you, but follow your gut instincts.

It was with this philosophy in mind that I threw the ball to Greg Blewett yesterday, just before lunch. Sourav Ganguly, an excellent player, was on strike, but something told me that Blewey's 'slippery' action might catch Ganguly off guard. I thought Blewey was a chance because he has a good change of pace and also has the ability to slide one away from the left-hander's bat, which might lead to a catch in the slip cordon.

It's great when a plan comes off and this is exactly what Blewey accomplished here in Melbourne, taking down Ganguly in identical circumstances in both innings. On other occasions, luck as well as intuition play a part in our success. Later in the day, I was working on trying to get a couple of quick overs in before tea, so we'd be able to take the new ball as quickly as possible after the break. To do this, I threw the 'cherry' to Mark Waugh, who isn't the most eager of bowlers at the best of times. He gave me the usual 'you're kidding' look and then proceeded to jag two important wickets with successive balls, which virtually guaranteed us the win.

January 1 SYDNEY

I BELIEVE THAT WINNING people surround themselves with inspirational, infectious types who are always positive and proactive. Consequently, from the start of this Australian summer I began inviting various guests to our pre-game dinners, to help us prepare for the battle ahead.

The search for our first guest, for the Gabba Test against Pakistan back in early November, wasn't that difficult. For in Brisbane town was a man with two US Open tennis championships to his credit, as well as a character full of admirable traits and qualities. It was as simple as a couple of phone calls being made and along came Pat Rafter to a small eatery on the fringe of the CBD. Not all our players were aware Pat was turning up, so his arrival caused quite a reaction when he homed in on our table and introduced himself to the lads. Then, to make the most of his knowledge and wisdom, we rotated his seat during the evening so all the boys had some access first hand to his thoughts.

One of the most comforting things to come from meeting a professional sportsperson from a different field is to learn that they sacrifice many of the same things we cricketers do in order to be successful. Time away from family, loss of privacy, overcoming injury and long hours 'on the job' seem to be common minuses in both top-level cricket and tennis, but overall the benefits certainly outweigh the negatives. Pat did, however, have a bit of a laugh when he discovered that we have to pay for our team dinners — the Davis Cup boys don't even consider reaching into their pockets while on tour. Still, if this is the biggest worry we've got we're doing okay!

The second Test of the summer, in Hobart, coincided with many of Sir Donald Bradman's 1948 Invincibles being in town. I saw a golden opportunity to pick their brains and to give the lads another first-hand feel of what tradition means to the game, so I invited along four members of that legendary team — Bill Brown, Doug Ring, Bill Johnston and Arthur Morris — who had made the trip south.

When we arrived at the Italian restaurant in North Hobart that had been recommended to us, our group split into three tables. Bill Brown, as usual, had the boys mesmerised with tales of the great Bradman and, as usual, played down his own ability by saying his only shot was the leg glance. I dare say he was a trifle better than that, as he averaged nearly 47 in Test cricket and hit a double century in a Test at Lord's in 1938. The table I was seated at featured the modern-thinking Doug Ring, a somewhat lesser-known member of Bradman's team but one of The Don's close friends and confidants. Doug's affection and admiration for Bradman remains immeasurable — in his view, Bradman was way ahead of his time in terms of his attitude to the game and his skill. Arthur Morris was also on our table, and I considered myself very fortunate to be in his presence. Arthur is incapable of saying a bad word about anyone; all we heard was praise for others and positive comments about any issue that was brought up. Sitting right next to him was Justin Langer, and I couldn't help thinking, as I reflected on Lang's stunning century in the Test that was played out in the days following that dinner, whether Arthur's words and inspiration might have been the catalyst for Lang's heroic deeds.

Over on our third table, the highly acclaimed left-arm bowler, Bill Johnston, kept our current-day quicks captivated from the calamari entrée through the lasagne main and on to dessert, discussing technique, touring and what tomorrow might hold. Overall, the night was a huge success and something I'd love to replicate each year. These champions played in an era where money wasn't an issue and their love of the game was the one and only motive for playing; for that reason alone we surely can only benefit from listening to their words and wisdom.

One of the highlights of the 1999–2000 season was having four members of the 1948 Invincibles join our team dinner in Hobart. This dinner normally takes place two days before a Test match, while on the evening before a match individuals are left to their own devices to decide how they want to prepare. Some like to relax, some go to the movies, some go to restaurants, but 48 hours out we get together. At right, you can see the leg-spinner, Doug Ring, on the right-hand side between Justin Langer (third from right) and Ricky Ponting (see also the photo below left). The great opener, Arthur Morris, is to Lang's right in the top right and middle photographs. In the bottom right photograph is the left-hand bowler, Bill Johnston, pictured here with Damien Fleming (centre) and Scott Muller. The fourth member of the '48 side at this dinner was Bill Brown.

The Trumper Caps

When I first came into the Australian cricket team back in late 1985 the side had just lost the great trio of Dennis Lillee, Rod Marsh and Greg Chappell. To compound this loss, more than a team of top players had defected to a rebel squad that toured South Africa. As a result of all this upheaval, the Australian team that remained was disjointed, and lacked experience and cohesion. The traditions of the past, along with the 'culture' of being an Australian player, had become less clear to those in the side, primarily because everyone was simply trying to survive.

Starting my career in such an environment wasn't easy. However, because of this tough beginning, I vowed that that if ever I became a senior player I would do everything in my power to make sure that the Australian team would again respect the game's history and uphold Aussie cricket's great traditions. As well, I hoped, we'd be able to create some of our own culture.

As part of this process, I arranged for Bill Brown to present Adam Gilchrist and Scott Muller with their baggy green caps after warm-ups on the first morning of the Brisbane Test. Bill appeared genuinely touched to be given this chance and his two-minute speech had the boys so proud and pumped up that everyone was sporting goosebumps by the time he finished.

'It is an honour to represent your country,' Bill told us, 'something that should never be taken for granted. The new boys have joined an elite club, which they have every right to be proud of, because I'm sure they have worked hard and deserve their selection.'

Later, the richly talented Brett Lee was presented with his cap by two former Aussie Test-match cricketers in Colin McDonald and Ian Meckiff. I was particularly pleased that Meckiff had this opportunity, as his career had been terminated by an infamous 'no-ball' chucking call in 1963. It seems to me that in today's game some of the superstars make Meckiff's action appear smooth and rhythmical, so it was satisfying to see him kick-start a quick bowler on his road to stardom.

The Australian team in front of the SCG Members Stand before the start of the third day's play. Left to right: S. Waugh, Warne, McGrath, Kasprowicz, Gilchrist, B. Lee, M. Waugh, Fleming, Blewett, Slater, Ponting, Langer.

This photograph was taken by Michael Kasprowicz, who is as thoughtful and considerate a teammate as I've had. Knowing that I like my photos and have a sense of history, he took my camera out of my bag and, when I came back from the toss, he met me at the gate to take a photo to mark the occasion.

In recent times, the numbering of our one-day caps and the fact that we as one always wear our baggy greens in the first session of a Test are very significant to us. Such gestures unify us as a team and make everyone realise that it's always a special occasion when you represent your country. To further drive this fact home, I decided that the start of a new millennium was a prime opportunity to link the current team with the past. The question was 'how?' Racking my brain, I was struggling for an answer until I thought of my favourite cricket photo – that famous shot of a classic Victor Trumper cover drive. But at this moment, it wasn't the exquisite artistry or beauty of the stroke that got me, but the 'skull cap' on his head that ignited my imagination. It is a very different cap from our current-day baggy green, but in many ways it is just as magnificent and has a definite aura.

On the same day as this idea struck me, I ran into cricket author and keen cricket historian, Gideon Haigh, in the lift of our hotel. I wanted to know more about the cap that Trumper and his teammates had worn in the first Test of the 1900s. My hope was that we'd be able to duplicate it for the first Test of 2000, so I asked Gideon to help me track down the history of the cap.

A short time later, with the necessary documents in place, I went to the chairman of the Australian Cricket Board, Denis Rogers, with the concept. Fortunately, he was also excited about the idea and when it was presented to the Board they happily approved it. Some more good work was done by the marketing arm of the ACB, so that by the final team meeting before the third Test against India, in Sydney, the first Test of 2000, I told the lads I had a bit of a surprise for them.

I must admit I was a little apprehensive, because as soon as I saw the new caps for myself I realised that anyone with a head above average proportions was bound to look like Herman Munster when wearing one. But thankfully the boys were rapt and excited about the caps, which are made of velvet, and are a slightly darker colour than our normal ones. Justin Langer, for one, was so captivated by the headwear that when he approached his Test century today he discarded his helmet so that he could reach triple figures wearing his newly beloved cap … and get a unique photograph to mark the occasion.

I've seen the team photo for this Test and it's a beauty. Sure, it's one we'll chuckle at a little in years to come, but another 100 years on, I wonder whether the Aussie captain might say to this troops, 'Let's wear the same caps worn by Joe Darling's 1901–02 side and Steve Waugh's 1999–2000 team.'

I hope they do.

The task of locating invitees for our pre-Test team dinner in Perth fell to local boy Justin Langer. For those who know Lang, it was no surprise that his choices were a little from left field, in that he opted for three identities who encompass three different sports and three different age groups. Mingled among the boys were the long-serving Hockeyroo star, two-time Olympic gold medallist and frequent captain, Rechelle Hawkes, aspiring Olympic swimmer Rachael Harris and the former Australian cricket captain Kim Hughes. Each one of these people gave us an insight into their sport and the era they play or, in Kim's case, played in, which gave the lads a more rounded view of professional sport and what is needed to achieve your ambitions.

The Adelaide Test saw us look to the legendary Barry 'Nugget' Rees to lift us once again. Here is a man who is loved, admired and respected by more people than anyone else I know. Nugget is a stalwart of the Adelaide Oval, having progressed from the somewhat menial role of room attendant to the heights of team motivator. Nowadays, he is often to be seen issuing instructions from atop of the home team's dressing-room table before the start of each day's play. A nicer gentleman you will never meet, to be in his company inevitably makes you a better person.

Warney took on the duty of identifying our guests of honour before the Melbourne Test, which took the form of a high-class barbecue at his home. Here we socialised with the hugely popular sportsmen-turned-media personalities, Rex Hunt and Sam Newman, who certainly gave us a different slant on proceedings. Then, last night in Sydney, we let the city take over, as our team dinner was held last night, on New Year's Eve, in full view of my hometown's famous Harbour. Our inspiration was simply the colourful way the new millennium's arrival was celebrated. The challenge for us is to welcome the new century in similarly spectacular style, with another big Test-match win over the Indians …

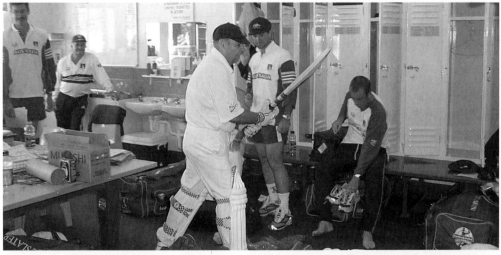

The legendary 'Nugget' Rees, the world famous room attendant from Adelaide, prepares for another successful innings. Nugget, as much a part of the Australian side as any other member, gives motivational speeches before games, runs errands during the match, and is the most courteous and polite guy you'll ever meet. When we won our Test in Adelaide against India early on the fifth day we invited Nugget to go out onto the ground for a bat, as he loves to do, and he peeled off a century. The baggy green Nugget is wearing was given to him years ago by the great Norman O'Neill, and is his most treasured possession.

Steve Waugh revealed that to mark the new millennium his Australian team would wear 1900-style skull caps during the third Test against India.

The first Test of 2000, the third of this series and Mark Waugh's 100th Test, was hampered on its opening day by rain, which kept the players off the SCG between 12.32pm and 3.08pm. There was time for 60 overs and in that time, India crashed to 8-121, with Tendulkar making 45 and Lee taking four more wickets to go with the seven he took in Melbourne ... Alan Davidson, President of CricketNSW, released the names of the 'Blues Living Legends XII', selected from all living players who have represented NSW. The team (in batting order) is: Arthur Morris, Bob Simpson, Sir Donald Bradman (captain), Neil Harvey, Allan Border, Steve Waugh, Keith Miller, Richie Benaud, Alan Davidson, Brian Taber, Glenn McGrath, Norman O'Neill (12th man) ... Australia A defeated the Pakistanis by 52 runs in a 50-over day/night match at the WACA. Matthew Hayden scored 128 for Australia A, and Shane Lee took 4-32. Saqlain Mushtaq took 5-40 and Azhar Mahmood hit an unbeaten 100 for the tourists.

January 2 SYDNEY

'There's no greater force on earth than your own personal will. So if you want to do something, anything, with all your will, find a way. If you don't, you'll find an excuse.'
— **Pat Farmer** (presented during day one, third Test v India, January 2)

'In battle, a courageous spirit is everything. Now the first roll of the drum tends to create spirit, but with the second it is already on the wane and after the third it is gone altogether. I attacked when their spirit was gone and ours was at its height.'
— **Sun Tzu** (presented by John Buchanan before day one, third Test v India, January 2. Sun-Tzu was one of China's greatest military strategists. His classic work, Ping-fa [The Art of War] was reputedly written around the 4th century BC.)

TO PLAY IN 100 TESTS not only proves that a cricketer has the skill to play the game, but is also an indication that that cricketer possesses the necessary mental toughness, physical durability and capacity to overcome adversity that are all essential if you want to succeed regularly at the highest level. It also reflects the cricketer's love for the game and that he has been prepared to accept that it's not always going to be a smooth ride.

Mark Waugh has deserved all the accolades that go with representing your country in 100 Test matches, a landmark he brought up today. However, in the back of his mind he must have been wondering whether or not it was going to be his last, considering the amount of negative press his perceived lack of form had attracted. It was a great thrill to let Mark lead the team onto the field in our skull caps for the first time. For Mark it was a moment in time that he richly deserved and one that can never be taken away.

During our many titanic struggles in the backyard, and for that matter frontyard and driveway, Mark and I never imagined that we'd play for Australia ... let alone achieve the feat of each playing 100 Test matches. That we've both had the chance to celebrate our century of Tests in front of our family and friends at the Sydney Cricket Ground (Mark this year, me two years ago against South Africa) must be a sign that fate is looking after the boys from Picnic Point Road, Panania, in a big way.

Many of our traits, skills and mannerisms were forged

during those years growing up as sports-mad kids from 'fibroland'. The fact that Mark is such a strong onside player may stem from the fact that our frontyard had a slope from the offside to the legside many times more severe than the Lord's outfield. Naturally, I'd be inadvertently bowling massive off cutters, which would be shipped across the line towards the front entrance of the house, usually ending up in Mum's pride and joy … the flowering 'Bird of Paradise'. It was here, too, that many heated arguments began. Occasionally, on the full into this area was out, but a recognition of this rule from the batsman would rarely be forthcoming and eventually a deal was struck that in order to stay in, the ball had to be retrieved from this spider-riddled obstacle. Bouncers were common and nasty in their intent, which, when coupled with the fact that quite often the ball would be taped with electrical tape to make it swing, meant it was a wise move not to get cleaned up.

This piece of bowling armoury was dangerous on our driveway pitch. It featured a steep incline, which favoured the bowler, and with a garage door and thick foliage surrounding the batsman there was no escape for the faint-hearted. This piece of bitumen almost ended Mark's hopes of any sporting future one sunny summer's day in the mid '70s. We'd have been around 10 years old, and didn't have the luxury of bikes, instead making do with a couple of sleek, streamlined scooters, with all the flashy accessories — stickers, bells and streamers off the handle bars.

Being very competitive at an early age meant everything turned into a contest. Scooter races down the driveway were notoriously dangerous, with a slick downhill start followed by a sweeping left-hand turn that had to be negotiated in order to miss that garage door. On this fateful day, the Waugh twins lined up, each with the head down, one foot on the ground and ready to be the victor. It was dead even as we flew down the first half of the course, but as we began to prepare for the dangerous left hander, it was obvious only one of us would be able to make it through safely. Being the oldest by four minutes and having the inside line I thought it may as well be me. It was then my right leg decided the outcome of this tussle when I clipped Mark's scooter just enough for him to lose his balance and dignity, sending him crashing to the ground while I carried on to collect the victory. My last recollection of the incident was seeing Mark tumble into the garage door, accompanied by a few loud screams and a flood of tears. For me, it was a proud moment!

We shared the same room, clothes and toys until we reached our senior years at school, when it became time for our greatest confrontation. We safely gained our driver's licences and though Mum and Dad were generous enough to let us both drive the family's white Ford stationwagon it did lead to one major problem. Who was going to pay for the petrol? We were earning around $30 a week each from indoor cricket umpiring, which meant we weren't exactly rolling in it. Mum suggested we take turns putting petrol in, but she didn't say how much. With a somewhat faulty petrol gauge it was pure folly to hop into the driver's seat and expect to not run out of petrol at some stage. The most obvious reason for this was the tank was only getting two dollars worth at a time and whoever put in the petrol made sure they got their value by driving the car until it was on the verge of running empty. It was a common sight to see us arguing as to who was going to get the jerry can filled up at the nearest servo and bring it back to the stricken vehicle.

But we survived these battles, and I also overcame the embarrassment of seeing Mark

Above: Mark Waugh in Ansett's Melbourne Golden Wing Lounge, answering more questions about his place in the national side. Each season, it's only a matter of time before someone comes under the scrutiny of the media in this way. Mark seemed to be under pressure for much of the summer, but I thought he came through it reasonably well and certainly did enough in tough situations to continue to justify his place in the side.

Right: Mark after taking the second of his two wickets in successive balls on the final day in Melbourne.

not being able to get back over the boundary fence at Waverley Oval in Sydney after retrieving a ball that had been hit for six during an under-16 game. And the time he pushed the sightscreen off its hinges at Rushcutters Bay Oval during an early game in first grade. Actually, all this does make you wonder how he got to line up for Test No. 100 this week!

As a player, Mark has the rare ability of being able to turn a match with his batting and fielding, and occasionally with the ball as well. Such gifts are priceless with our overall team structure. Mark has a good cricket brain and a simple but very logical outlook on his game and strategies. An excellent example of this came during a team meeting before a confrontation with the West Indies. 'Their strength is also their weakness,' he exclaimed. 'If we can get used to their pace and hostility, they haven't got any variation to get you out!'

He often suffers from observers thinking he gives his wicket away too easily, but in reality he values his time in the middle as highly as anyone else. It's just that his style lends itself to these criticisms, as he is an elegant and graceful player, and 'elegant' and 'graceful' are two adjectives that can easily get mixed up with 'lazy' and 'carefree'. Australia is lucky to have him and we should be very thankful I didn't kick him so hard that his head went through that garage door!

A proud moment. Going out for the toss with Sachin Tendulkar at the MCG. This was my first Test as Australian captain in Melbourne.

Above: These days, because of Test and one-day commitments, I rarely get the chance to don the NSW blue cap. My only Shield game in 1999–2000 was at the WACA between the first and second Tests against India, but it developed into one of the best wins I've been involved in for a long time. Beating WA on their turf is never easy. It was also the first time I played in a Pura Milk game with Brett Lee (at the bottom of this photograph, holding the competition sponsor's product), which was a very exciting experience. Brett had the WACAs on the back foot, taking eight wickets for the match as we completed a 115-run victory. Our win probably put the West Australians out of contention to win the competition, but sadly this was the Blues' only success of the season.

Below: A rain-soaked MCG during the Boxing Day Test. In a way, the time lost because of the lousy weather was a good thing for us, because it forced us to play positive cricket if we wanted to get a result out of the match.

Above and below: The brothers Waugh hit through the offside during the second Test against India.

Left: Brett Lee introduces himself to Test cricket with a dynamic five-wicket effort. I'm not sure the Indians knew what had hit them.

Below: Justin Langer, savouring a Test victory with his kids in the MCG dressing room. To the Langer clan's left is Michael Slater.

Left: The little champion, Sachin Tendulkar, at the SCG, playing as only he can.

Below: Sachin before the Sydney Test, framed by the ground's light towers and the focal point of the Indians' preparations.

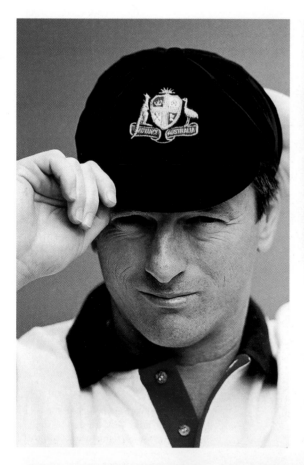

Our 'Victor Trumper' caps, as modelled by yours truly (left and below) and Michael Slater (above). Slats is wearing a very modern pair of sunglasses, designed to brighten gloomy conditions, which offers an interesting contrast to his 1900-style cap.

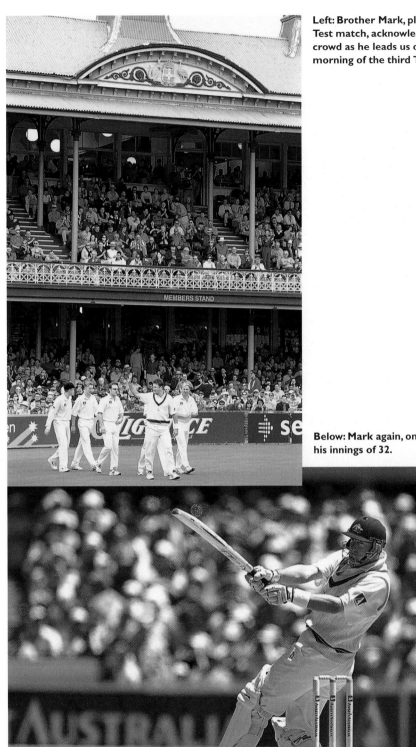

Left: Brother Mark, playing in his 100th Test match, acknowledges the Sydney crowd as he leads us out on the first morning of the third Test against India.

Below: Mark again, on day two, during his innings of 32.

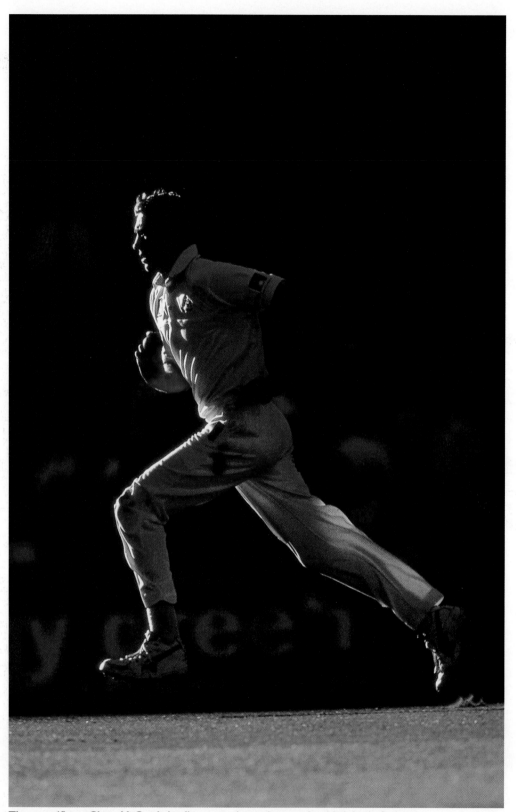

The magnificent Glenn McGrath, leading us to victory late on the third day in Sydney.

January 3 SYDNEY

SO OFTEN IN OUR recent past we have seen Warney not only win Test matches for us but also grab most of the headlines. During this series against India, however, our quicks — Glenn McGrath, Damien Fleming and Brett Lee — have really put their hands up. They have applied unrelenting pressure through their quality bowling, following the game plans for each of the Indian batsmen exactly and working superbly as a unit. Yesterday's effort, restricting the Indians to 8-121 on a day abbreviated by rain, was a classic example. McGrath finished with three wickets and Lee four, and although Flem went wicketless he still managed to bowl 13 overs for just 24 runs and ensured that the pressure was never relaxed for an instant. In fact, it was somewhat strange to see Flem miss out today, because to this point he has taken 29 Test wickets this Australian season. By comparison, Pigeon had gone into this Sydney Test with 22 wickets for the summer, and Warney had 20.

In the same way that the batsmen have meetings, so do the bowlers get together to share information and strategies. In this way, they are always pulling in the same direction and the opposition batsmen feel under constant threat. The remarkable consistency of McGrath, combined with the raw pace of Lee and swing and guile of Fleming have proved to be a combination capable of winning us matches just between the three of them.

When play resumed today, Pigeon snapped up the final two wickets, to give him another Test five-for. And then our batsmen, or more specifically, Justin Langer, went to work …

I'm a firm believer in the adage, 'there is no such thing as luck'. Rather, you create your own destiny by stamping your authority on the situation you find yourself in. However, being bowled on a no-ball is the closest thing you'll ever get to being lucky as a batsman. Fortunately for Lang and Australia he had the good fortune of seeing his bails dislodged by

Pat Farmer, who came into our dressing room during the Sydney Test, is a champion who never gives up. This was a motto we all, particularly Justin Langer, adopted during the match.

By the close of play on day two of the third Test, Australia had moved into a close to invincible position. Justin Langer, with his third century of the summer and with strong support from Mark and Steve Waugh and later Ricky Ponting, steered the Australians' total to 4-331 at stumps, after India had added 29 runs to their first innings total when play resumed. Earlier, Glenn McGrath had taken the final two Indian wickets, to give him 5-48 for the innings … Pakistan Cricket Board secretary Shafqat Rana, in response to questions about Shoaib Akhtar's banning, suggested other players were escaping similar scrutiny. 'It's only against the Asian cricketers … why not against the others?' Rana said in a radio interview. 'Why not go against Brett Lee when he bowls the faster one? Why Pakistanis, why Indians?'

Javagal Srinath just as Darrell Hair's arm was outstretched to signal the bowler's indiscretion. Lang was not long past his 50 at the time.

It was as if Lang had been cleared of a crime while he'd been sitting nervously on death row. He began to play without inhibition, using freedom and aggression as his guides. His first 50 had been a real scratchy affair, featuring inside edges, mistimed drives and plenty of playing and missing. But these events quite often signal that a big innings is on the way because it forces you to concentrate harder, apply yourself and dig in, whereas sometimes when you're going along in overdrive, smashing everything into the gaps, you become complacent and liable to play a careless stroke. Lang's biggest assets are his determination and great powers of concentration and he certainly made the Indians pay, demoralising them with a marathon innings.

The moment I'll most remember about Lang's innings was something that demonstrated his undying love for the baggy green. It came when he reached 96. Instead of wanting to celebrate with his helmet on, he called for his skull cap. It was a bold gesture, for I would never tempt fate in the 90s, but it was also a sign of his love for Australia and the increasing confidence he now has in his game.

Yesterday, as the rain continued to fall and we were confined to our dressing room, we had a very welcome visitor in the shape of ultra-marathon runner Pat Farmer. Pat said a few well-chosen words to the lads, which I know had an impact on me, but were especially important to Justin Langer. As I looked over Lang's shoulder tonight, while he was writing his latest entry for his Internet diary, I saw what he wrote about Pat's visit and thought I couldn't have put it any better myself. This is what Lang wrote:

As the rain was falling during the afternoon Pat Farmer, Australia's truly inspirational ultra, ultra long-distance runner, visited the changing room. Having seen him on This is Your Life *I was ecstatic to have had a chance to meet the man face to face. What a fantastic bloke and Australian he is. Among other things his message was that you can achieve whatever you set out to achieve by giving it your all and never giving up on your dream. He also shared with us that he gets through his immensely long runs by always picturing the finishing line in his mind. By seeing the finishing line, it helps him get through every tough moment along the way*

Lang made sure he was wearing his Trumper cap when he reached three figures at the SCG.

and you can be sure there would be plenty of those as he is running his two marathons per day.

His words of motivation helped me get through a few tough periods during my first century at the SCG. There were times early on day two where I felt terrible with my bat in hand, but I kept telling myself to hang in there and if I did there would be a Test century for the taking. My finishing line was initially the hundred, but that turned into a bigger and more productive innings with the words of Pat Farmer ringing through my ears. Scoring a Test century is a marvellous feeling, especially when it goes a long way towards putting your team into a commanding position ...

The partnership between Lang and Punter has already reached 64, and our lead is nearing 200. The challenge now is to maintain our intensity for the remainder of this Test, because, though we find ourselves in a strong position, complacency must never become a factor. The Indian batting card remains one rich in talent, and I will never forget lessons learnt back at the start of my international career, when the Australian team was a long way from the top of the cricket tree. I remember, for example, my first Test at the SCG, against India in 1985–86, when we spent the final day trying to avoid what would have been an

The Australians produced an extraordinary display to win the third Test of the series in three days, after taking an extra half hour to end the Indians' second innings. The winning margin was an innings and 141 runs. The victory gave the Aussies a second successive 3-0 series win, an unprecedented achievement in a single Australian summer. It was also their seventh Test-match victory in a row, one short of the Australian record held by Warwick Armstrong's Australian teams of 1920–21 and 1921. From their overnight total, Australia had gone on to 5-552 declared, with Justin Langer finishing on 223 and Ricky Ponting staying undefeated on 141. For both, it was their third Test century of the summer. Langer's score was the highest by an Australian against India, and he and Ponting added 190 for the fifth wicket. When India batted again, VVS Laxman played a heroic lone hand — eighth out for 167, from 198 balls, after opening the innings. Glenn McGrath took five more wickets, while Agit Agarkar was out for a second-ball duck, to go with the four first-ball noughts he'd suffered in his previous four Test innings ... Australia A defeated the Pakistanis by six wickets in a day/night 50-over match in Adelaide.

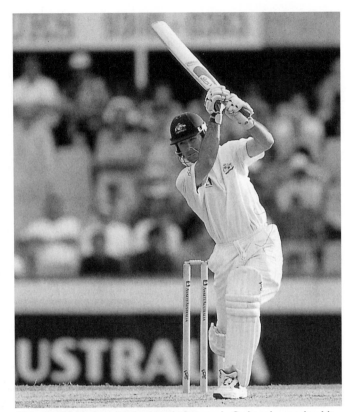

Ricky Ponting, who matched Justin Langer in Sydney by scoring his third Test-match century of the Australian summer.

embarrassing loss, after being forced to follow on. Admittedly, those days seem long ago, but they stay in the back of my mind. I want to enjoy *all* of the good times, so there is no way we'll be relaxing early.

Certainly, the Indians have seemed dispirited at times during this match. Touring is always hard when you start losing and things stop going your way. With the exception of Sachin Tendulkar and to a lesser extent Sourav Ganguly, their batsmen haven't scored many runs, and because we've bowled so well at them, they've stayed under pressure. This was the case throughout the entire first day, and then Lang was relentless when he got his chance, riding his luck early and grinding the bowlers down throughout the second afternoon.

I'm proud that to date we've done our new Australian caps justice. We've all enjoyed wearing them, as they gave us a feeling of great pride — that we were walking proudly along the same path that legends such as Trumper, Darling, Hill and Noble strode so famously down a century ago.

Occasionally, I stopped and pondered what it would have been like back then, playing for Australia in front of a full house at the Sydney Cricket Ground. We should all be thankful cricket has such a rich and wonderful history.

The SCG crowd for this match has been fantastic. I was amazed when someone mentioned that the 42,000-plus who attended on day one was only 4000 less than the total attendance when Australia last played India in a Test match here, back in early 1992. When Brett Lee charged in to attempt a hat-trick, the noise was as loud as I have ever heard on an Australian cricket ground. It's not easy for the away team to bat against that sort of din, but it was great for us to have that level of excitement all around us.

January 4 SYDNEY

WHAT A COMEBACK! Who would have imagined that Ricky Ponting could come back from three successive ducks to post three Test-match hundreds in four Tests. And it wasn't only the statistics today, but the way in which he scored his runs — exquisite strokeplay, fearsome shot selection and unrelenting positivity. This was a great lesson to all of us: never doubt yourself, trust in your ability, and keep working no matter how tough it gets. With Justin Langer, who didn't reach his finish line until he'd powered on to 223, Punter put us in a totally unassailable position.

From there, I'm proud to say, we demonstrated a new-found feature of our make-up, by grinding our opponents into the SCG dust. In seasons gone by, we had developed a frustrating habit of losing 'dead' matches — in England at The Oval in 1993 and 1997, and against the Poms again at the MCG last year; against the West Indies in Perth in 1996–97; against South Africa at Centurion Park in early 1997. However, this summer, against Pakistan and now India we have decisively turned 2-0 series leads into clean sweeps, a fact that suggests a new 'ultra-hardness' in Australian cricket, a fact I enjoy.

This final day of this series was highlighted by some magnificent batting, by Lang, Punter and Adam Gilchrist. And then by VVS Laxman, who belted us all over the park while playing what might even have been the Test innings of the season — though he was aided to some degree by the very aggressive field placements I employed during that innings. But through all Laxman's magnificent shots, Glenn McGrath was superb, completing the second '10-for' performance of his Test career — a feat made even more pleasurable for him because it occurred on his home ground.

Significantly for India and importantly for us, Tendulkar looked mentally fatigued and uncomfortable at the crease. It was obvious that the strain of both the captaincy and the enormous expectations about his run-scoring ability had taken their toll on him. His soft dismissal — caught by Justin Langer in the covers off Damien Fleming after playing a tired drive — confirmed what his negative body language had already told us, and it wouldn't surprise me if he does poorly in the upcoming one-day series. To me, he definitely needs a break from the pressure he's currently under.

There are times when you sense that you must lift the intensity or tempo of the match to press home an advantage that you have created. Late today, I felt as if we could win the match by claiming an extra half an hour. To do this you must tell the umpire of your intentions at least an over before the scheduled close of play. Pigeon was due to bowl that

After the Sydney Test win we were joined in the dressing room by the Australian Prime Minster John Howard (right), who we regularly see at the cricket and who quite often comes into the dressing room to have a chat with the boys. Here, the Border-Gavaskar Trophy is in the foreground, amid the usual dressing-room mess.

last over. When I let Darrell Hair know, he told me that the umpires wouldn't grant our wish for an extension unless we happened to claim a wicket in the over. Of course, Pigeon obliged, as he so often does, which enabled us to go on and achieve victory in what would have definitely been the last over of the day.

We all had two reasons to try and win in three days — firstly, you never know what the weather might do, and secondly we all wanted as many days' rest as we could find before the start of the World Series. Our win was achieved courtesy of a farcical run out, which saw us erupt as one to celebrate another great win and a historic home season.

The quality of our play has been downplayed by some people who say our opposition was of poor quality. But less than six months ago Pakistan were our adversaries in the World Cup final and widely regarded by keen cricket authorities as the second-best Test-match team, while big things were expected of an improving Indian team under the leadership of arguably the best batsman in the world.

To decimate both these sides to a point where they were mentally shattered and unable to fight back was a great credit to our planning, quality training, camaraderie, positive attitude and enjoyment of representing our country. One of the most encouraging features of this summer has been the way in which men such as Langer, Ponting, Gilchrist, Fleming and, lately, Brett Lee have stepped up and made such major contributions to our effort. In my view, we now have a side that could remain at the forefront of world cricket right through the first decade of the 21st century. Long after I'm gone, I think the Australian XI will be a dominant force in the world game.

So now we get a couple of unexpected but gratefully accepted days off, before the World Series begins in earnest in five days' time in Brisbane. Perhaps I should be tired, and looking for a longer break, after what has been a relentless period of cricket since we left for Sri Lanka back in mid-August. But now is such an exciting time to be playing cricket for Australia, let alone leading this team into battle, and I'm eager and ready for the challenges that lie ahead.

PART FOUR:

THE WORLD SERIES

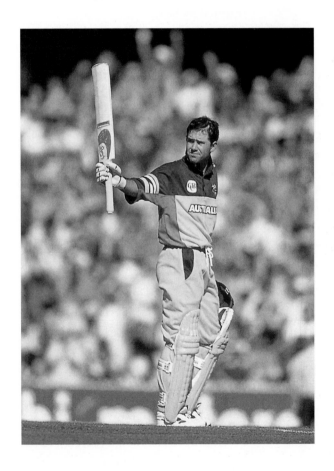

January 6

Sri Lankan match referee Ranjan Madugalle revealed that he had passed the bowling action of Brett Lee after studying slow-motion replays. 'There is nothing to report, it's okay,' Madugalle was reported to have said, before he departed for home after officiating in the recent series involving Australia, Pakistan and India. In other news, the ICC explained that Pakistan's request to review Shoaib's action had been referred to President Jagmohan Dalmiya of India and Clyde Walcott, the West Indian head of the ICC's cricket committee. 'The request from Pakistan for the decision to be suspended is unprecedented, as no formal procedure currently exists,' the ICC said in a statement ... Queensland defeated the Pakistanis by four wickets in a day/night 50-over match at the Gabba. Moin Khan, batting at No. 7, hit an unbeaten 77 out of 167 for the tourists.

January 8

Wasim Akram was quick to respond to reports that a statement from Australian umpires, refuting allegations that they were racially biased, had been read at the previous day's pre-tournament meeting. 'They gave a statement to the referee that they were not biased, and we don't think they are biased,' the Pakistan captain said.

HARDLY HAVE WE HAD time to take in the glory of our successful Test summer, and the one-day internationals are upon us. Things move so quickly in cricket these days, but we are all aware of how things work, so there can be no excuses, and for us, no drop in our intensity. We must never treat any match as being anything other than special.

Typical of cricket these days, no sooner had we gathered in Brisbane and tried on our new gold-and-green-with-a-dash-of-blue uniforms, than we were embroiled in another contentious issue. This one has been prompted by recent comments from a few areas that some of the decisions that have gone against touring teams in recent times have been inspired by racism.

As is the customary procedure before the start of any Test or one-day series, the match referee calls all of the competing teams' hierarchies and the umpires together for a general chitchat. During this meeting, we talk about relevant issues and question marks over rules in an open session where anyone can raise any matter they would like. From our squad, I attended along with manager Steve Bernard and vice-captain Shane Warne, while India and Pakistan sent along their managers, coaches and captains. As I said, the umps were there as well.

Match referee Cammie Smith from the West Indies is a man with a strikingly similar voice to the one that features in the Kit Kat advertisements. He began proceedings by welcoming everyone, then asked gently, 'Would anyone like to raise any issues before we get down to the basics?'

Immediately umpire Darrell Hair raised his hand and said, 'Yes. I would like to make a statement on behalf of the umpires.'

This was a surprise. I can't remember an umpire jumping up in this way, but his actions had me interested. The gist of what he had to say was that he and his fellow umpires were not racist or biased, which is how they believed they had been portrayed by certain players and officials in the media. His statement was, I believe, fair if slightly inflammatory. The umpires' accusers will probably be keen to have the last word. But as always, Darrell said what he believed, even though he must have known that his words were going to cause some friction.

From where I sat, you could see the Pakistani and Indian management moving uneasily in their seats. Then one of the Pakistani officials stood up and made sense of the whole issue, stating, 'Let's get on with the cricket and remember that the bond between all countries is the most important issue. It's only a game.'

He went on to say that he didn't believe that there was any racism or accusations of bias coming from any side, and that we should just get out there and play hard but fair. It was a timely intervention and all parties, including the umpires and match referee, seemed more relaxed about these touchy issues. I wouldn't say the umpires' concerns had been resolved, but I for one was keen for all the aggrieved parties to try for a fresh start …

January 9 BRISBANE

IT HAS SEEMED so far this season as if the dawn of each day will inevitably bring with it a new controversy, or at least an issue that will make headlines for the wrong reasons. Chief among these stories has been the contentious issue of throwing, which culminated in Pakistan's Shoaib Akhtar being suspended until his action was cleared. Shoaib, we were told, was to fly home before the World Series began. With this seemingly resolved, at least in the short term, I thought we'd be going into the World Series one-day competition against Pakistan and India with playing cricket being the major thing on the agenda. I was wrong.

Two days before the opening one-dayer, in Brisbane, everything changed very quickly. To this point, the International Cricket Council's committee that had been established to examine suspect actions had revealed that it had reason to believe that Shoaib's delivery was sometimes not as it should be according to the laws of the game. As a consequence of this finding, he was required to work with an ex-international player to make his bowling action acceptable. I had heard, but had not had confirmed, that he had been working with the great Dennis Lillee but, whatever the case, a decision announced by the ICC on the evening leading up to the Brisbane one-dayer was amazing.

It seems that the president of the ICC, Jagmohan Dalmiya, overruled his expert

Shoaib Akhtar is mobbed by reporters as he arrives at the Gabba after his flight from Perth. The circumstances surrounding Shoaib's sudden re-emergence were interesting to say the least.

The Carlton & United World Series opened in Brisbane with the Australians suffering a shock first-up loss to a rejuvenated Pakistan at the Gabba. The tournament began on a controversial note after Shoaib Akhtar, who was cleared to play by the ICC only hours before the toss, played a major role after Wasim Akram won the toss and batted. Pakistan made 8-184 from their 50 overs, and then bowled out the home team for 139 in 39 overs, with Shoaib taking 3-31 from seven overs. Abdur Razzaq, who took 4-23, was man of the match. Australian vice-captain Shane Warne batted with a runner, after hurting muscles in his side, below his left shoulder, while bowling earlier in the match.

Pakistan won their second straight match in the World Series, with a thrilling last-ball victory over India in Brisbane. India had made 195 from 48.5 overs, and Pakistan, fined an over for a slow over-rate, finished at 8-196 from 49 overs, with man of the match Yousuf Youhana making 63. When Youhana was dismissed in the 43rd over, Pakistan still needed 43, but Saqlain Mushtaq (27 not out) and Waqar Younis (13 not out)

committee and gave Shoaib a last-minute clearance to play. In my view, the basis of this decision was ridiculous. The ICC argued that the deliveries under scrutiny were Shoaib's short-pitched balls, which are deliveries that cannot be bowled in one-day internationals without being no-balled. If he wasn't going to bowl these types of deliveries, he was clear to play.

I reckon this argument has more holes in it than a block of Swiss cheese. The most obvious is that many bowlers still bowl short-pitched stuff in one-day cricket, despite the no-ball threat. As well, it is my understanding that most of Shoaib's deliveries that have been examined and questioned have, in fact, been fast yorkers or at least balls of a very full length. Nevertheless, the decision was out of our hands.

In the hours before the World Series opener, I still believed the Shoiab affair would have an impact on our preparation, for this game at least. My understanding was that he was still in Perth, where he had been preparing to fly home. But then, around 45 minutes before the start of the match, umpires Daryl Harper and Steve Davis entered our dressing rooms to reveal that they had just received a request from the Pakistani management, seeking permission for Shoaib Akhtar to play. As Harper and Davis explained, as Shoaib had been 'cleared' by the ICC in the previous 12 hours, he was clear to play. But there was a problem: the Pakistani quick was at that moment on a flight from Perth to Brisbane, and wasn't expected to arrive at the ground until at least 30 minutes after the start of the match. The umpires, it seemed, were seeking permission from *me*, as the Australian captain, to allow Shoaib to play under these circumstances.

If a team wants to change its line-up after that line-up has been nominated in writing prior to the toss, then it must get the okay from the opposing captain. But that wasn't the case here. So why was my permission being sought? In my view, if there was conjecture, then the matter should have been resolved by the match referee, who is, after all, paid to adjudicate on such issues. But the match referee had passed the conundrum on to me, via the umpires. For a number of reasons, I didn't need this hassle prior to the toss. Firstly, our game plan for the match had been developed on the basis that Shoaib wasn't going to be in their line-up. Secondly, it wasn't my decision to make. And thirdly, it put me in a classic 'no win' situation. If I said 'no', it would have been called an 'unsportsmanlike' decision, and probably 'racist', too. But by saying 'yes', I could have been seen to be endorsing the ICC's original ruling concerning Shoaib's right to play in the competition.

I was only a captain and player, my job was to prepare for the game, so I left it to the officials. My understanding was that the rules prevented him from playing in a situation such as this, but in all honesty, it didn't worry me whether or not he played, because I believed we had Shoaib's measure and had handled him successfully during the Test series. In the end, officials ruled that he could play, citing the 'exceptional circumstances' of Shoaib's case.

Certainly, these were exceptional circumstances, but a more appropriate phrase might have been 'farcical circumstances'. From this outrageous start, the day and night didn't pan out the way I had imagined it would, with an Australian batting collapse triggering a first-up loss. For me, everything was capped off by my dismissal, first ball, by ... guess who ...

Shoaib Akhtar!

January 10 BRISBANE

AT A DINNER PARTY, held by Australian rugby captain John Eales and his wife two nights back, I had the good fortune to sit next to one of Australia's leading sporting poets. Jason 'Rupert' McCall first made a name for himself and his craft by reciting his verses — much to the delight of the boys and girls in the outer — atop a flagpole at the Gabba until the local constabulary dragged him down. So positive was the response to his ballads and the remarkable manner in which he presented them, Rupert cut short a career in the legal world to pursue his love of sport and poetry.

I was looking for a novel way to kick off our one-day series, and here was my chance. I invited Jason to address the team on the field before the start of play in today's match against Pakistan. He had a mere 12 hours to pull a special poem together, but he managed to capture the moment brilliantly and delivered his epic masterpiece by not once looking at his notes! Instead, he looked around the gazing eyes in our huddle, inspiring everyone with his passion and skill.

I've always believed that little surprises such as Rupert's unexpected appearance help keep players on edge and focused on the job by feeling alive and ready for the challenge ahead. That we didn't go on to win tonight was no fault of his. It's nice to know that the Australian team means so much to individuals such as Rupert McCall, and that we are looked up to by many people. We are fortunate to be in such a highly regarded position ...

January 11 MELBOURNE

IT SEEMS AS IF the opening game of the World Series is a cursed game for us. For the second year in a row, Australia collapsed in their quest for a small total. Perhaps, we pondered after this season's loss, we struggle to adapt to the change in format from the Test to the limited-overs games? We'd also lost the first one-day international in the West Indies in April 1999. Maybe we need a couple of one-day practice matches, as our adversaries have? Certainly, as the results show, we are at our most vulnerable first-up.

Above: Shane Warne at the Gabba, before a damaged side muscle forced him onto the sidelines for the major portion of the preliminary matches.

Below: Glenn McGrath clashes with Abdur Razzaq during the Pakistanis' innings in Brisbane.

got them home ... Shane Warne admitted he would probably miss all Australia's World Series matches before the finals, because of the side strain he suffered in Australia's opening match against Pakistan ... Former Australian cricket coach Bob Simpson, a member of the ICC committee that ruled against Shoaib Akhtar late in 1999, admitted he was 'shocked and disappointed' that the panel's verdict had been overturned. 'The view of the panel was that it wasn't just the bouncer, it was also his faster delivery,' Simpson said of Shoaib's bowling. 'It was unanimously agreed that his action needed remedial work.'

Dream of the Backyard Basher

And so today we gather for another cricket game,
The uniform is different, but the ticker's just the same.
So too, I guess, the pressure and the weight of expectation,
But I know that you'll enjoy it 'cos you're playing for my nation.
Warney, Flem, Marto, Bev and never seen before …
Underneath the Southern Cross — the brothers Lee and Waugh.
Punter, Pigeon, Buck and Chippen, Gilly's pumped as well.
And Symo — fresh and eager from the fishing trip from hell.

Ask me as Australians why I'm standing here today,
Ask me why I'm nervous — why I'm not sure what to say.
Ask me, if you like, why there's a shiver down my spine,
Why a doctor had to diagnose this nasty rash of mine.
Ask me and I'll tell you, and I'll tell you with a passion —
It began with taped-up tennis balls in days of backyard bashin'.
Those afternoons your backyard made the perfect cricket ground,
When you dreamed the dream — the dream that said this day would come around.
Now when I, the humble cricket fan, can see you live those dreams,
That's the shiver — that's the rash — the tear that sometimes streams.
'Cos from the Gabba here in Queensland to the sweeping shores of Broome,
On the Harbour banks of Sydney, where the waratah's in bloom,
From Uluru at sunset to the mighty Tasman Sea,
In the Adelaide cathedrals, at the roaring MCG,
From the Great Australian Bight to the Gulf of Carpentaria,
The medical profession calls it 'Green and Gold Malaria'.
But forget about the textbooks, boys — the truth I shouldn't hide,
The rash that we've contracted here is good old Aussie pride.
I'm afraid that you were born with it, and one thing is for sure —
You'll die with it alright, because there isn't any cure.

— **Rupert McCall**

The only positive way to look at the situation we now find ourselves in is to say that we can only get better. If we were going to lose a match, it was better to do so now than later on in the final series. The defeat also provided us with a reminder that every team will be out to better us simply because we are the World Cup holders. We have to stay a step ahead.

Last season, I suffered a leg strain, which resulted in me having a severely disrupted World Series campaign. This time it was the vice-captain's turn, as Warney tore a muscle in his side after trying to bowl through the injury. This is a huge loss for us — Shane, with Glenn McGrath, has been our most dependable and decisive bowler in one-day cricket. We can only hope that toasted cheese sandwiches — Warney's staple diet — will hasten his recovery, because we don't want him out of the team for very long.

On the positive front, Warney's injury gives the hugely talented Stuart MacGill an opportunity to prove that he can perform in the shortened version of the game. Before Warney's great success, many believed that there wasn't a place for leggies in one-day

January 11

ACB Chairman Denis Rogers criticised the ICC ruling that cleared Shoaib Akhtar. 'I am worried about the processes involved and the precedent it sets,' Rogers told a press conference in Melbourne ... Ricky Ponting was named as Australia's fill-in vice-captain, while Shane Warne remained sidelined with injury. NSW leg-spinner Stuart MacGill was added to the Australian squad.

January 12

Australia had their first win in the World Series, with a 28-run victory over India at the MCG. The home team, batting first, hit 7-269 from their 50 overs, with Ricky Ponting making 115. The Indians mounted a credible reply, and reached 3-177 in the 40th over before Sourav

cricket, because their control and economy rates wouldn't be acceptable. Now wrist-spinners are seen as a huge bonus, because, provided they are accurate enough, they can win you games as the opposition is forced to take them on. Unlike a Test, where batsmen can 'sit' on a spinner and wait for the loose ball, in the one-dayers it is a very different proposition. 'Magilla' has the 'spinningest' fingers in the game and may well become a trump card!

January 12 MELBOURNE

'Sometimes it's easy to see another one-day game as a dime-a-dozen,
And to treat them as Test cricket's poor, unfortunate cousin.
But we all know that playing for Australia is special any time you do it,
That when you put the cap on and look at the emblem,
If there was a brick wall, you'd be able to run through it.
For since that day at Lord's and our whole World Cup campaign,
We've shown this team's got character, personality and can endure any hardship or pain.
Every time you put the cap on, every time you run out, every shot, every throw, every ball, every catch ...'

— **Dave Misson** (read before World Series match v India, January 12)

Some Indian fans in Melbourne, on the night that a crowd disturbance temporarily stopped play during the visitors' innings.

ONCE AGAIN THE MENTALITY of some people who frequent one-day games came into question as they showed their displeasure at India's Sourav Ganguly's run out tonight by throwing whatever they could lay their hands on onto the arena. These imbeciles showed a complete lack of respect for the game and lack of knowledge of the rules, and in the process stopped the match for a good half-hour.

Some of the blame for the fiasco must go to the technical system, which produces a green light for not out or a red light for out. Almost immediately after our appeal was referred to the third umpire, the green light flashed on, to the delight of the strong Indian contingent of supporters at the ground, most of them situated adjacent to the scoreboard at the Great Southern Stand end. It was a crucial decision, as Ganguly had just reached his century, was in great form and was getting better with each delivery. The match at this point could have gone either way.

What the crowd didn't realise was that there had been an electronic error, and in fact a decision hadn't been reached yet. What the third umpire was actually seeing was Ganguly failing to ground his bat, preferring to casually stroll into his crease with his bat in the air, unaware that Andrew Symonds' throw had caught him short of his crease. As soon as the red light appeared, after a couple of replays that clearly showed Ganguly's foot short of the line and his bat over the line but still airborne, a small section of the crowd also saw red and lost the plot.

If there is one thing that really bugs me about one-dayers, it's the fact that the crowds can't seem to handle anything that adversely affects their team without disrupting the game. It's only a minority who cause the trouble, but they ruin it for the majority. Unfortunately, this has become the norm rather the exception, and one day we might have to show our displeasure by walking off. Then they'll have something to really whinge about. I know two wrongs never make a right, but how else can we make our point?

January 15 MELBOURNE

MANY PEOPLE BELIEVE that a captain's job is solely about getting the results on the park, which, of course, is part of the overall picture. These days, however, that role has been somewhat overtaken by off-field duties, including dealing with the media, liaising with the Australian Cricket Board, making sure the mechanics of the team are running smoothly and keeping an eye on issues that might affect the team. After the recent crowd fiasco at the MCG, when the game was held up for around 30 minutes, the ground authorities' embarrassment at the perceived lack of security was sufficient for them to mount a campaign to warn potential troublemakers of the serious ramifications if they were caught behaving badly.

In order to help get this message across, I was asked to attend a press conference with security chiefs, the hope being that we'd be able to get the message across that if anyone was going to the cricket to make trouble they were going to the wrong place. My cameo performance was whittled down to a couple of mundane, routine answers, while the police chief revelled in the bright lights, lapping it up as if he was auditioning for a TV pilot. Still, it was a necessary part of my job and something I wanted to do — each day brings a new angle on what it's like to lead your country at cricket.

Left and below: Michael Bevan during the World Series — still in my view the most effective batsman in international cricket.

January 12 (continued)

Ganguly was run out immediately after reaching his century. This dismissal led to a crowd disturbance, after Indian supporters reacted to a temporary malfunction in the third umpire's dismissal lights by throwing bottles and other objects onto the field — despite the fact that video replays clearly showed that Ganguly was out ... The Pakistanis defeated an Australian Country XI by 37 runs in a 50-over match in Canberra.

Stuart MacGill at the SCG, during his highly successful first appearance in international one-day cricket.

If nothing else, the captaincy is becoming a great preparation for life after sport. Playing diplomat on delicate issues, gaining confidence in front of the media, and needing an awareness of things going on around you rather than just in front of you are all part of the honour of captaining your country …

January 19 SYDNEY

OUTSTANDING, MATCH-WINNING PERFORMANCES in one-day cricket tend to blend into one another, purely because of the large number of contests happening around the world every year. However, Stuart MacGill's effort against Pakistan in Sydney last night was one that stood out, not only for his superb figures of 4-19 from 10 overs, but also by the way in which he had such an impact on the match. Not only did he change the tempo and direction of the game by taking wickets at vital stages, he backed himself and achieved his success in his natural, uninhibited way. Stuey didn't just try to do a job, be conservative and economical; rather he wanted to leave his mark by spinning the ball prodigiously and attacking each and every batsman. He was confronting, intimidating and enticing, much to the delight of his home town crowd, and it was a joy to watch him operate in such an enthusiastic, decisive way.

Good as Stuey's bowling was, it wasn't the biggest thing to happen in Australian cricket during the past week. That No. 1 position went to the announcement of the 'Team of the Century', a best Australian XII selected from all the men who've worn the baggy green cap over the past 100 years. The final selection has created much debate, which only confirms what I believed from the start — that we could easily have chosen three or four teams of the highest possible standard. Such events are a wonderful reminder of the rich history of our game, and what an important responsibility we have to ensure that the work of the champions of the past is never forgotten.

Australia joined Pakistan at the top of the World Series table after beating India in a low-scoring encounter at the SCG. After India were reduced to all out for 100 in the 37th over, the home team stumbled to 5-59 before Andrew Symonds came out to score an unbeaten 28 from 32 balls. Earlier, Symonds had taken 4-11 from 3.3 overs and Glenn McGrath 4-8 from 10. At the end of his first spell of seven overs, McGrath had three wickets for five runs. 'I would back him against any side in the world,' Steve Waugh said of his great fast bowler.

Australia defeated Pakistan by six wickets in their World Series match in Melbourne, thanks largely to an unbroken fifth-wicket partnership of 85 between Steve Waugh and Damien Martyn. Earlier, Abdur Razzaq had scored 51 from 54 balls to allow the visitors to reach 9-176 after they had been 7-106 in the 31st over.

The ACB released the names of Australian cricket's 'Team of the Century' at a function in Sydney. The team was Arthur Morris, Bill Ponsford, Sir Donald Bradman, Greg Chappell, Neil Harvey, Keith Miller, Ian Healy, Ray Lindwall, Shane Warne, Dennis Lillee, Bill O'Reilly and Allan Border (12th man).

Adam Gilchrist, whose move to the top of Australia's one-day team's batting order was one of the most significant developments in the team's progress to the top of the world rankings.

It was great to see three of my contemporaries — Allan Border, Ian Healy and Shane Warne — in the squad. They joined Arthur Morris, Bill Ponsford, Sir Donald Bradman (captain), Neil Harvey, Greg Chappell, Keith Miller, Ray Lindwall, Dennis Lillee, and Bill O'Reilly. The team was announced at a function in Sydney where a vast number of the living former and current Australian internationals got together. Just to have these men under the one roof was a wonderful thing for the game, and for me a magnificent chance to chat with legends of past eras, to talk cricket and discover what made these champions tick.

January 22 MELBOURNE

INDIA'S LOSS TO PAKISTAN in Hobart yesterday has left them needing to win their remaining matches to make the finals. But, in truth, the way Tendulkar's men are playing, such a winning run seems unlikely. To me, it seems as if they are resigned to the fact that they will be going home early. It's been a tough tour for them, during which they've suffered from a lack of depth in their batting and an inability as a unit to adapt to the bouncy Australian wickets. They've been relying on too few players to get them through, and have missed a couple of key, experienced men who have

Above and below: In the World Series match at the MCG on January 16, Pakistan's Abdur Razzaq took to Glenn McGrath, smashing him for five fours in one over.

NSW leg-spinner Stuart MacGill made a spectacular one-day international debut by taking 4-19 from 10 overs as Australia defeated Pakistan by 81 runs at the SCG. Batting first, Australia made 286 from 49.4 overs, with Michael Bevan making 77, Damien Martyn 50, Andrew Symonds 47 from 26 balls and Damien Fleming 26 from 13 balls. In reply, Pakistan got to 2-100 in the 13th over, before MacGill was introduced to the attack.

Pakistan defeated India by 32 runs in their World Series match in Hobart. Pakistan made 7-262, including 67 from Ijaz Ahmed and 70 from 52 balls by Abdur Razzaq. Despite an innings of 93 from Sachin Tendulkar, India were all out in the 47th over. Abdur Razzaq finished with 5-48.

Australia won a tight World Series match against Pakistan in Melbourne, after Michael Bevan, with 83 from 101 balls, spearheaded the home team to 9-260 from their 50 overs. The Pakistanis reached 4-201 in the 41st over, before the last six wickets fell for 44 runs in 8.4 overs. The win meant that Australia had safely qualified for the World Series finals. Glenn McGrath missed the game to be with his wife and newborn son.

been absent because of injuries. But perhaps their most noticeable weakness has been their fielding, where they have lacked men capable of getting that critical run out, or taking a difficult half-chance that might turn a game. That's been our strength in recent times, and also a distinguished feature of South African teams, the thing that has set us apart from many of our opponents.

India are not the first side to learn that an Australian tour is a tough one when things start to go wrong. But it is important that they play well in their remaining matches, so that there will be something positive to come from their experience. Pakistan, on the other hand, are playing with a lot of confidence. They are a very good side, with dangerous hitters all the way down their batting order and a bowling attack capable of knocking over any team. A very aggressive team; on their day they can beat anyone.

A satisfying feature of our displays through the tournament to date has been the contribution of players such as Andrew Symonds, Shane Lee, Stuart MacGill and Damien Martyn, who in the past haven't had the same high profile as some other members of the squad. We know now we have the all-rounders, such as Symonds, Lee and Adam Gilchrist, to match any other side in the game and the depth to cover even Glenn McGrath and Shane Warne. We're also encouraged by the evolution of our late-order hitting, which in this competition has been akin to anything Simon O'Donnell managed so successfully for Australia in the mid-to-late 1980s.

January 26 ADELAIDE

THERE ARE MANY elements that make up a great catch. It must be inspirational. It usually is only a 'half chance' at worst. It should have a major impact on the game, maybe even turn the whole nature of the match around. It can be spectacular, most probably it will be athletic, it more often than not will be instinctive and certainly it will be technically perfect and require a high level of skill.

Bearing these features in mind, the effort of Stuart MacGill to claim Sachin Tendulkar's wicket here in Adelaide — running at full pace from deep third man, which culminated in a defiant one-handed leap, mirroring the 'Statue of Liberty' — was a marvel. The moment the ball left a flashing Tendulkar's blade it had boundary written all over it, but the

Mark Waugh in Adelaide, scoring yet another one-day international hundred.

deceptively quick and soft-handed 'spin whiz' homed in on it like a dog would to a bone. It brought the house down, not to mention us as a team, because it was the wicket that drained the life out of the Indians in their quest for a massive 300-plus total.

It must have been a gem, because Stuey refused to smile or even vaguely acknowledge his feat. We've worked out with him that the better he performs the more intense his facial expressions and body language become. Of course, the other explanation may have been that he was in shock, but I doubt that because this guy is a big-match player who thrives on pressure ...

January 27 ADELAIDE

AS I WAS READING OUT the Australian batting order to the Adelaide Oval scoreboard attendant yesterday, I successfully got through the first six, and then came to numbers seven, eight and nine — Shane Lee, Ian Harvey and Brett Lee ...

Lee ... Harvey ...

Brett Lee, formerly known as 'Bing' or 'Binger', is now known as 'Oswald'.

January 29 PERTH

BEING ON TOUR FOR long periods at a time means constantly eating from room-service menus or in restaurants, which can be excellent or awful, but nothing beats a home-cooked meal or a barbecue. Consequently, we have tried to encourage the boys to take advantage of such offers whenever they arise, and to even organise such events when in their home town. This breaks the monotony and stops us from being lazy and taking the easy option — the club sandwich and fries.

India kept alive their slim chances of reaching the World Series finals with a 48-run victory over Pakistan in Adelaide. Sourav Ganguly made 141 from 144 balls for India, and when Pakistan batted, Azhar Mahmood hit 67 from 50 balls and Anil Kumble took 4-40.

Australia thrashed India by 152 runs in their World Series match at the Adelaide Oval. Batting first, Australia raced to 5-329 from their 50 overs, with Gilchrist (92) and Mark Waugh (116) adding 163 for the first wicket in 29.2 overs. India were never likely in reply, struggling to 177 all out in the 47th over. Brett Lee took 5-27 from 8.5 overs. 'This is as good as it gets,' Steve Waugh said of the Australians' effort. 'The best thing was Mark's return to form, and I was very impressed with the way we continued to push the Indians throughout the match.'

Pakistan confirmed their place in the World Series finals with a 104-run win over India in Perth. Pakistan made 8-261 from their 50 overs before bowling out India in 46 overs.

Our recently retired coach, Geoff Marsh, invited the boys around to his house for a traditional Aussie barbecue, together with some yabbies caught at the family's dam and some fresh crayfish he'd collected from a buddy of his. What a sensational feed! Just the sort of relaxed get-together we needed before our one-dayer against India tomorrow. Swampy's strength was always his ability to unite the players and promote team harmony, as well as having a real skill for creating an environment in which everyone could make the most of their ability.

Individually, for the Australian guys there's a lot at stake in tomorrow's match. We have 13 in-form men in our squad, all of whom want to play a significant role in the finals. Over the past week, we have mixed the teams up a bit, to give everyone an opportunity to stake their claim to a spot in the starting XI in the finals, but rather than this settling anything it has confused the issue to some extent, because everyone has taken their chance and performed exceedingly well.

There is currently a great deal of respect for each other among the squad, and a great commitment to each other to play well at all times. We have developed extremely high standards, and have come to appreciate the psychological value of winning consistently against all our opponents. Hence our great desire to beat India once again, to ensure that we stay unbeaten against them throughout the entire Australian summer.

For this Perth game, we welcome back Shane Warne, for what will be an important game for him. He needs a good hit-out before finals, as he's been out for three weeks, which has been tough for him. Hopefully he'll enjoy a productive and confidence-boosting 10-over spell at the WACA. Of course, with Shane back there is no longer a place for Stuart MacGill, who is very unlucky to be omitted, as he bowled superbly when called upon. However, he knew, as we all did, that Shane would be straight back in once he was right. It is extremely comforting for us to know that we have more than just the one high-class leggie to call on at any time — yet another example of the wonderful depth of talent we have available at present.

For Australia, two highlights of the past week have been the performances of Mark Waugh and Brett Lee. It was good to see my brother back in form. He was relatively cautious

It wasn't often that an opposition batsman got the ball back past Brett Lee during the 1999–2000 season.

early on in Adelaide, but after a ball or two hit the middle of his bat he went along nicely to register another one-day international century. In many ways, cricket can be a fickle game — you only need to get one or two shots right and your confidence and good form can come right back.

Brett Lee was almost impossible to play in Adelaide when he was operating with the old ball. The poor batsmen could hardly see it at the pace he was bowling. He's made quite an impression, and I am looking forward to seeing him bowling on the WACA track. He was outstanding here in Perth when NSW played Western Australia last month, and now, after his excellent debut in international cricket, his confidence is sky-high.

In many ways, Brett typifies the aggressive style of one-day cricket that we have tried to play in recent times. In this sense, it is ironic that he is so new to international cricket, because it has taken us two years of hard work to reach our current level. The rewards for all our effort are now there for all to see, however, especially in our fielding. It has always been my belief that if you can be the best fielding team in one-day cricket, you will be close to the most successful team in one-day cricket. Nowadays we rarely miss the chance to get that crucial run out, or take that difficult half-chance.

And the energy and confidence we get from our performances in the field are now being transferred into every aspect of our game, not least the way we are going past 250 as often

Shane Warne returned to the Australian side as the World Series favourites extended their winning run to seven matches with a four-wicket defeat of India at the WACA. India made 6-226 from their 50 overs, a target the Australians reached with three balls to spare. Michael Bevan, with 71 from 92 deliveries, was named man of the match.

Glenn McGrath was named the inaugural Allan Border Medallist at a function at the Crown Casino in Melbourne. The award was given to the man judged Australia's best international cricketer for 1999. McGrath was also the Test player of the year, while Shane Warne was the one-day player of the year.

Australia won a decisive six-wicket victory in the first final of the 1999–2000 World Series, at the MCG. Batting first after winning the toss, Pakistan were 3-4, then 4-12, then 5-28 before a Moin Khan-led resurgence got them to 154 all out. Glenn McGrath dismissed three of the top four Pakistani batsmen for ducks. Although Adam Gilchrist and Mark Waugh fell early, Ricky Ponting (50) and Michael Bevan (54) steered Australia to victory.

as not. It seems that if we get in a spot of bother during our innings, these days there always seems to be someone prepared to back themselves, to try to take charge.

February 3 SYDNEY

DESPITE OUR OUTSTANDING cricket and emphatic victory in the first match of the finals series yesterday, for me the moment that best indicated that we are at present an extremely powerful and successful team came when we were forced to announce that Damien Fleming would not be in our starting XI for the match.

Flem has been an integral member of our Test and one-day sides over the past 12 months, best remembered by fans, perhaps, for his coolness under extraordinary pressure in the 1999 World Cup semi-final against South Africa. We have been most grateful for his valuable and successful performances, day after day. And he will continue, I'm sure, in that role for many seasons to come. But right at the moment, with our all-rounders bowling so well and Brett Lee in such dynamic form, Flem was the unlucky guy to miss out when we picked our side to face Pakistan at the MCG. And given that we went so well in Melbourne, unless the SCG for game two is a greentop, it will be difficult now for us to change the team to fit him in.

I have been asked if I am happy with the way the team is playing at the moment, and the answer is happy, yes, but fully satisfied, never. We want every team we're playing against to not want to face us. Our ambition is to keep improving, to the point that we have an aura of invincibility about us, similar to what the West Indies carried through the 1980s and Bradman's famous Australian side must have worn against England in the late 1940s.

While we thought Pakistan might have been revved up to try to get some revenge for their loss to us in the World Cup final, we came into the finals treating this series as a completely new event. Still, it was impossible afterwards not to ponder the similarities between this first final and the game at Lord's back on June 20. Once again, Wasim Akram won the toss and sent us in. Once again, our new ball bowlers were superb, crashing through the Pakistan top order. Our fielding was top class on both occasions. Pakistan again set us a modest total, which we handled relatively comfortably.

Above: We liked our chances of getting Pakistani opener Saeed Anwar caught behind or in the slip cordon early in the first World Series final. Brett Lee put the ball in the right spot, Anwar fended at it, and Shane Warne at first slip did the rest.

Below: Whether batting, bowling or fielding, Andrew Symonds is a human dynamo, whose energy and enthusiasm are infectious. This photo was taken during the first World Series final.

Team Meeting: The Captain's Notes*

BEFORE WORLD SERIES FINALS, v PAKISTAN

ONE DAY THEME: NEVER SATISFIED

Batting

- Partnerships are the key!! Don't lose two quick wickets.
- Rotate strike.
- Keep batting tempo up — all players to back themselves.
- Give yourself a chance when you first go in (they have a few danger bowlers)
  - — attack key bowlers (eg. Saqlain)
  - — respect certain bowlers (eg. Razzaq — extra pace)
  - — maintain communication! — in the centre, in the rooms, and between
  - — put pressure on their fielders — they will crack! Anwar, Razzaq, Waqar, Inzi — (slow to ball).

Bowling

First 15 overs

- Tight overs — dot balls — first and last balls.
- Spin option.
- Minimise extras — best for the summer (less than six).
- Take early wickets (eg. Afridi — test line, hit deck).

Middle overs

- Hustle between overs.
- Break partnerships.
- Communication with the captain.
- Sum up the situation — attack?

Last 15 overs

- Run outs.
- Bowler back to stumps.
- Change of pace/length.

General

- Bowl in partnership (stack up overs conceding less than three).
- Anticipate run outs.
- Pressure in middle overs.
- Work on the ball for Irish swing (punter with bowlers — don't rub it too much.
- Maintain high standards.
- Keep mood even and balanced.
- Recognise and reward good efforts.
- Team orientation over individual need/success.
- Delight in everyone's success.
- Bowlers: think clearly about fields if Pakistan is going!

* *based on notes to team from John Buchanan*

As has been their custom throughout this one-day tournament, the tourists' late order batted very well, with Moin Khan at the forefront again. This just reminded us that, whatever the scoreboard might say, Pakistan are never completely beaten.

Glenn McGrath was magnificent, producing one of the finest opening spells I've seen in international cricket. Ironically, two weeks earlier the same Pakistani batting line-up was smashing him all over the park, but here he was fantastic. I heard afterwards that Wasim Akram reckoned Glenn must be one of the best three bowlers of the past 10 years. High praise, indeed, when you think about all the great performers of the decade — Wasim, of course, included — but who am I to disagree with the Pakistan captain's verdict?

For us, there was much to be satisfied with. Brett Lee was very quick, justifying his selection, while Shane Warne was excellent, too, demonstrating conclusively that he is completely over his recent injury by producing a clever spell. And Ricky Ponting and Michael Bevan batted very well and very sensibly, defusing a potentially tricky situation when we lost Adam Gilchrist and Mark Waugh for just 27.

Now we are just one win away from completing what would have to be the most decisively successful season by an Australian team in recent years. We are extremely proud about the way we are playing, but remain fully aware that if we ease off even a fraction, then Pakistan are capable of coming back and ruining our summer.

February 5 SYDNEY

FOR MOST OF THE one-day series we have been emphasising the fact that, while we've been winning, we can play better. This was especially true of our batting, which has been improving through the World Series, and it was very rewarding to be able to produce as close to the perfect one-day batting performance as I have been involved with in what proved to be the World Series finale. To get 337 from 50 overs against a quality bowling attack, without one player making a big, fast hundred, was a fine team achievement.

Bowling-wise, we were satisfied, too, with Glenn McGrath and Brett Lee leading the way, just as they did in the first final. Pakistan were never a chance, and our eventual winning margin was 152 runs. Glenn really has had the most amazing 12 months, and the most amazing past couple of weeks — with a son being born, being named the Australian Test cricketer of the year and winner of the inaugural Allan Border Medal. A five-wicket haul at the SCG iced his season perfectly, and his place in the roll call of truly great Australian pacemen is now assured. Last night, Shane Lee also did a good job, while Shane Warne stemmed the run flow at an important stage. Over the series I thought our bowlers were consistently outstanding.

Summing up, we really enjoyed ourselves during the finals and got great satisfaction from the way we stuck to our game plan. A very satisfying performance.

Although our main focus was on maintaining our very high standards, we were conscious of the fact that a win last night would give us some time off before our New Zealand tour. You don't get much time off in this 21st-century world of cricket, and we certainly haven't been spared any spare time in the past few months. So the next few days, while only a 'mini-break', will be grabbed enthusiastically.

The only downer to victory was Ricky Ponting's disastrous slide in the boundary boards

Australia clinched the World Series trophy with an emphatic 152-run victory in the second final, at the SCG. After Steve Waugh won the toss, the home team hit 7-337 from their 50 overs, the highest ever score by an Australian team in international one-day cricket, and the highest one-day international innings total ever made by any team in Australia. Adam Gilchrist made 51 (from 42 balls), Mark Waugh 53 (from 73), Ricky Ponting 78 (80), Andrew Symonds 45 (45) and Steve Waugh 37 (30). In reply, Pakistan's innings was broken by Glenn McGrath, who took 5-49. 'They are definitely worthy world champions,' was how Wasim Akram described the Australian team afterwards. Ricky Ponting won the man-of-the-match award, while Abdur Razzaq was named the player of the tournament.

The new pavilion at Bankstown Oval, in Sydney's south-western suburbs, was named in honour of two of the district's most famous cricketers, Steve and Mark Waugh. 'Bankstown people seem to have a great spirit and character,' said Steve. 'An example is this cricket club, the way it sticks together and helps people out. It's a real family atmosphere. My roots are here, it's a great area.'

— a brave but unrealistic effort to save a run — that left him injured and now in doubt for our tour of New Zealand. His attitude and commitment were, of course, first class, but his misjudgment yesterday may prove very costly. It appears to be quite a serious injury and looks to have put a temporary stop on his career just when he was conquering all before him.

What a tumultuous season it's been for him — six international centuries, six ducks, a run as vice-captain when Warney was injured and now this serious injury.

Our World Series triumph will still be a sweet one for Ricky, and for all of us, particularly as we have been winning with some style. Our successful batting in the tournament's latter matches has been built on a policy that requires each new batsman to begin as the previous one finished, ensuring that we don't lose momentum and are continually putting pressure on the opposition to perform for each and every ball. This isn't easy to do, because you must be pro-active from ball one and not waste any time settling in. In yesterday's second final, we demonstrated the fruits of this approach — it was like watching a snowball gather momentum as it races down a slope, crushing everything in its way. Then our bowling was again well executed, occasionally punctuated by a mini-resurgence from the Pakistani line-up, but consistency and persistence eventually won the day for us.

Glenn McGrath, inaugural winner of the Allan Border Medal as Australia's international cricketer of the year for 1999–2000. I thought the introduction of this award, a joint innovation of the Australian Cricket Board and the Australian Cricketers' Association, was a real feature of the summer.

Above left: The Lee brothers on home turf in Sydney during the second final.

Above right: Damien Martyn and Ian Harvey help the injured **Ricky Ponting** off the **SCG** after the post-match presentations. Ricky had damaged his ankle when he slid into the fence while trying to prevent a boundary.

In my opinion, the primary reasons for the chasm between us and Pakistan and India are our running between the wickets, our superiority in the field — in terms of both skill and agility — and our strict adherence to our game plan. That plan revolves around a tight theme, but still allows for individuality and moments of inspiration. I can see no reason why team togetherness and a desire to be the best won't see this side continue to improve and become even more united in the times ahead.

February 10 SYDNEY

SO WHERE NOW IS the Australian one-day team, compared with where it was back last June, when we were crowned world champions? In comparing the current Australian one-day team with the one that won the World Cup, the one area in which we are undoubtedly better is fielding. Not that the World Cup team was a bad fielding side — far from it — but the infusion of Andrew Symonds, especially, has taken the present team to a new level. Against this, the current side hasn't yet been tested under the type of intense pressure the World Cup team encountered during that tournament. So to say one team is better than the other … it's probably too early to judge.

One other difference between these two sides is, of course, that we now have a new coach. There is no doubt that John Buchanan has had a positive impact on the side, but I believe it would be unfair to give him *all* the credit for the way the current team is playing. Many aspects of the way we go about things were in place before he came along, so our previous coach, Geoff Marsh, should take some of the glory, too. But we have been grateful for the manner in which John leaves absolutely no stone unturned in his quest for us to perform at our very best. He is extraordinarily meticulous and attentive during a match, forever noting all sorts of things that might be useful in analysing how we performed, or where we might improve.

Like Geoff Marsh, John is a coach who stresses that Australian cricketers have to be their own men, and play in the manner that got them into the team in the first place. He is also keen, as was Geoff, to get all the players involved in developing overall game plans and specific strategies to counter opposition players. And he's very clever with his 'quiet words' to individual players, to make them always feel an important part of what is going on, and able to perform to the best of their ability.

Our confidence was a feature of the Australian summer, whereas often our opponents seemed unsure of their ability. India, especially, were disappointing. Much more was expected of them by the Australian public, the Australian team, and, I imagine, themselves than what was eventually delivered. Throughout the one-day series, they lacked players who would consistently take the fight to the opposition. Perhaps I should exclude Sourav Ganguly from such an assessment, for he was a standout, having a reasonable series with the bat and making a couple of hundreds.

I thought Sachin Tendulkar was mentally gone on this tour from as early as when the third Test began. He looked out of sorts in that Test match and I remember predicting at our team meeting prior to the one-day series that he wouldn't score too many runs in the tournament. To me, it looked as if he was struggling under the pressure he and his team were under, and under the colossal expectations he always carries with him; by series end he was reduced to the same level as we mere mortals.

PART FIVE:

INTO THE RECORD BOOKS

The opening match of Australia's one-day international series in New Zealand, in Wellington, was abandoned without a ball being bowled, after umpires ruled the bowlers' run-ups were unsafe. No toss was made. Officials ruled that the match would be played on the following day, the designated reserve day ... Steve Waugh slammed the ICC's handling of the Shoaib Akhtar chucking affair. 'The whole thing is a joke, and all the players think it's a joke,' Waugh told AAP. 'We've got no faith in the system. We're very professional in what we're doing on the field but off the field it just doesn't seem to be working.'

The Australian team's game plan for the tour of New Zealand found itself in the wrong hands in Wellington, after copies of it were inadvertently pushed under the wrong hotel door. From there the papers were delivered to a local radio station, which told listeners of the Australians' analysis of the Kiwi players' strengths and weaknesses. Among a host of comments, many positive, about the home team, was an instruction to 'intimidate' the New Zealanders with 'controlled aggression,' but to control 'sledging and body language'. New Zealand captain

February 20 AUCKLAND

THE FIRST FEW DAYS here in New Zealand have been interesting, to say the least. At our initial press conference, in Wellington four days back, the major talking point seemed to be the Shoaib Akhtar affair, which was a pity given that I would much rather have been talking about our recent excellent form.

Then came an intriguing story, when our team notes for the one-day series against New Zealand found themselves in the wrong hands and were then quickly broadcast on a local radio station. The media tried to beat this up into a major incident, but we weren't overly concerned. If the reporters thought that our analysis of the Kiwi players might cause some sort of rift between the two teams, or inspire our opponents to greater heights, they were way out. I'm sure the players mentioned in the papers would have looked at our brief comments on each of them and thought, 'yeah, that's pretty right'. Our manager, Steve Bernard, was spot on when he was asked about the papers.

'Everybody has a game plan,' he replied. 'Our side has to know what they have to do and though we would prefer the opposition not know the plan, it's not the end of the world.'

The bottom line for us is that New Zealand are a good, tough side who will be very confident after their recent matches against the West Indies, when they won both Tests

Why is manager Steve Bernard dressed like this? The answer is on page 184.

Above: Justin Langer in the Sydney dressing room after his marathon innings in the third Test against India. The locker changing rooms at the SCG have changed remarkably over the last couple of years. The bottom section of the dressing room, where Lang is sitting here, offers quite small spaces, but up a couple of stairs at the back of the room are spaces that are twice as wide. Those larger spots are for the members of the NSW XI; the smaller ones are left for the other members of the state squad.

Right: Indian opener VVS Laxman playing a sensational lone hand on the final day of the series. Out of an innings total of 261, Laxman scored 167.

Above: The end of an extraordinary home summer of Test cricket — six matches, six wins. Back row: Slater, B. Lee, Gilchrist, Blewett, Kasprowicz, M. Waugh, Ponting. Front: S. Waugh, Warne, McGrath, Fleming, Langer.

Right: Our three match-winners from the Sydney Test — Ricky Ponting (left), Glenn McGrath and Justin Langer — with the new, much improved Border-Gavaskar Trophy.

Left: Ricky Ponting was in cracking form during the World Series.

Below: Michael Bevan works the ball into another gap, as the scoreboard ticks over and he builds another important innings during a one-dayer against Pakistan.

Gotcha! It's hard to believe that Brett Lee was a virtual unknown at the start of the summer.
By season's end, his victory leap had become a trademark.

STEVE WAUGH

With Shane Warne and the World Series trophy, amid the fireworks, after winning the finals series 2-0, in Sydney.

Above: The moment Shane Warne knew he'd finally broken Dennis Lillee's Australian Test wicket-talking record. Adam Gilchrist (furthest left) has taken the catch, off Kiwi No. 11 Paul Wiseman.

Right: Warney in the Eden Park dressing room afterwards. Reaching this landmark was a huge relief for him. He'd wanted to achieve it during the Australian season, but couldn't quite get there. Ironically, Shane didn't bowl particularly well in this game — it appeared he was distracted by all the coverage the impending record was causing.

A classic Michael Slater off-drive during the New Zealand Test series.

Some of the results of the team's 'ugly shirt' competition. My outfit (right) was a nice little black-and-white, flowery number. Shane Lee (below left) actually liked his top, which I purchased and cost NZ$2.50. Dave Misson (centre) wasn't quite as keen on his 'John Travolta' silk shirt with the white tie, while Andrew Symonds appears to be wearing some sort of lady's nightgown. In the photo above, John Buchanan is framing a market as to who will win the 'daktari', an always appalling outfit that is awarded to the team member who commits the silliest act or makes the stupidest mistake during the previous week. Steve Bernard was a short-priced favourite and after he won the vote, he was obliged to wear the ensemble captured on page 176 — a wig, a pair of sunnies and earrings, striped purple-and-brown top and striped black-and-white silky pants — out for the evening.

and all five one-dayers. In players such as captain Stephen Fleming, dynamic all-rounder Chris Cairns, spinner Daniel Vettori, keeper Adam Parore and batsmen Nathan Astle and Craig McMillan they have the nucleus of an excellent cricket side. Anything less than our very best form won't be good enough on this trip.

As to the cricket itself, the tour got off to a slow start, as constant rain resulted in the first one-dayer being first washed out without a ball being bowled, and then when it did get going the following day, the game was abandoned after just 23 overs. About the only bloke who had a good time was Matthew Hayden, who revelled in the simple fact that he was back in Australian colours as Ricky Ponting's replacement, and then marked his return by racing to 64 from 68 balls in the time available when the game did finally start.

From Wellington we journeyed north to Auckland, where yesterday we did get to play, but not for too long as we won comfortably. The game was a day/nighter, but so quickly did we bowl the Kiwis out and then knock off the winning runs that the sun still hadn't set completely when the post-match presentations were being made. In the field, we took four excellent catches, while all our bowlers were impressive as the home team crashed to 122 all out. Then Haydos continued his outstanding start to the tour by making 50 at better than a run a ball.

February 23   DUNEDIN

QUITE OFTEN AFTER a victory, the members of the Aussie team will manage to convince each other that they deserve a little treat on the journey home. After steamrolling New Zealand in Dunedin last night, the lads were somehow magnetically drawn to the golden arches for a midnight feed of burgers, fries and shakes.

While waiting for the orders to be filled, a couple of students from this university town decided to make a name for themselves by mouthing off at us and generally being a bit too

The damaged tyres on our team mini-van, and the note that quickly led the local constabulary to the perpetrator of the crime.

Stephen Fleming was described as 'a bit lazy early,' while under the heading 'Mental/Current Form', Chris Cairns was summarised as: 'Fragile. A good front runner, but lacks confidence if you get on top of him ... their key player, others feed off him.' Spinner Daniel Vettori was labelled a 'good bowler [who] turns the ball, gives the ball good flight, good arm ball'. Craig McMillan was a 'good confident player but prone to silly mistakes', while Adam Parore was called 'a dangerous player coming in down the order, can hit straight away'. .... The first one-dayer of this series was declared a 'no result' after the match was restricted to 23 overs.

February 19

Shane Warne apologised after being involved in an off-field incident during the rained-out Wellington one-dayer, when he objected to two boys taking his photograph while he was smoking. 'I believed the matter had been resolved,' Warne said in a statement, 'but if there has been any misunderstanding I apologise and I will meet the boys in Wellington to sort this out.' ... Australia won the second one-day international against New Zealand, in Auckland, by five wickets. The home team was all out for 122 in the 31st over, and Australia reached their victory target in 24.4 overs, with Matthew Hayden scoring 50 from 49 balls.

smart for their own good. None of us wanted to make a scene, so initially the boys just let it slide, but as the criticism and crudeness continued Haydos gave it to one of the young loudmouths by sledging his mid-1980s Adidas tracksuit, to which the uni student fired back with, 'Yeah pal, thanks very much, it only cost me 10 bucks from the op shop!' And that was it.

Thinking nothing more of the altercation, the team headed back to the hotel for a few hours' 'shuteye' before an early departure in the morning. After checking out and paying the bills, we got on board our mini-bus, but from my seat I could see that some of the tyres on our other bus were looking decidedly flatter than they should have been. A closer inspection revealed that a knife was wedged into the front right tyre, with a note attached that read, 'Hayden, your family will suffer, mate.' And it was signed 'Adidas Three Stripes'.

Clearly, this lad was bored with life. It didn't take long for the local authorities to track him down, with the film from the McDonald's video surveillance camera a useful piece of evidence. We learned later that he actually turned himself in when word got around town that the police were after the 'Adidas Three Stripes' man. Now he has to repay the Budget hire company the money to cover the cost of the replacement tyres, do 20 hours' community service and write apology letters to Budget, the hotel and to our team management. Maybe next time he'll limit his sledging to when he's sitting in the outer ...

February 24   DUNEDIN

A RULE THAT MUST be changed to enhance one-day cricket is the one that concerns limits to short-pitched deliveries. As things stand at the moment, you can't bowl anything that bounces over shoulder height, which takes the unexpected bouncer or throat ball out of the fast bowler's armoury, as well as depriving the batsman of any chance to play a hook shot.

Brett Lee, being the 'young pup' and 'new kid on the block' that he is, rightly wants to make his mark. And I, as captain, have always reckoned that if you want to unsettle a batsman or change his thought process then I don't mind seeing the odd bouncer, because the one-run penalty for a no-ball might be paid back in other ways. During yesterday's

Occasionally during our New Zealand tour, with ball and especially bat, Chris Cairns played as if he was another Ian Botham.

Dunedin one-dayer, while I was icing my ankle in the freezing conditions up in the grandstand, 'Binger' produced a delivery that stunned everyone and incited the ire of the crowd. He cranked up his pack to somewhere near 100 mph and hurtled down a lethal nut that climbed quickly enough to catch Kiwi keeper-batsman Adam Parore unawares. The ball crashed into Parore's thumb on its journey towards his helmet, and from there onto the stumps for a hit-wicket verdict.

The crack of leather on helmet was audible to everyone at the ground. The ambience of the Kiwi team, sitting on the viewing area next to ours, changed as if they were a group of tourists who had just been told they had to make a compulsory bungee jump. The mood went from frivolity and laughter to fright and silence in one split second. The effect it had on the crowd was predictable, particularly after Parore hung around, looking for an escape clause in the form of a no-ball because the ball was above shoulder height. The no-ball call wasn't forthcoming, because the ball had clearly struck the batsman's glove first, but a barrage of bottles and rubbish onto the field was. Most of this debris was thrown by the many university students who clearly felt invincible because there were so many of them.

That delivery represented a significant moment, not only in the message it gave to the Kiwis that Brett Lee is quick, mean and a force to be wary of, but also because it put a major dent in Adam Parore's pride, confidence and ego. He is seen as a leader in the New Zealand team, a guy who can get things going, and a player who likes to verbally mix it with the opposition. But this heavy blow will not only affect him physically, it might also be mentally quite damaging …

The third game of the one-day series resulted in an Australian win by 50 runs. The catalyst for the visitors' big total of 4-310 was an opening stand of 114 in 19.6 overs between Adam Gilchrist (77 from 65 balls) and Mark Waugh (75 from 109). Later, Andrew Symonds hit 34 in 12 minutes from just 13 balls after Steve Waugh had to retire hurt. New Zealand's reply featured good innings from Roger Twose (62 from 61 balls) and Nathan Astle (81 from 83), but the result was rarely in doubt, the innings ending in the 45th over.

The ACB sought and received assurances from New Zealand Cricket regarding the control of crowds after a series of incidents during the recent one-day games and an overnight attack on the team vehicles in Dunedin. Play in Dunedin was held up for 10 minutes after the crowd objected to the dismissal of Adam Parore, who was out hit wicket to a short but legitimate delivery from Brett Lee.

February 26 CHRISTCHURCH

INSTINCTIVELY, A PLAYER KNOWS when he or she has just entered the world of continuous ice packs, repeated deep friction treatment and endless hours of rehabilitation. For me, it happened right in the middle of a batting onslaught that I was revelling in, during the third of our one-day matches over here, in Dunedin three days back. Taking Kiwi quick Chris Cairns down isn't an easy task to accomplish, but I was on fire, smashing him around the park, when I gave myself a bit of room to try to blast him through the offside. Cairns might have seen my movement and speared in an attempted yorker which ended up making a beeline for my midriff. As I tried to extricate myself from this vulnerable position, I went over on my left ankle in a way that left me feeling as if someone had shoved a knife through the joint. This led to the first 'retired hurt' of my career and a long night of treatment on the ankle ahead. We eventually won the match, thanks largely to a massive batting total, but the event was marred by what has become the now customary crowd disturbance and a number of examples of loutish behaviour by spectators.

For me, the hard slog ahead had already started — ice packs at regular intervals and keeping the ankle elevated to stop the bleeding. These measures are so crucial in the first 24 to 48 hours. With the next one-dayer in Christchurch only two and a bit days away, I needed a miracle, and as luck would have it, we had just the man in team physiotherapist, Patrick Farhart.

Patrick was with the team because long-time physio Errol Alcott was back in Sydney recuperating after major knee surgery. He had slipped and fallen awkwardly during a game of touch footy in Adelaide, tearing the cruciate and medial ligaments in his right knee, as well as both cartilages. First estimates were that Errol would be out of action for at least six months.

The mission to be fit again began immediately, even before the game was over. It was a new ice pack every 45 minutes, each one for 25 minutes and then 20 minutes where my leg was encased in a compression bandage to stop the swelling and bleeding. This process continued all night, with a little shuteye being had around 4am, but just for two hours until our wake-up call at 6am to prepare for

Team Meeting: The Captain's Notes

BEFORE ONE-DAYER IN CHRISTCHURCH

THE DIFFERENCE BETWEEN BEING GOOD AND GREAT

Preamble: I raised this concept to give us an idea to focus on, and to give everyone connected with the squad a target we can aspire to and — when we get there — something that we can maintain.

This is a topic we haven't discussed before, or even been in a position to consider. But I feel, given our recent run of success, that it is now appropriate for us to embrace the concept. What I did was raise the issue, and seek responses from all the players. This is a summary of our conclusions.

To be great we must have:
- Talent.
- Skill.
- Passion.
- Discipline.
- Respect (for ourselves first, then the opposition; and also the traditions of the game).

And we must also want to:
- Be prepared to 'raise the bar'.
- Identify and rectify barriers in our way.
- Know each other.
- Be honest (to self and teammates).
- Be ruthless.
- Enjoy each other's success.
- Champion things we do well.

the trip north. To give you some idea of Patrick's dedication to the task, he carried ice bags on the bus to the airport and had some more ready for the flight. The moment we reached the hotel, he immediately set himself up in the designated team room in preparation for what lay ahead.

Over the course of the next 24 hours, we worked together on the injury for at least 15 hours. It was a continual cycle of treatment — beginning with the dreaded ice (which I feared would shortly lead to frostbite), followed by deep tissue work and mobilisation of the ligaments around the ankle. After this, we got to work with the 'Thera-Band' (elastic tubing) to strengthen up the weakened and injured muscles. And finally I was walking, which became running later in the night. We didn't finish up until 12.45am, by which time we were both knackered, but the improvement in my ankle was quite incredible — from being no chance, I felt I was now a 60-40 chance of playing.

As I hobbled off to my room, Patrick gave me the good news. 'Tugga,' he said quietly, 'I'll give you a bit of a rest. How about we start at seven in the morning.'

Wow, I smiled as I continued on, this guy should have been in the army. But he assured me that I needed another five hours in the morning before I'd be right for this afternoon's game which will start at 2.30pm.

Australia clinched the six-match one-day series with a third win (plus one no result), in Christchurch. Batting first, Steve Waugh's team established a new record innings total by Australia in limited-overs internationals — 6-349 from 50 overs. Adam Gilchrist slammed 128 from just 98 deliveries and with Mark Waugh (70 from 88) added 189 for the first wicket in 27.6 overs. Steve Waugh hit 54 from 44 deliveries, and Damien Martyn smashed an unbeaten 29 from 14 at the end. The Kiwis also passed 300, being 9-301 at the end of their 50 overs. Captain Stephen Fleming made 82, and Chris Harris 59.

The treatment was again intense, but I could feel the benefits coming my way with each cycle of work. The great feature of Patrick's effort is that he takes each case so personally — he isn't happy until he's got someone back on the park. That sort of dedication from the support staff is priceless. Eventually, I felt as if I would play the Christchurch one-dayer with the aid of strapping, even though the ankle was still short of being 100 per cent right. But if you wanted to play every game feeling 100 per cent you'd never play at all ...

When we batted after losing the toss, we proceeded to put on a run-scoring exhibition that I thought was as close as we'll ever get to batting perfection. We amassed 6-349 from our 50 overs, to register our country's highest-ever score. It was like watching a highlights package, and included a world record 15 sixes (which, in fact, was 16, but the third umpire ruled incorrectly — as they so often do — on a shot that sailed well clear of the fence but was only called a four).

Gilly's 128 from just 98 balls was a scintillating display. He even looked set to be the first man to make a one-day double hundred, until he actually mishit one. Based on

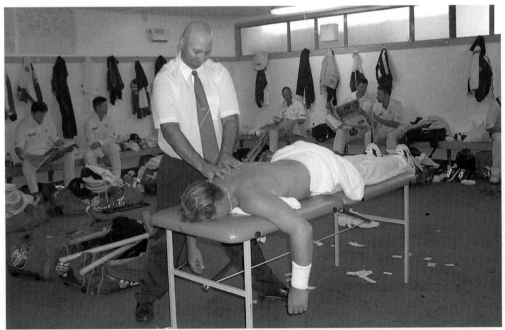

Team physio Pat Farhart works on the famous right shoulder of Shane Warne. This photograph was actually taken on the morning of day two of the first Test, in Auckland, just after we'd had our team photo taken. This is why Pat is wearing suit pants, shirt and tie rather than training gear.

what he did today, he'll be the first to make it to 200 in a one-day international; he was simply awesome. Our clean hitting and continuous assault was like being in a dream — we just couldn't make a mistake. The magic fingers of Farhart got me into the game and enabled me to smack five sixes in a 44-ball knock of 54, which made all the pain and suffering worthwhile.

Our batting ensured another comfortable victory, which stretched our winning sequence to 13 matches and a new world record. Count the washed-out game in Wellington and we've been unbeaten in our last 14 games. It is fantastic to be a part of a team that is so positive and prepared to back itself. It feels as if we're on automatic pilot.

February 27 CHRISTCHURCH

THE DEMANDS ON INTERNATIONAL cricketers seem to be ever increasing in recent times. This has been brought on by the large number of games being played each year — and resulted in us having to endure an enormous amount of time away from family and friends — and has also meant that our team needs some flexibility so it can deal with issues that might otherwise destabilise the team.

One strategy that seems to have gained acceptance is the 'rotation' of the quick bowlers during a one-day tournament, with bowlers being 'rested' from some matches, to make sure they're at their peak when we really need them. This was a touchy one in years gone by, as the bowlers all wanted to play every game, and feared that by giving up their position to someone else they might actually have been putting their long-term place in jeopardy. However, during recent series — including this one — it was made clear that the quick bowlers would be rested on occasions, to recharge the batteries and take care of the inevitable niggling injuries that crop up. Once the situation was made clear, it didn't present any problems and I believe was actually welcomed by the players. A similar strategy prevailed upon the three genuine all-rounders in our squad — Ian Harvey, Shane Lee and Andrew Symonds — who all expected at one time or another to have a breather on the bench.

One of the reasons this policy works for us is that at present we have such a talented squad that I believe than no matter what our final XI is, we will be just as competitive and strong. Last year I was missing because of injury, this year it was Shane, but the team hasn't missed a beat. I have always believed that one of the greatest hindrances to trying to maintain excellence and staying at the top is staleness and a lack of variety. By this, I don't mean that you should continually change the side and get new faces in just for the sake of it, but it is important not to leave a player with the same tasks and duties in every match.

To bring out the best in people, you have to sometimes force them out of their comfort zone by giving them a new situation or experience to deal with. Batting at No. 6 for my first 100-odd one-day internationals was great in many ways, because I knew what to do in certain situations, my role was defined and I became fairly adept at my tasks. However, I believe that if I had been given opportunities elsewhere, my game would have flourished and climbed to a new level. The benefit of having batsmen, bowlers and fieldsmen trying new positions is that it might open up more options, tactically, in the future, give you more flexibility and keep the opposition guessing.

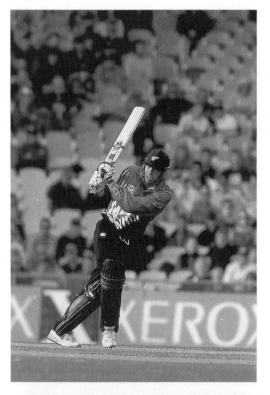

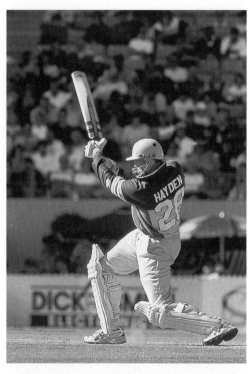

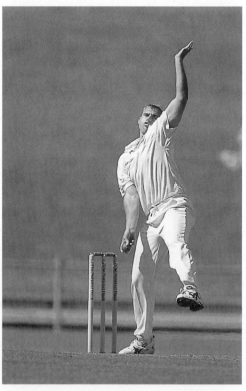

Four photos, three cricketers. The two Kiwis at left are captain Stephen Fleming (above) and their excellent spinner Daniel Vettori. The cricketer at right is Australia's Matthew Hayden, on the attack during the one-day series (above) and having a rare spell at the bowling crease (below) during our tour game against Central Districts.

STEVE WAUGH

Examples of this include Andrew Symonds being injected during the first 15 overs of our batting, or as happened yesterday, when he batted at No. 3 after Gilly and Junior put on 189 for the first wicket. Another case is Michael Bevan sliding up and down the order to suit the occasion, trying to have a left-hander and right-hander batting together as often as possible, leaving Brett Lee at first change, bowling Shane Warne in the first 10 overs, moving regular infielders such as Ricky Ponting and Symonds to the outfield during the last 15 overs so they are always in the game. It also creates an air of excitement, because players may be called on to do something they don't normally do or are given a chance to show their full potential.

Away from the game we are trying to make playing international cricket for Australia as 'family friendly' as we can. Having the Australian Cricketers' Association work with the Australian Cricket Board has been tremendously beneficial in many areas. One long-suffering group has been the families, who have long been ignored and neglected. Thankfully, the Board now caters for them by providing its players with apartment-style accommodation, single rooms instead of twin share, designated seating areas at the grounds, even crèches at certain grounds. This comes on top of a general awareness that if the family is looked after, then the player will be more comfortable in his attitude towards playing and performing. In line with this is a more understanding attitude to one-off personal circumstances — such as when Shane Warne was allowed to briefly return home from an Ashes tour after the birth of his daughter, when Glenn McGrath missed a one-dayer during the recent Australian season because his wife was due to give birth, or letting someone fly home from a tour for a funeral, as happened earlier on this trip when Slats returned home.

To a certain degree, these personal moments weren't considered important by the officials in past years, but now the ACB agrees with me that a happy and contented individual makes for an even better sportsperson.

February 29 NAPIER

THE AUSTRALIAN TEAM'S social committee of Gilly, Warney and Haydos have the job of organising our after-match activities, days out and other assorted entertainment. Not long after we arrived in Dunedin a few days ago for the third one-dayer, the boys came up with the concept that in broad terms involved each player drawing out a teammate's name from a hat, with that player drawn becoming your personal target for embarrassment. The objective was to locate the worst, most incriminating shirt you could find for your victim, with everyone's new shirts to be worn on our next team night out. The only selection criterion was that all shirts needed collars.

The next morning, the boys were quickly out looking for a cheap and nasty purchase. Favourite haunts around Dunedin were St Vincent de Paul, the local church opportunity shop, the Salvation Army shop and any other establishment where a bargain-basement buy might be on offer. Some magnificent items were purchased, but little did we know that we'd actually got more than we bargained for.

It's almost impossible to keep anything involving a high-profile sportsperson a secret these days, especially in a big country town such as Dunedin. Still, you can imagine how hard we choked on our corn flakes the day after this shopping extravaganza, when the

Australia extended their undefeated run in one-day internationals to 13 with a comfortable five-wicket defeat of New Zealand in Napier. Nathan Astle hit a century for the locals and Damien Fleming took 4-41, before Australia replied with 5-245 in 45.4 overs. In at 2-34, Michael Bevan scored 107 ... Damien Martyn was included in the Australian Test squad to face New Zealand, after Ricky Ponting was ruled out because of his ankle injury.

Australia lost only their third one-day international since the 1999 World Cup (in 24 matches: 20 wins, three losses, one no result) when they were defeated by seven wickets by New Zealand in Auckland. Steve Waugh rearranged his team's batting order, which allowed Damien Martyn to bat through the innings for 116 not out from 135 deliveries, out of 191 all out in 46.2 overs. The Kiwis' successful run chase was led by opener Chris Nevin, who made 74, and Stephen Fleming, who remained undefeated on 60.

headline 'AUSSIE CROSS DRESSERS' leapt from the front pages of the local paper. It turned out that someone had seen Adam Gilchrist looking at a frilly lady's blouse and overheard him mention that it appeared to be a 'good buy'. From there, the rumour mill went into overdrive. First, the eavesdropper called a local radio station, which quickly broadcast a report questioning our sexuality and behaviour. And then the papers had a go. This was only a small distraction with the match still 24 hours away, but on game day the locals turned it into something to rival the Trevor Chappell underarm affair. The jibes came thick and fast as the team's mini-bus made its way through the town centre to the ground.

Our efforts at setting each other up culminated in a barbecue at Napier today. The food was magnificent — cooked fish that had been caught by our self-titled 'Rex Hunts', Hayden and Symonds, and meat purchased by the lads at an excellent local butcher. It was a real team effort, with salads to be made up, bread to be buttered, guacamole to be created and onions to be superbly sliced (by yours truly). After the feed and amid raucous laughter, we presented one another with our shirts. My favourites were Buck's delightful tank top and rub-on tattoo, thoughtfully purchased by Brett Lee, and Pat Farhart's silky see-through number, which highlighted his thick Merv Hughes-like body carpet. Fortunately for me, Marto knew where his bread was buttered and didn't slip the boot in too much. Still, the black-and-white flowery top was something I couldn't imagine anyone ever wearing for real, even if I heard one or two comments behind my back that 'it didn't look half bad'.

Not being satisfied with keeping our little team night to ourselves, we set off in search of the nearest pub, which was located close to our hotel, right in the middle of town. You can imagine the looks we received when we strode in as a group, ridiculously outfitted in tank tops, leather jackets, frilly blouses and an assortment of '70s style shirts. For me, it was worth the whole exercise just to see the locals' jaws drop, especially when the boys began competing on the video car-games and pool tables situated right next to the bar and restaurant. We play hard on the field, but off it we try to enjoy our time as much as possible, and in doing so we generate a few laughs and a lot of memories.

Mark Waugh struggles to regain his ground during the final one-day international of our New Zealand tour. The defeat ended our unbeaten streak at 14 games (13 wins and one game abandoned).

March 4 AUCKLAND

WE HAD NAMED THIS limited-overs leg of the tour 'Operation Blackout', a reference to New Zealand's national colours. Coming into yesterday's fifth and final one-dayer, our winning sequence in limited-overs internationals stood at 14, and trying to achieve a 5-0 clean sweep remained our priority. Buck and I had also decided to use the game as a chance to offer different opportunities to many of the players. With this in mind, we put Damien Martyn and Matthew Hayden at the top of the order, I went to No. 3, followed by Michael Bevan, Mark Waugh and Adam Gilchrist. It was a move bound to stir controversy, but we needed to give Marto an extended hit before the Tests and we also believed that both he and Haydos could do the job. The move was also made with half an eye to the future, just in case our regular openers couldn't play due to illness, poor form or injury.

The plan was part success, part failure, with our batting generally being of a poor standard — except for a gem of a knock by Marto, who scored an unbeaten century. This was the first time an Aussie had carried his bat through a completed innings in a one-day international. The resounding defeat, though, wasn't what we were after, and the predictable media questions came at the post-match press conference.

'Why did you tamper with the batting order?'

'Why did you change a winning formula?'

And so on and so on. Perhaps the press guys had a point, but in all honesty we would still have won if we had played to our abilities. I don't think it was the change in the batting

Northern Districts were 9-295 at stumps on the first day of their match against the Australians in Hamilton.

Justin Langer (155) and Damien Martyn (109) were the stars of the second day of the Australians' tour match in Hamilton. Shane Warne declared the tourists' innings at 4-383, after Northern Districts were all out for 300. At stumps, the home side was 1-48.

The Australians won their tour match against Northern Districts by eight wickets. Glenn McGrath and Colin Miller each took three wickets, after which Greg Blewett (83 not out) top-scored as the visitors hit the 198 runs needed for victory in 46 overs.

New Zealand finished the first day of the first Test, in Auckland, precariously placed at 4-26, after earlier bowling out Australia for 214. Justin Langer (46 from 47 balls) and Mark Waugh (72 not out) were the only batsmen to get past 17 in the Australian innings, in which Daniel Vettori took 5-62. Brett Lee claimed two wickets in the late New Zealand collapse, and Glenn McGrath and Shane Warne one each.

order that made our approach complacent, lazy and soft. Anyway, the fact that Marto scored his first hundred for Australia was a major breakthrough, and I now expect him to really kick on. From personal experience, I know how important that first century is, because it allows you to settle down and play with the confidence and style you had when you were scoring the runs that got you into the team in the first place.

Even though we've managed to establish some records during our winning one-day run, I think there is still room for improvement. We're certainly not looking at this tour as being the end of our adventure. We want to set new standards. We believe we can play better and we believe we can keep winning. Sure, we're playing cricket to a high standard and maybe to a standard that very few teams in the one-day game have ever reached, but I felt that the South Africans were at that high point a few years ago and the West Indies most definitely were in the early and mid-1980s.

But our team is really growing together well, which is encouraging given that the bulk of this side can stay together until at least the next World Cup in 2003.

March 9 AUCKLAND

ONE OF THE BIGGEST challenges an elite cricketer will face during his career is whether he can he come back from being dropped, and even more important, will the experience make him a better person and player. In the case of Damien Martyn, the answer to these questions is a resounding 'yes'. Marto has shown great poise and maturity in his cricket over the past couple of years, to first establish himself in the one-day squad and now, with Ricky Ponting's injury, regain his place in the Test team.

Marto has always been an enormous talent, and was being groomed for the highest positions from very early in his first-class career, but a mixture of complacency and lack of direction saw him plummet out of the scene after taking on the Windies with some success back in 1992–93. Today, he is a complete cricketer, composed and classy on the field, and a major contributor to the team off it. It's a pleasure to see him back. Based on the way he has handled himself, I confidently predict that his future will be littered with success.

Damien Martyn during his lone hand in Auckland, when he scored an outstanding century and became the first Australian to carry his bat through a completed innings in a one-day international.

I see our series against New Zealand, which begins in two days' time at Eden Park in Auckland, as being a real challenge for us, given that the Kiwis are coming off their highly rewarding Test-match victories over the West Indies. I am fearful, too, that a jaded feeling might have swept over our team. We have been playing cricket for 20 of the past 22 months and I know that I am starting to feel the effects. As a result, we've backed off on our training sessions and even spent some days completely away from the game, visiting wineries and golf courses to chill out and get recharged.

On the field, we intend to continue with our policy of being aggressive, but patient, and to continually make the opposition feel the pressure. We've identified the top of their batting order as being suspect and their bowling does seem to revolve around paceman Chris Cairns and the left-arm spinner, Daniel Vettori. With this in mind, when we bat we know there are going to be moments that will need to be identified as being key times to go on the offensive.

March 11 AUCKLAND

EVEN THOUGH LANG only made 46 in our first innings of the first Test in Auckland here today, it was the manner in which he scored them that counted. On a pitch that was already turning at an alarming rate, Lang took the 'bull by the horns' to try and give our whole team a psychological boost. The man on the receiving end was New Zealand's premier bowler, left-arm orthodox spinner Daniel Vettori, whom we all feel is the key man if the

Shane Warne moved to within one wicket of Dennis Lillee's Australian Test wicket-taking record, as the visitors took a slight advantage during day two of the first Test. The home side was all out for 163 in their first innings, with Glenn McGrath taking four wickets and Warne three, and by stumps Australia's lead had grown to 165, with five second-innings wickets remaining.

At stumps on day three, New Zealand were 5-151, needing 130 more runs if they were to win the first Test. Craig McMillan was unbeaten on 57, Chris Cairns not out 20. Earlier, Daniel Vettori had taken 7-87, giving him 12 wickets for the match, including his 100th in Tests, and Adam Gilchrist had played an important hand of 59 to get Australia's second innings up to 229. Then Shane Warne had bowled Nathan Astle for 35, to bring him level with Dennis Lillee on 355 Test wickets. Astle, with McMillan, had steadied the New Zealand ship after four wickets — three of them to Colin Miller — had fallen at the start of the innings for 43 runs.

No play was possible on the scheduled fourth day of the first Test, because of consistent overnight rain and then another heavy downpour in the early afternoon.

Kiwis are to extend their undefeated run against Australia in Auckland beyond 24 years.

Lang is renowned for his long net sessions, and is a confessed 'bataholic'. He has been putting Buck's throwing arm through hell with the hundreds of throwdowns he's requested from the coach after our regular team sessions. Hitting over the top has become the latest skill that Lang has been trying to improve, and the early evidence is that all the practice has certainly been beneficial. Fearing neither the quality of the bowler, nor the match situation, Lang repeatedly lofted Vettori over the infield to the boundary, a strategy that forced the Kiwis to change their tactics and bring on the right-arm offie, Paul Wiseman. It was a significant victory for the batsman, as he had quickly thrown the opposition team off their game plan; that Lang did it against their premier bowler was not an easy thing to do.

Another crucial innings of a different style came from Mark Waugh. They say class is permanent and form is temporary and today Junior proved it when he guided us beyond 200 after it looked for a period as if we'd struggle to reach 150. Mark is increasingly motivated by the situation these days, and seems to thrive on the tough times. His skill at deflecting the turning ball off his pads and his timing through the field was a lesson for all of us. It was a dig that won't attract all the headlines but, if we win, it will be one of the major reasons for our success.

Obviously, we weren't happy to be bowled out for only 214, but our bowlers and fieldsmen put in a stunning display before stumps to give us an advantage. One thrilling moment came when Marto pulled off an acrobatic full-length diving catch to get rid of Kiwi opener Chris Spearman. It was an astounding effort that tilted the events of the day ever so slightly in our favour.

Then, as he has so often done in the past, Warney concocted a plan with one delivery remaining in the day's play. With Brett Lee, operating at full tilt to nightwatchman Paul Wiseman, we had a very attacking field in place — plenty of slips for an edge and a close-in fieldsman either side of the pitch, each hoping for a tentative prod to a short-pitched delivery. Of course, there was plenty of encouragement from the lads for Brett to test out the middle of the pitch, and we hoped such a thought was entrenched in Wiseman's brain, and maybe a bit of fear, too. To further make him sweat, Warney dashed across to me in the gully and suggested that the mid-on be moved to a leg-gully position and our fine leg come up to leg slip. Now, he hoped, the batsman was sure to be thinking that a searing bumper was going to finish off the proceedings.

At the same time, we were thinking that — because Wiseman was sure to be on the back foot — it would actually be an ideal time to pitch one up. But for this to happen we needed to have a bowler thinking on the same lines as we now were. Such a 'cricket brain' is something you can't teach; it's a born trait, and fortunately for us, Binger has got it. He obliged with a full-length 'in-ducker' that shot between the bemused Wiseman's bat and pad, crashed into the stumps, and ended our day on a high …

March 16 AUCKLAND

'We play it tough, we play it hard, we always play to win,
'Cause in our hearts and in our eyes, you can see the passion within.
We compete in green, we compete in gold, now it's time to play in whites,
This standard that we speak about is being lifted to new heights.
From ball one today, to the last ball bowled and the remainder left in NZ,
We owe it to us to back ourselves and leave the Kiwis for dead.
If I can say just one more thing, if we make it up this hill,
There's a trophy waiting right at the top with a message engraved — "Australia 3-nil".'

— **Brett Lee** (read before day three, first Test v New Zealand, March 13)

I ALWAYS SAW THIS first Test, at Auckland's Eden Park, as being our greatest challenge. The pitch is low and slow, with some turn, and as such is well suited to their team. Eden Park has also been something of a 'hoodoo' ground for Australia, as we have not won here in nearly 25 years. If ever there was a team to break the mould, however, I felt that this one was it — statistics such as these are treated now as a challenge rather than an obstacle.

Everyone was tremendously proud and mightily relieved when Warney inched past Dennis Lillee as Australia's highest Test wicket-taker by getting the final wicket of the Test, Paul Wiseman caught by Adam Gilchrist. In my view, the pressure involved as he inched

Brett Lee in Napier during our tour match against Central Districts. The reason this part of the dressing room is particularly messy is that Bing made the mistake of parking his gear right next to mine.

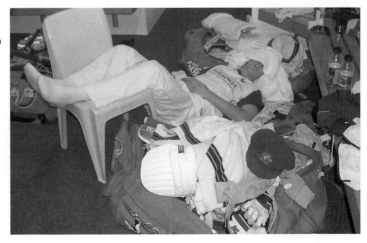

Play was delayed until 11.30am, but Australia finally won the first Test and Shane Warne got his record-breaking 356th Test wicket, when last man Paul Wiseman was caught by Adam Gilchrist. The winning margin was 62 runs. Colin Miller took 5-55, his best figures in Test matches, and Craig McMillan made 78. The man-of-the-match award went to Daniel Vettori. The win was Australia's eighth straight in Test matches, equalling the record set by Warwick Armstrong's Australian teams of 1920–21 and 1921.

The Australians were 4-118 in reply to Central Districts' 160 at stumps on the first day of the tour match in Napier. Damien Fleming took 5-21 for the tourists, and Mark Waugh reached 46 not out by the close.

The Australians struggled to 207 all out (Mark Waugh 93 not out) and Central Districts were 4-207 at stumps on day two of the tour match in Napier.

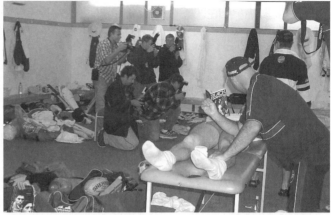

On day four, which was eventually completely washed out, the press came into our dressing room seeking a snap to send back to their editors — something to fill the sports pages. To help them, we started up a game of mock cricket, with Slats (below) batting left-handed to give the bowlers a chance and the photographers something to get excited about.

towards this milestone has certainly affected Shane's bowling in recent times. He got away from his great strengths — consistency and patience — and became a little wayward in his quest to get the wickets in a hurry.

Watch out for him in the next two Tests when he gets back into the rhythm and control that have made him one of the all-time greats.

Here in Auckland, with Warney a little off his game, we needed someone else to step up to the plate. Who better than the man who defies all of cricket's stereotypes to fill the void, the caterpillar turned butterfly, Colin Miller?

Funky, as he is affectionately known, has been a revelation and continues to improve with every game. So much so, I believe he can become the best off-spinner in the world during the next 12 months if he can fend off the perils of his art, injury, and defy the bowler's curse, age. He is unique in his action, as he is self-taught, giving the ball an enormous rip combined with a speed that is much quicker through the air than the average tweaker. Miller has been great for the whole team with his refreshing attitude, relishing every day on tour as one he never expected to have.

The story of Colin Miller, cricketer, is a great one. A journeyman pro, he played for three states in pursuit of the ultimate dream of representing his country. For over a decade he bowled only medium-pace outswingers, until he 'saw the light', turned to off-spin, and miraculously became one of the best in the world. Not long before he finally made the Australian team, I'm pretty sure 'Funky' would have thought his time was gone, but now not only is he wearing the baggy green; he's played a major role in each and every one of the Tests he's appeared in.

This Test was probably Funky's toughest examination. Going into the game, I expected him to be a match-winner because it seemed that the playing surface, with its clay base, was going to suit his much-quicker-than-normal off-spin. These conditions, I thought, should have enabled him to make the ball grip, turn and hopefully bounce. I wasn't far wrong.

Such is my faith in Funky, I elected to open the bowling with him alongside Glenn McGrath. I did so for a number of reasons. I believed that it would upset New Zealand's opening batsmen's thoughts and plans, because they'd be expecting Brett Lee to take the new ball. Secondly, with the harder ball and raised seam, I banked on Funky being able to get that extra bounce, and perhaps more turn than usual, too, as the seam gouged into the surface. Thirdly, the top three Kiwi batsmen are all considered pretty good players of the new ball but in our view they are suspect against the turning ball.

As things turned out, Funky did more than just

Colin Miller had plenty to get funky about during our first Test victory, in Auckland.

The tour match in Napier
ended in a draw. Central
Districts declared their second
innings at 9-320, and then
the Australians batted out
time, to be 4-186 when play
ended. Justin Langer scored
79, and Damien Martyn was
61 not out.

At stumps on the first day of
the second Test, at the Basin
Reserve in Wellington,
Australia were 2-29 in reply
to New Zealand's first innings
total of 298. Chris Cairns hit
a stirring 109 from 138
deliveries for the Kiwis, after
they had fallen to 5-66.
Shane Warne took four
wickets for the Australians.

acquit himself admirably; he went on to take a five-for in the second innings and lead us to victory. A crucial moment came in the first over of the fifth day, when he claimed the vital wicket of Chris Cairns.

One part of our strategy throughout this Test was obvious: whenever a left-hander came in we wanted Miller bowling at him; when a right-hander arrived we wanted him facing Warney. The ball spinning away is always harder to play. Of course, this isn't always possible, so Funky began day five bowling to the right-handed Cairns. I wasn't too concerned, though, because I felt that Cairns didn't like being tied down and Miller had been very economical throughout the game to this point.

There must be something about spinners and their diets, because Warney is a living miracle, having survived 30 years on toasted cheese sandwiches, bread rolls, chips, sauce, spaghetti bolognaise, nachos, tomato and cheese pizzas, Burger Rings, Pizza Shapes and Twisties. Funky, in contrast, just plain doesn't enjoy food that much — except for his specialty sandwiches of cheese, chips, ham and a Kit Kat all squashed together.

Whatever their tastes, our two spinners were both

The great Shane Warne departs Eden Park after breaking Dennis Lillee's Australian Test wicket-taking record.

instrumental in Australia's Eden Park Test win, along with the ever-blossoming Justin Langer, the ageless younger Waugh and the deadly duo of the Porsche-like Brett Lee and the Bentley, Glenn McGrath. And for me, the Test had a moment I will always cherish, that occurred straight after the match.

I had the honour of leading the team into our much-loved *Under the Southern Cross* after the absent Ricky Ponting passed the job on to me. I dragged Warney up onto the bench to help me out, while Punter and Geoff Marsh listened in via a telephone hook-up.

March 23 WELLINGTON

IT HAS ALREADY BEEN a historic couple of weeks for the Australian one-day and Test squads, and the Test here in Wellington gives us the opportunity to further rewrite the record books. A win in the second Test will see us become the most successful Australian team in both one-days *and* Tests in terms of consecutive wins.

Records, of course, are made to be broken and I'm sure in time we will be eclipsed. But it gives me an enormous sense of pride to have done so well since we arrived in Zimbabwe last October. For me, the greatest joy has not been our results but the way we achieved them. They have come from positive, aggressive cricket with every member of both squads growing in stature in the process ...

March 24 WELLINGTON

OVER THE PAST 12 months we have tried to constantly come up with fresh ideas to keep us on track and motivated. Before this Test, Buck decided he would ask each of us to write down what we wanted to get out of the match and how we were going to go about achieving our objectives. So a plain sheet of butcher's paper hung in our team room for two days before the match, with each player putting his thoughts down whenever he felt he had something appropriate to offer.

Eventually, each player and each of our support staff, too, had contributed. Then, as a gentle reminder, Buck stuck our words to the dressing room wall, just in case we couldn't remember what our goals were. It was a clever move, which should ensure that we never lose focus throughout the Test, even though the weather will be cold and I can feel a certain lethargy and staleness seeping into the squad.

Stephen Fleming won the toss and elected to bat, but we got off to a terrific start as Brett Lee took a wicket in each of his first two overs and then Funky Miller trapped Mathew Sinclair lbw to have the home team reeling at 3-18. Fleming and Nathan Astle mounted something of a fightback, but then we had the good fortune to witness a magical hour of spin wizardry from Warney. You could literally hear the ball fizzing through the air; the drift, flight and dip of the ball's trajectory had the likes of Nathan Astle and Craig McMillan groping and searching for the ball as if it was mysteriously disappearing, then re-emerging from nowhere. It was Warney at his best — the shoulder was in perfect position and the energy he was generating at the crease was enabling him to really give the ball a rip. It was a spell the like of which he hadn't produced since his shoulder operation in 1998, but it gave a clear indication that he still has many great years ahead of him if his desire remains strong.

This was certainly one of the most joyous Test celebrations I've been involved in. Not only had Australia won a Test at Eden Park for the first time since 1977 and Shane Warne broken the Australian Test wicket-taking record, but it had been a really gutsy, satisfying victory, during which we'd shown great strength as a unit to win a match we could easily have lost.

March 25

Michael Slater and Steve Waugh took command on the second day of the second Test, after Australia were initially struggling at 4-51. Both men made hundreds — Slater 143 and Waugh 109 not out — in a partnership of 199. At stumps, Australia were 5-318, with Damien Martyn 41 not out.

March 26

New Zealand held a lead of 78 with five second-innings wickets in hand after the third day of the second Test. Australia had been dismissed earlier in the day for 419, with Damien Martyn out for 78 and Steve Waugh unbeaten on 151. Waugh thus became the first man to go past 150 against each of the eight possible Test-match opponents.

When McMillan fell the scoreboard showed New Zealand's innings in tatters at 5-66, but led by Chris Cairns, who bludgeoned a remarkable Botham-like century, the Kiwis recovered admirably to reach 298. Then, before the close, Greg Blewett and nightwatchman Shane Warne were both dismissed, which I'd say definitely had the locals feeling better about the day's events than we did as we pondered the state of play late into the evening.

March 25 WELLINGTON

THINGS WERE LOOKING tricky. We had slumped to 4-51 chasing 298. Slats and I were in the middle. Our task was looking especially difficult because Daniel Vettori, hot off his 12-wicket haul in the Eden Park Test, was troubling both of us with his subtle changes of pace and varying degrees of flight. However, suddenly Vettori's back went into a spasm — a direct result, we learned later, of a suspected stress fracture. The release in pressure was immediate, the handbrake was off. It's times such as these that you have to up the tempo and, as the legendary coach of Essendon's AFL side, Kevin Sheedy, once told us, 'Seize the moment.' From this point onwards, we took control and basically put New Zealand out of the match.

Slats and I went on to add 199 and set the match up for us. It was exhilarating watching Slats lay into them, like William Wallace of *Braveheart* fame. In the face of adversity and uncertainty, he showed again that attack is so often the best form of defence. As a captain, I love it when we have to get our hands dirty before we come out on top …

March 26 WELLINGTON

THE BEAUTY OF HAVING a genuine strike bowler is that such a weapon can turn a game on its head in an instant. This was precisely what Binger did late on day three, when in consecutive balls he destroyed the stumps of both Horne and Sinclair with two of the most ferocious in-ducking yorkers you'd ever have the privilege of seeing. These wickets came at a time when we were struggling to get that critical initial breakthrough and when I was very conscious of the fact that everyone appeared a little flat. But after this spectacular over, we were back on track and hungry for more success …

March 27 WELLINGTON

WHEN WAS THE LAST time Glenn McGrath bowled an ordinary spell? The answer is, 'I can't remember.'

It don't think I have ever played with a bowler who carries out instructions or who can follow a plan better than Pigeon. Before play started today, we set ourselves the task of stopping Chris Cairns from scoring quickly, which is the way his natural instincts dictate to him to play. This job was executed magnificently by Glenn, who sent down eight overs and conceded barely a run, which set us up for the session in exactly the way we wanted it to pan out. With Cairns unable to score quickly, you could sense the pressure transferring directly onto his partner, which created a situation where we were able to control what was happening from both ends. Only great control and concentration from your bowlers can allow you to do this.

The end of the Test came soon after 5.30pm, after our bowlers ended the Kiwis' second innings with a real workmanlike performance in the cold, blustery conditions and then we knocked off the 174 runs needed to win in our now trademark fashion — aggressively and quickly. It was an Australian record-breaking ninth straight victory. Afterwards, our celebrations took on a special verve.

During the early weeks of this tour, I had given Ricky Ponting a call — to check up on his recovery from his damaged ankle and see whether he'd be available for the second half of the tour. Unfortunately, the news wasn't good: he told me that the ankle wasn't right, and he'd have to miss the entire New Zealand experience. Then he stunned me. 'Tugga,' he said, 'I want you to take over the honour of leading the boys into the team song.'

I had expected Punter to give this privilege to one of the younger guys. He had been

Australia won the second Test by six wickets, to take a 2-0 lead in the best-of-three series. New Zealand were bowled out for 294 (Stephen Fleming 60, Chris Cairns 69), leaving Australia needing 174 to win. Justin Langer made 57 and Mark Waugh remained 44 not out as the victory target was achieved in 54.1 overs. Michael Slater was named man of the match ... The West Indies' Courtney Walsh became Test cricket's leading wicket-taker when he captured his 435th wicket, against Zimbabwe in Jamaica. 'It's great he's got it,' remarked Steve Waugh. 'He's well respected and dedicated and it's a great effort for a fast bowler to stay fit and keep going for over a decade. He's played it tough and competitive but he's a good man as well.'

handed the role by Ian Healy, who in turn had received it from David Boon, who had had it passed on to him by Allan Border, who got it from Rod Marsh. For me to join this illustrious band, however temporarily, was a career highlight.

The whole experience of standing atop a dressing room table in front of the lads after a one-day series win or a Test-match victory, is something I'll never forget. To see the boys, arm in arm, screaming the words out together and for me to be their 'conductor' is a unique feeling.

Here in Wellington today, after we'd taken the second Test and in the process surpassed the eight-match winning streak of Warwick Armstrong's great Australian side of 1920–21 and 1921, I decided I wanted to share this experience. So I called upon each of the boys to take the stand, share a favourite memory from any one of our nine wins and lead us into one verse of *Under the Southern Cross*. To hear Matt Hayden's thoughts on what the baggy green means to him, to watch Justin Langer individually give each player a huge wrap, to see Flemo deliver his message in his birthday suit, and to feel the passion of physio Pat Farhart and fitness trainer Dave Misson as they explained their special feelings at being part of the squad, made this a very special occasion.

The motivation we gave each other for future challenges was priceless. The most important aspect to come out this experience from my point of view was that it emphasised the fact that every player can contribute to team strength in his own way. It may only be one comment, even a sentence, but everyone should be heard. We each have different strengths and assets that can help bond the squad and take our performances to a higher level.

March 28 WELLINGTON

MY LOVE FOR THE ballads and music of John Williamson is well known within the Australian cricket side, but I'm not alone. Andrew Symonds, Justin Langer, Matt Hayden and Adam Gilchrist are also big fans, and brother Mark is on the verge of becoming a convert. Even Warney has reached the point where he sings *and* enjoys *True Blue*. Damien Fleming is next in my sights, but how do you turn around the opinion and taste of a man whose CD collection features the entire Kiss collection, plus albums by bands such as Metallica, Grateful Dead and Grinspoon? However, I've got an inkling

Brett Lee in full cry at the Basin Reserve in Wellington during the second Test.

Flem really is a closet admirer, who secretly plays *The Best of John Williamson* in his headphones when nobody is around.

Fortunately for all of us, John just happens to be in town, so I got on the 'blower' and invited him around for a drink. Jokingly, I said to him, 'Why don't you bring your guitar along and give the lads a mini-concert?'

A few beers into our post-Test celebrations later, John strolled into our room with his guitar under his arm. Two hours on, and his set ended with *Waltzing Matilda*, the climax to a performance we'll never forget. Old favourites such as *Old Man Emu* and *Crocodile Roll* were interspersed with gems such as *The Cootamundra Wattle* and *Galleries of Pink Galahs*.

The guy who probably enjoyed the night the most was Brett Lee, who gained some coaching and tips on playing the guitar, an art at which it must be said he is already pretty useful. 'Binger' is currently in the all-cricket-player band 'Six and Out' (playing alongside brother Shane, Brad McNamara, Gavin Robertson and Richard Chee Quee) and for relaxation takes his guitar on tour to try to polish his skills and/or torture the hotel-room occupants next door.

Matthew Hayden was brought into the Australian Test XI for out-of-touch opener Greg Blewett for the third Test of the Australians' New Zealand tour. 'It was a real tough decision,' explained Steve Waugh. 'It's never a great policy to change a winning side, but if you think you can improve a side then you should make changes.'

Australia sent New Zealand in to bat and then saw the home side dismissed for 232 on the first day of the third and final Test, in Hamilton. At stumps, Australia were 1-4. Brett Lee, with five wickets, and Glenn McGrath, with four, were the chief destroyers for the visitors. The chief run-scorer was Craig McMillan, who made 79.

After crashing to 5-29, Mark Waugh, Adam Gilchrist and Damien Martyn mounted a recovery that saw Australia with a slight advantage after day two of the third Test. Waugh and Martyn added 75 for the sixth wicket, and then Martyn and Gilchrist put on a further 119, as the Australians gleaned a first-innings lead of 20. Gilchrist made 75 (from 80 balls) and Martyn remained 89 not out. New Zealand were 3-58 at stumps.

March 30 HAMILTON

FOLLOWING ON FROM our successful idea of making each player accountable for his actions in Wellington, it was decided, at our last team meeting before the third Test, that each player would explain to his teammates what it was going to mean to him to play this match.

For me, it is an exciting time, as I believe that, while we haven't played our best cricket yet on the tour, I have a feeling that this is going to be the match we will excel in. At the meeting, I stressed to the lads that here was a chance for us to be ruthless, professional and clinical and to show everyone in world cricket that we are the team to beat. I also reminded the team that while we'd beaten Armstrong's team's record, there was still the world record — currently held by the West Indies — for us to pursue. Finally, I said, it was important that we enjoy ourselves and finish the season on a high note; after all, there's eight months to our next Test match. On these subjects, everyone had much the same thing to say; it's great knowing all the lads are committed to finishing off the job in style ...

April 1 HAMILTON

'It'll be eight months till we play a Test again,
Eight months until we pull on the baggy green.
Never forget that you are the chosen few,
That most blokes in Australia wish they could be you.
Sometimes it's a labour of love, especially when your form
   gets rough,
But you love it deep down and you're here because you have
   the right stuff.
So let's enjoy the feeling of being a team close and true,
And of extending our boundaries to levels bold and new.
And as times get hard, as they inevitably will,
Put your cap in your hand, take a moment and be still.
Look around at your mates, the blokes whose pain and
   success you share,
And know they'll be there for you wherever you dare.
For you are playing for Australia, our country, our home,
Take the field today with pride and play better than you've
   ever known.'
— **Dave Misson** (read before day one, third Test v New Zealand,
   March 31)

OVER THE PAST 12 months we have found ourselves in many challenging situations. Whatever the circumstances, our belief in each other has always been strong and our positive attitude has seen us overcome many obstacles. But perhaps our sternest examination came this morning here in Hamilton, the second morning of the third Test, when we slumped to 5-29 at the hands of a fired-up Chris Cairns and Shayne O'Connor. On most occasions, such a scoreline would spell disaster. Here, though, none of us felt any fear or negative vibes — we all knew that we could recover; that someone would confront the crisis head on. On cue, Damien Martyn and Adam Gilchrist stemmed the 'blood flow' and then proceeded to put the pressure back on the Kiwis.

It was a brilliant counterattack. From facing the prospect of conceding a significant first-innings deficit, we ended up with a first-innings lead. However, the value of such a comeback can't simply be measured by bare statistics. Our opponents' body language late in this great partnership suggested that Marto and Gilly had inflicted some deep psychological wounds. Marto's 89 was a gem of an innings, while Gilly's inspirational dig again displayed his priceless ability to play the same way no matter the situation. It is a rare gift and one I hope he never loses.

April 2 HAMILTON

'It's time to dig deep and to search within,
To show our inner strength, if we are to win.
This is the challenge we all must embrace,
Showing courage, commitment, poise and grace.
These are just some of the traits we will need,
And don't forget to throw in a healthy dose of greed.
When the final ball has been bowled,
History will ensure our story will be told.
Underneath the Southern Cross I Stand, Khe Sanh and True Blue,
These are the precious memories, shared by the chosen few.'
— **Steve Waugh** (read before day three, third Test v New Zealand, April 2)

DURING A SEASON there are going to be times when the team is a little flat or the players' minds begin to wander from the task at hand. I could definitely sense this before we went out to bowl in the second innings of this Test, so I let the boys know of my frustrations in the 10-minute break before we took the field. After such a tirade, I needed someone to lead the way when we got out on the field.

The source of this brilliance was a surprise to everyone. With a cordon full of slips, a bat-pad fieldsman and a man at leg-gully in place, the entire cover region was left to the fieldsman we sometimes call 'Edward Scissorhands' or 'Blandy' (an ironic nom de plume, after Colin Bland, the famous South African fieldsman of the 1960s) … Colin Miller. Quick as a flash, Funky swooped on the ball as the Kiwi openers tried for a short single, and his underarm throw broke the stumps with Phil Horne short of his ground. Had a master fieldsman such as Jonty Rhodes or Ricky Ponting performed this feat, we would have acclaiming their enormous skill, but for Funky to pull it off bordered on the miraculous. It was just the tonic we needed, a good laugh and a joke and even more importantly a breakthrough to set us on our path for victory.

Australia appeared to be near to a record-breaking third straight series clean sweep and 10th straight Test win at the end of the third day's play of the third Test. Thanks largely to Chris Cairns' 71, the Kiwis were able to set the visitors 210 to win, but by stumps Australia were 3-137, with Justin Langer 71 not out. During the new Zealand second innings Adam Gilchrist completed five catches, giving him 10 for the match, a new Australian Test wicketkeeping record.

Australia won the third Test in spectacular style, by six wickets, courtesy of a vibrant Justin Langer century off just 102 balls. He finished unconquered on 122. Afterwards, Steve Waugh commented: 'At the moment — today — Lang is the best batsman in the world.' The Australian second innings of 4-212 lasted just 41.3 overs, and 179 minutes. Steve Waugh had to retire hurt after being struck above the wrist by a delivery from Test debutant Daryl Tuffey. Adam Gilchrist was voted man of the match.

April 3 HAMILTON

ONE SATISFYING ASPECT of our recent run of victories has been the way we've been able to dispel some beliefs about the team. One of the best examples is one I keep coming back to as I reflect upon this amazing season — the argument that we don't play well or win the so-called 'dead rubbers'. This theory has been well and truly dismantled by the way we've achieved impressive victories in the final Test of our last three series, even though we've gone into all three games leading 2-0 with one to play.

Even more significant, in my view, has been our

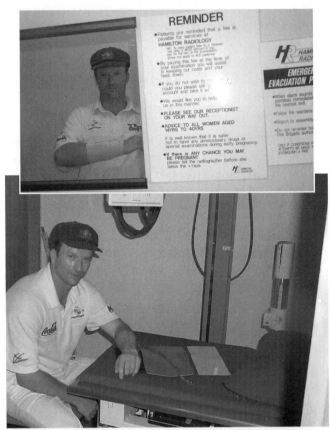

It's funny to think that I started our run of Tests in 1999–2000 in a hospital in Colombo and ended it in a hospital in Hamilton. I was here to have my arm, struck by a delivery from Test debutant Daryl Tuffey, x-rayed. This was the first time I'd retired hurt in 128 Test matches. When I was struck, I immediately thought I'd broken my wrist or the lower part of my arm — there was a loud cracking noise, it was very painful and I couldn't hold the bat. Fortunately, it was just a bone bruise. I had my camera with me, so I thought I might as well take a photo of myself in the mirror (above) while I waited to be x-rayed.

breakthrough when it comes to chasing targets, however big or small, in the last innings of a match. Earlier in our campaign, we had that memorable record-setting win in Hobart, and then came our victories in Wellington and now here in Hamilton. In this Test, the manner in which we scored the runs was the most impressive feature. It was total aggression, in stark contrast to some of the previous efforts in years gone by when we have been too cautious. Justin Langer's 122 off as many balls was a gem of an innings — if he didn't feel 100 per cent comfortable at this elite level before this innings, surely now he knows that he belongs.

Our six-wicket triumph meant that Adam Gilchrist didn't get a bat today, but judging on his form in this Test I'm sure that if had he would have done something spectacular. What a debut season he's had! Not only has he met the enormous expectations and standards left by Ian Healy, he is now being recognised on his own merits — not an easy thing to do when you take the spot of a legend. His Australian record 10 catches in this Test were not only of the highest quality, they also gave a true indication of his overall attitude and performance during this match. He worked hard in the lead-up and at our pre-Test meeting voiced strong thoughts on how he wanted to end the season with a big performance. His first nine Tests have seen him score a century, five fifties, build up a Test batting average of more than 57, and complete 41 dismissals. And to think, with this experience under his belt, he's only going to get better.

There was a stage during this amazing season when I was reported as saying that I believed this Australian side was the best of all time. But I didn't actually say that. What I said was that this team could definitely *compete* with any other Australian side. Whether we'd beat them is for more experienced observers to say, but I'm sure we'd give anyone a game.

Before this Test, I'd stressed to the guys that you can never take winning for granted. I thought it was a little ironic that I was savouring this mightily successful season in the same country where I experienced my first tour as an international cricketer. When Australia toured New Zealand in early 1986 we were coming off a very ordinary period, having lost heavily to the West Indies at home and away, lost the Ashes in England in 1985, and then been beaten at home by New Zealand and been fortunate to square a home series, 0-0, with India. The second match of that India series was my debut Test. We lost that New Zealand Test series in 1986, too, by one Test to nil, and I came away wondering if I'd ever play in a winning Test team

To emphasise the point, I donned the cap I wore during that series for this match. I thought it was important that I passed on the message that you should never get complacent. Winning a Test match is always a big achievement.

April 4 HAMILTON

MANY INDIVIDUALS NEVER get the chance to experience it and those who do never forget the moment it is reached. To be part of a Test-match winning team is something that can never be taken away from a cricketer and is what we as international players strive to achieve. Victory is so special to an Australian side that we join, arm in arm, and rejoice in our team song in the dressing rooms for hours afterwards to further strengthen our bond and to celebrate what has been achieved. Put simply, winning a Test match for your country is as good as it gets.

As I sit back here now, the New Zealand tour over and only three one-dayers against South Africa to come before we can have an extended break, I can't help but savour all that we have achieved. To have won 10 consecutive Tests is a feat that was thought to be almost unattainable among cricket folk. To be a part of a team that has done just that has brought me a joy I never thought I'd experience in my playing days. To be the captain of such a great unit gives me immense pleasure and satisfaction, while also filling me with a sense of pride and patriotism. Now, my aim is to do my bit to make sure we forge ahead to a new world record for consecutive Test-match victories, now only two wins away. Coming on top of our recent world one-day record of 13 consecutive wins, this Test feat would cap off one of the great periods of Australian cricket and ensure our place in history as a team that achieved an impressive run of sustained excellence.

Test cricket is exactly what the title suggests. It is a test of many skills and attributes, that can be exposed or eroded if you are not up to the challenge at any given time. Many people think it's a test of just your natural talent, which, of course, forms a piece of the overall jigsaw. But to me Test cricket also entails words such as dedication, sacrifice, commitment, unselfishness, camaraderie, courage, pride and passion. To win, you must have all these plus more. You have to be able to handle pressure better than your adversary over a sustained period of time. You have to be able to seize the moment when a game is in the balance, but more importantly know when this moment is upon you. As captain, you have to pull together 11 different personalities and characters and get them all going in the one direction. Everyone within the team has to believe in each other when those outside of the team have doubts. You have to strive to continually improve your own game, both mentally and physically, while at the same time suppressing any egos that may cause problems to the 'karma' of the team.

Cricket can be, in many ways, much more than a game. It can teach you a lot about yourself and gives you the opportunity to continually improve and grow as a person. The game exposes you to many different scenarios and situations that not only have an effect on the match or your career, but later on in life may lead you in a certain direction or influence your judgment.

To me, it is not just superior talent that makes a cricket team a winning one. A successful team is one that features a combination of people, each of whom is mature enough to take responsibility for his or her actions and decisions and live by them. Having said this, no one is perfect and we all make our fair share of mistakes, but I believe this current Test squad is full of good people and human beings as well as talented at playing the game and this has contributed enormously to our success.

PART SIX:

TWO MORE PLANE TRIPS

Police in the Indian city of Delhi announced that they had laid charges relating to the alleged 'fixing' of cricket matches, against South African captain Hansie Cronje and three of his teammates, Herschelle Gibbs, Pieter Strydom and Nicky Boje. They also released transcripts reputedly of a conversation between Cronje and an Indian businessman they alleged was also a bookmaker. In Johannesburg, South African cricket chief Ali Bacher rushed to Cronje's defence, stating that he was certain the claims of the Delhi police were false. In a statement issued by the United Cricket Board of South Africa (UCBSA), Cronje said he was 'stunned' by the allegations, which were 'completely without substance'.

South African cricket officials and the South African media were quick to support Hansie Cronje. Newspaper reports claimed Cronje was framed. 'We remain adamant that our players have never been party to match fixing,' Ali Bacher said.

Soon after Hansie Cronje publicly reaffirmed his innocence at a Durban media conference, Steve Waugh, talking to reporters prior to the Australia team's departure for South Africa to play three

April 12 Durban

HANSIE CRONJE'S LIAISON with an Indian bookmaker has cast a shadow over every game of international cricket in the past decade. Initially, I had the gut feeling that Cronje was innocent and I was genuinely upset to learn of his admission to an association with an Indian bookmaker.

I'm disappointed because I know that every game I've played I've given 100 per cent. But people will be saying: 'This has obviously been going on for a long time and how regularly is it going on?' All I can say from my point of view is that the Australian team has never been involved in match fixing or throwing a game and that sort of thing.

There have been a lot of questions raised but no real answers given as this story has escalated in the last two years. From my point of view I think it's frustrating. I want to know whether or not whomever I'm playing against is fair dinkum. Cricket doesn't need this sort of stuff. We've had our fair share of controversies over the last couple of years and this one's added to it.

I'm realistic enough to know that this is a big story. It makes papers sell and all that sort of stuff. Now, for the good of cricket, it's got to be sorted out. It is a major issue. It's got to be addressed. You can't just sweep it under the carpet. Like everyone else I'm shocked and disappointed. I feel sorry for Hansie's family. They've been dragged through this. I guess the people who supported him during the week have probably been the worst done by in this whole issue.

Hansie was a man who played the game hard out in the middle. I never had any problems with him; in fact, I would have said I was pretty good mates with him and I certainly enjoyed playing cricket against him. He seemed to bring the best out of my cricket. Looking back over our battles, I reckon we're pretty even. And despite these allegations and his confession, I always knew he was out there trying when he was playing against Australia.

Today, it would be wrong to call cricket a 'gentleman's game', as it once was. The onus is very much on the game's administrators to get all the way down to the bottom of this insidious story and make the tough decisions that will clean up the sport. I appreciate that it is hard for the ICC, because so much of what is out there is merely gossip and innuendo, rather than solid fact. But when genuine evidence comes before them, they must act, for the game's sake.

I am sure that 99 per cent of international cricketers are clean. The future of the sport lies in its ability to rid itself of the tainted one per cent.

April 14 CAPE TOWN

'The poem I write is about one thing, and one thing only: <u>desire</u>.
This is the drug that will keep us on fire.
For the season's been long, hard and plenty tough,
One final hurdle to see if we've had enough.
A special season to date, in fact, more than special, truly the stuff of dreams,
To keep that dream alive must be our next theme.
Do we want it more than they do, have we got what it takes?
Desire is the word, not skill or good breaks,
For we know we've got them covered in every single way.
We must look deep inside for the desire to make them pay,
Ask yourself the question, "Are you still there for your mates?"
I'll give you 100 per cent, right here, right now, this is the time, the place, the date.
We write our own destiny and decide what we want, we are the ones who control the passion
    and the fire,
Two words spring to mind — Enjoyment and Desire.'

— **Michael Bevan** (*second one-day international v South Africa, April 14*)

Victorian all-rounder Ian Harvey staked a claim for a permanent place in the Australian one-day team with some impressive performances in South Africa.

one-dayers, said that any cricketers who were found guilty of the charges should be banned. 'If you are found guilty you are not playing the game for the right reason, you are selling the spectators short and your teammates,' the Australian captain said. 'There is no room for it in any sport, so if the charge is serious enough, then they should have to pay the penalty.' Later, on the team's arrival in South Africa, Waugh preferred to concentrate on the cricket. He suggested this current Australian team might be superior to the side that won the 1999 World Cup, and said he was looking forward to the 'tough competition' the South Africans always provide.

April 11

In a development that shocked world cricket, Ali Bacher announced that Hansie Cronje had been sacked as South African captain for the three-match one-day series against Australia, scheduled to commence on April 12. Bacher revealed that Cronje had admitted being 'not entirely honest' with the UCBSA over his activities in India. Bacher claimed Cronje had acknowledged receiving money for providing information and forecasting, but soon after Cronje issued a statement denying he had done so. Bacher also indicated that the South African government would be launching an inquiry into the allegations.

Shane Lee, Adam Gilchrist and I celebrate the dismissal of Jacques Kallis, one of a world record equalling six catches taken by Gilly during South Africa's innings in the second game, at Cape Town.

DESPITE OUR STRONG victory tonight, all the talk at the post-game media conference was about the match-fixing issue. Almost immediately, the press guys wanted to know if I'd dob in a bloke if I knew he was guilty. 'Why not?' I replied. 'If you've got information, then yes. If one of the Australian team was doing something and I knew about it, then I wouldn't want to play with that guy. If there are people out there taking bribes or fixing matches, they should be exposed.'

End of story. It seems this line of questioning was motivated by a rumour that one of Hansie Cronje's teammates had tipped the authorities off about the former captain's links with the Indian bookmakers. Lance Klusener has even gone public, denying that he was that player.

I was then asked if the Cronje affair had somehow lessened the quality of our two victories over South Africa in the 1999 World Cup. I thought this was unfair, although I understood, in the current climate, why someone would suggest this. People were quick to point to that infamous 'catch' that Herschelle Gibbs had dropped during my century

The incomparable Glenn McGrath, who by the conclusion of the New Zealand Test series was moving in on 300 Test wickets, with the promise of many more to come.

Team photos of different kinds.
Top: The boys in Wellington after our second Test win, which gave us nine straight Test wins. Middle: The boys in the middle of another team bonding exercise, wearing weird, ugly and crazy headgear bought for each other after names were drawn out of a hat. Bottom: The official team photo, taken in Auckland. Back row: Misson, Martyn, Miller, B. Lee, Kasprowicz, Hayden, Fleming, Gilchrist, Farhart; Front: Langer, Blewett, McGrath, Bernard, Warne, S. Waugh, Buchanan, M. Waugh, Slater, Mike Walsh (scorer).

Chris Cairns at Wellington during the second Test, making a blockbuster of a century.

Above: The scene in Hamilton during the third Test, with the steam and mist giving the ground a somewhat eerie feeling.

Right: Justin Langer demonstrating once again the aggression that has become typical of his batting.

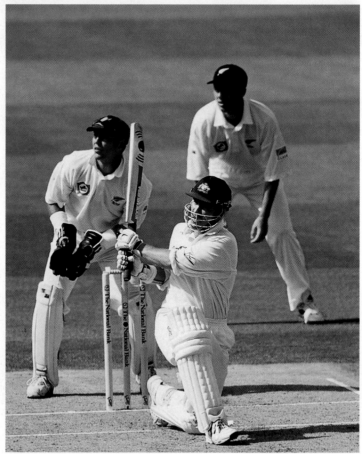

Above: Brett Lee, wowing them in South Africa as he had already done in Australia and New Zealand.

Right: Damien Martyn, our best batsman in the one-dayers in South Africa.

Above: One of the most impressive sights I've seen in my travels around the world is Table Top Mountain in Cape Town. Here, Andrew Symonds is sitting on the edge of a cliff, looking out over the city. Behind him is the mountain, with what they call the 'table cloth' of thin cloud covering the peak.

Right: During my press conference in Calcutta, I turned my lens against the media and their cameras, to get this player-under-scrutiny view. I was there to try to promote Udayan, but all the questions were about the Hansie Cronje scandal.

Left: Some of the girls in the Udayan children's home in Barrackpore, outside of Calcutta, a charity I get great delight from supporting. I went there straight after the South African tour. There have been some amazing changes in the girls' personalities since I first met them in 1999. They appear more relaxed and comfortable, and are happier and healthier. It seems the home is achieving its objectives.

STEVE WAUGH

The scene at Colonial Stadium in Melbourne, during international cricket's first indoor series, in August 2000.

My hundred in the first indoor one-dayer was very satisfying, given that I managed it despite having hardly picked up a bat since the games in South Africa in April. These two hits, not quite conventional but right off the middle of the bat, helped me get to my hundred in just 91 balls.

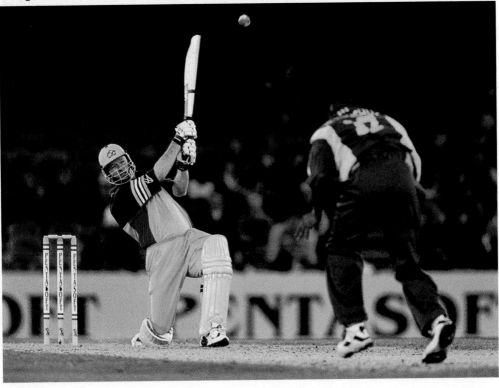

at Headingley — the one where he threw the ball in the air in triumph before he'd caught it. I was not long past 50 at the time, and went on to 120 not out as we won with two balls to spare and thus qualified for the Cup semi-finals. But the cynics forget that Gibbs made a hundred himself in that game. I know, as a heavily involved participant, that every game we played in that tournament was fair.

Looking back now, there have been, in years gone by, one or two games that I've played in where our opponents perhaps weren't quite fair dinkum. But every game I've been involved in, and the Australian team's been involved in, we've played with 100 per cent intensity. I'm sure the Australian public know that. This said, we've all now got to go out there and prove to everyone that the sport is clean and that it is still a great and unique game.

April 17 JOHANNESBURG

WE KNEW THAT THE South Africans were going to provide a tough test — despite all the off-field dramas, that they will still be a good side without Hansie Cronje, just as we are still a good side despite the fact that champion players such as Ian Healy, Mark Taylor, David Boon and the like have retired in recent years. No one cricketer is bigger than the game.

The cricket during this short tour was tough and enjoyable, but the media scrutiny off the field was so persistent — understandably, given the Cronje story — that an edge was taken off the series. It was almost as if getting into the dressing rooms and onto the field was our only escape from the story. We were probably distracted a fraction, and I certainly don't like being hounded by the press about issues that are not directly related to the cricket, but I don't want to use any of that as an excuse. The South Africans have probably suffered more than we have, both in terms of the amount of cricket they've been asked to play and the ramifications of the match-fixing saga in recent days.

I feel that, as a one-day outfit, we peaked in New Zealand. Still, there were some excellent Australian performances in the matches here. Gilly's effort in Cape Town, taking six catches to equal Alec Stewart's world record for most wicketkeeping dismissals in a one-day international, was a highlight, as was Pigeon's bowling in the same match — 10 overs for 13 runs and two wickets. His first six overs cost just seven runs, and made me look like a genius after I'd sent them in. Marto's batting was also excellent — his development as a top-class international batsman has been one of the highlights of the season.

Now, I'm eagerly looking forward to some time off. Before I get home, I will go to Barrackpore, near Calcutta, to help celebrate the opening of a home for the

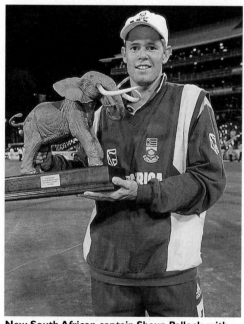

New South African captain Shaun Pollock, with one very impressive trophy.

Amid the great controversy and gloom of the match-fixing scandal, South Africa won the first one-day international of their three-game series against Australia by six wickets. Adam Gilchrist (51) and Damien Martyn (74) made half centuries for the visitors, but Gary Kirsten was named man of the match, after scoring 97 from 126 balls to anchor South Africa's successful reply.

Hansie Cronje, while admitting he took money from bookmakers for information, repeated his denial of any involvement in fixing or manipulating match results. 'I always played to win,' he said in a prepared statement, which he read to the media in Bloemfontein. 'I know of no member of any side that I have led who has done anything reprehensible or wrong,' he added, before ending with the comment, 'I find myself in an awful predicament brought about by my own foolishness and naivety.'

Australia levelled the one-day series against South Africa with a five-wicket victory in Cape Town. Glenn McGrath (10-1-13-2) was the bowling star, as the home team were limited to just 9-144 from their 50 overs. In reply, Australia slumped to 3-21 before Damien Martyn smashed a 50 from 32 balls.

female children of leprosy sufferers. This is a project I've been close to for the past two years, and it is a source of great satisfaction to know that the efforts of a lot of people have come to something worthwhile and substantial. Once home, I probably won't pick up a cricket bat again until the beginning of August, to prepare for the indoor matches against South Africa at the new stadium in Melbourne. In the meantime, I'm sure I'll be busy — there is always so much for the Australian captain to do and so many issues to comment on — but I'll still find time to look back with enormous pride on the success we achieved during the 1999–2000 season.

I remember back to that time in Brisbane when John Buchanan got up before the first Test against Pakistan, his debut Test as Australian coach, and said, 'Today is the first Test of our journey to the "Invincibles" — let's make the ride enjoyable and attainable.' As I've said before, I was taken aback a little by this statement — there will only ever be one Invincibles, and it is inappropriate in my view for any team to try to compare themselves to Bradman's immortal side. But in the games that followed that we did manage to forge our own story and build our own identity as an excellent cricket side.

Now, we must raise the bar still further. More challenges await the team — the West Indies at home, the Ashes in England in 2001, the 2003 World Cup. Personally, I don't want to look too far ahead. Plan for the future, play for the moment. And at the moment, things are looking pretty good. I am so grateful to have been given the chance to be a part of this Australian cricket team.

The bags are packed for one last flight home!

What a Team by Dave Misson

We arrived in Cape Town for the second one-dayer tired and disappointed, as much because we felt let down by our scheduling, as because we'd lost in Durban. However, our spirits were lifted as we approached Cape Town itself and the bus reverberated with stories from Rory Steyn (our security officer; a man who guarded Nelson Mandela during Mandela's five years as South African Prime Minister), Dougie (a very thirsty liaison officer) and veterans of past tours about how this place was the jewel in the crown of South African touring life.

As we drove along the six-lane motorway, past a shantytown that resembled a scrap-metal yard, the mountain appeared. Sitting on the bus, exhaustion engulfing me, the thought that I would be her conqueror tomorrow was the furthest thing from my mind. Training came and went but, once sighted, it seemed the mountain followed our every move, stalking us, the new predators in town.

The stadium at Newlands, with the mountain ever present in the background, behind the veil of the clouds and the fog, is a perfect marriage of man's fleeting achievements and nature's powerful permanency. We planned an expedition to scale Table Mountain the next day. Buchanan, Misson, Farhart, Steyn and Brian Murgatroyd, the ACB's media manager. Many words have already been devoted in the literature to the beauty of Table Mountain, but the sheer exhilaration can only be conceived through actually being there. Our climb was five very personal experiences, shared together.

'Murgers', the human mountain goat, leaping and bounding ahead, regardless of terrain, only ever being stopped by man's equivalent to the animal kingdom's buzzing gnat — the mobile phone. As media manager, he was conscious of wanting to appear the consummate professional to his peers, by making himself available to all and sundry, even during a mountain trek. Unfortunately, the incongruous ringing of the mobile phone reinforced a subconscious disrespect for the experience, as well as really annoying his mates. Finally, he succumbed to the heartfelt cries to turn it off ... or have it thrown off the mountain ... wherein he was then able to clear his mind of the clatter of media-generated 'mundanities'.

Patrick Farhart, lacking hair on his head but more than making up for it on the rest of his body, was Cape Town's version of the Yeti that morning. Physically struggling with the arduous climb, but buoyed by the team support around him, he refused to let the mountain beat him. Humour, musical trivia and many, many water stops led to his unbridled declaration of amazement as he reached our Holy Grail — the summit.

It didn't disappoint us. It took us one-and-a-half hours of climbing, on steep and rocky terrain but it was always going to be worth it. For me, the African morning left me invigorated, as much by the journey as by the destination. After our tour of the summit, the cafeteria and souvenir shop presented themselves to us in the name of progress and crass commercialism. We succumbed meekly, although we can always say we ate breakfast while admiring one of the great views of the world.

As we were about to leave, we stumbled upon Steve Waugh and Andrew Symonds, who had caught the cable car up. The skipper had managed to convince 'Roy' that abseiling off the mountain presented no real danger and would probably be a great way to get the adrenalin pumping for today's match. Like our own trek up, Roy's journey down the mountain on the end of a rope is something he will never forget.

April 16

South Africa won the deciding third one-dayer, in Johannesburg, by four wickets, thanks to an undefeated seventh-wicket partnership of 87 between Lance Klusener and Mark Boucher. Earlier, Australia had made 205, with Steve Waugh scoring 51 and Shaun Pollock taking four wickets. During the South African innings, Australian pace bowler Brett Lee bowled a delivery that was timed by a radar gun at 156 kilometres per hour, reputedly the fastest bowling since Jeff Thomson was timed at upwards of 160km/h in the nets in the mid-1970s.

April 17

UCBSA chief Ali Bacher revealed that the South African side was allegedly offered US$250,000 to throw a game against India in 1996. The matter, Bacher said, would now be the subject of a UCBSA investigation.

April 20

In Calcutta, Australian captain Steve Waugh admitted that the match-fixing scandal had tarnished the game's image, and that it was now up to cricketers and administrators to clean the mess up. 'A lot of unfortunate things have been happening,' Waugh said. 'If somebody has done something wrong, he will pay the price at some stage.'

Two mornings later, now looking out over Johannesburg from the window of my 20th floor hotel room, the only thing that came to mind was, 'I wonder how many people were murdered out there last night?' The city with the highest murder rate in the world is probably the best (or worst) example of the problems of truly unifying disparate cultures, economies, and social structures. In any case, I wouldn't be leaving the hotel (except for the game) over the next couple of days.

The third and final game in the series saw us in a position to win, but probably needing another 30 runs to really be able to turn the screws. It seemed that we were always one wicket behind and when Klusener and Boucher put on 87 for the seventh wicket, we didn't quite get across the line. It was the end of a long 20 months for most of the support staff and a large contingent of the team. Starting in Pakistan in August 1998, we had been through two entire home summers, plus tours of the West Indies, the UK for the World Cup, Sri Lanka, Zimbabwe, New Zealand, and now, finally South Africa. In that time we had probably had a total of 10 weeks break and six of those were after the World Cup. To be honest, everyone was stuffed.

However, in the best Aussie tradition, we still had enough energy for a major party. Gathering in the team room for a signing session and tour debrief, everyone had that 'end-of-road' look about them. Five of the guys were heading to county cricket (Glenn McGrath, Shane Warne, Michael Bevan, Matthew Hayden and Ian Harvey), Damien Fleming was getting married, Steve Waugh was going to India for a few days to open another wing of the children's home he sponsors before finally heading home, Mark Waugh was heading back to his trotters and Sky Channel, Brett Lee was going back to Wollongong, and Andrew Symonds was going 'bush' for a about a month. Most of us were heading back to our families and friends, keen to return to a life of normality.

Our last morning on tour saw us carry the piano from the lobby into the bar, where Brett tinkled the ivories and Shane played the guitar. The Lee brothers were on fire. We drank copious amounts of alcohol, oblivious to the 36-hour journey home we faced the next day. A couple of the South African team management were in the bar witnessing this spontaneous display of camaraderie. They left astonished and amazed, muttering, 'You guys are great, what a team.'

That pretty much says it all.

EPILOGUE:

CRICKET GOES INDOORS

August 22

WE CAME INTO THE HISTORIC one-day 'indoor' series, played at Melbourne's new Colonial Stadium in August 2000, very conscious of the hammering our sport had taken in the preceding months. The publication of Justice Qayyum's report into match-fixing in Pakistan, which left some players banned for life and many others with their reputations tarnished, was followed by a highly-publicised commission of enquiry conducted by Judge Edwin King in South Africa. That latter investigation brought to light the full extent of the Hansie Cronje affair and did nothing for the former South African captain's reputation. It also exposed a few other players as having been guilty of at least providing information, and highlighted the extent to which match-fixing, illegal bookmakers and 'under the table' payments had infiltrated the game. At the same time, some astonishing developments in India saw a number of players' homes being raided by police, tax and banking records checked, and more reputations sullied. In Australia, the Australian Cricket Board appointed a former National Crime Authority member, Greg Melick, to head an investigation, which came up with no evidence of Australian involvement in cricket bribery or match-fixing.

In July, not long after the King Commission had concluded its hearings, came news from the ICC that the validity of Brett Lee's bowling action had been questioned. Here was another example of the game's ruling body handling a difficult matter in a very ordinary way. It took many, many weeks for the ICC to respond to an initial report that had come out of our matches in New Zealand in March. When they finally did announce there was a problem, Bing's future seemed to be hanging in mid-air, and it was left to the Australian Cricket Board to take a lead by demanding a quick resolution. When the matter was finally considered, Brett was cleared as I believed he should have been immediately, but I was left wondering why it had been approached the way it had, especially after the appalling way the Shoaib Akhtar problem had been mishandled a few months before.

Within the Australian team, we had a major change when Shane Warne was replaced as vice-captain by Adam Gilchrist. I know that Warney was extremely disappointed to have the position taken away from him. He saw the vice-captaincy as a huge honour, and I had valued his support and input, but I knew that he'd take the decision on the chin and come back as good as ever. Similarly, I had no doubts that Gilly would do a tremendous job as his replacement, just as Ricky Ponting or any other member of the team would have done so had they been appointed.

Amid these gloomy stories, we were determined to put on a good show in the indoor series. I knew that Shaun Pollock and his men were similarly motivated, and we all realised that the best way to boost the sport's image was to go out and play good, positive cricket. We could only give our best and be judged on that.

Back to the cricket. Entering game one, we had a real dilemma — who to leave out? Of the 13 players in the squad, 12 had performed superbly throughout 1999–2000, and the

13th, Jason Gillespie, was a proven international campaigner on the comeback trail. I kept tossing around the 13 names and came up with a strong combination whoever we picked — whichever pair missed the first game would be very unlucky.

The first question we had to work out was whether to play three fast bowlers (Glenn McGrath, Brett Lee and Gillespie) plus Warney and just one all-rounder (out of Andrew Symonds, Ian Harvey or Shane Lee), or leave a quick out and play two of the all-rounders. Making this choice harder was the fact that we didn't know how the Colonial Stadium pitch was going to play. In the end, we opted to go with just two quicks, Pigeon and Bing, to give Ian Harvey a game in front of his home crowd, and to play Shane ahead of Symmo.

As things turned out, our win in game one was outstanding, with the feature being our batting performance. To score nearly 300 first up from a spell, on a deck that we had to be a bit suspicious of (but which actually played magnificently), was a brilliant effort. I was delighted with my own batting, though disappointed to miss out on scoring the first international century indoors — Michael Bevan beat me to that landmark by one delivery. The honour of hitting the first indoor six went to Shane Lee, who actually hit two during his brief, unbeaten dig of 28 from 15 balls.

Before Shane strode out to the middle, Bevo and I had added 218 in 35.1 overs for the fourth wicket, with Bevo finally out for 106 and me undefeated on 114 at the end of our 50 overs. As I've said many times, Bevo is great to bat with. He turns the strike over very well and turns a lot of ones into twos, which helps him, his partner and, of course, the team. As a pair, we hustled really well, a feature that was duplicated when we went out to field. Our intensity was first class, in particular our backing up, which I thought was a major highlight of the team effort. The eventual winning margin was 94 runs.

The following day, Bevo and I woke up feeling as if we'd run 10 miles through sandhills. My thighs, groin and hips were so sore that if I even touched them it felt as if a massive weight had been dropped on them from a 20-storey building. Later on that night, after dining at a Japanese restaurant with my wife Lynette, I was unable to move from my chair, such was the stiffness and soreness in my legs. It was embarrassing — being watched by people as I lifted each leg out separately from under the table with my hands, until I was free to hobble away back to the hotel for a late-night swim. The only consolation in being so sore was that it meant that I had played well; if I'd woken up feeling fresh as a daisy it would have meant that I hadn't done much.

As good as our victory in game one was, in my opinion the biggest plus to come for us from the entire series was the successful return to international cricket of Jason Gillespie in game two. Dizzy had been off the scene since that still-painful-to-think-about collision in Kandy, but he returned to take 3-40 from his first 10 overs back. His form in the nets leading into the matches had been good, and he was clearly ultra-keen, so it wasn't a huge surprise to see him go so well. He started by getting his first delivery past the outside edge of Gary Kirsten's bat, and was quickly surprising the visitors with his pace and bounce. I gave him a rest after five overs, but mid-innings he came back to knock over Jacques Kallis with the second ball of his new spell, and then took two more good wickets — Lance Klusener and Shaun Pollock — near the end of the South Africans' 50 overs. Dizzy also could have had a fourth wicket, when Mark Boucher was dropped at deep square leg.

As I watched Dizzy do his thing so well, I couldn't help thinking, with a smile, that Australia's pace-bowling options are remarkably broad at the moment, with Dizzy part of a 'stable' that also includes Glenn McGrath, Damien Fleming, Brett Lee and Michael Kasprowicz.

Game two was the most exciting of the series — a last-ball thriller that ended in a tie. It was a game we probably should have won, but we stumbled somewhat in the final overs and in the end were happy to come out of it with something. At 1-105 in the 24th over and then 3-164 in the 39th over, chasing 227, we were travelling comfortably. But the South Africans bowled very well at the death, especially Andrew Hall, who took 2-8 from three overs, having not come on until the 45th over.

The equation came down to us needing 13 from the final over, with two wickets in hand and Shane Warne on strike. Warney handled the pressure admirably, immediately blasting a ball over cover, and finally the game came down to the last possible ball. This was the perfect script for the hometown boy — one ball remaining and his team needing one to tie and two to win. After the enormous controversy surrounding Shane's demotion from the vice-captaincy, this seemed the ultimate way for him to extinguish those bad memories. I must admit that at the time I thought an Aussie victory was meant to be and that Warney was a certainty to take us through to victory. Unfortunately, though, it didn't quite work out, but we did end up escaping with a tie, which wasn't a bad result considering that Pollock, in my view the world's No. 1 one-day bowler, was delivering the South Africans' final over.

In fact, Shane rebounded from the vice-captaincy controversy well, batting very sensibly here and bowling cleverly and economically in all three games, to show everyone that he has many more years left in him.

Early on in game three, it seemed that we might take the series easily, after Glenn McGrath and Brett Lee each took two wickets as South Africa crashed to 4-19. But Lance Klusener (49 from 74 balls) led a fightback that saw our target climb, and though Adam Gilchrist hit 63 from 67 balls at the top of our order, we struggled to force the pace, especially against their left-arm spinner, Nicky Boje. We eventually finished up a frustrating nine runs short of what was required to win. It was a poor performance by our batsmen — our theme of 'no mercy' wasn't taken on board enough by each individual. We must learn from our carelessness. I guess we could claim that many of us were in our off-season and, as such, were slightly out of knick and lacking in intensity and routine, but as the No. 1 side in the world this is a lame excuse in my opinion. Quite simply, we weren't good enough. For the second time in a row we had thrown away the chance to win an international match.

One curious point came right at the finish of this game, when Andrew Hall was called upon to bowl the 47th over. Nothing unusual about that, you might think, except for the fact that Hall had kept wicket in the absence of the injured Boucher for the previous 46 overs. When the over began we needed 22 from two. Kirsten took over the gloves for six balls, Hall conceded just five runs (including a first-ball wide), and captain Pollock looked like a genius. I learnt later that this was the first time a wicketkeeper had bowled in a one-day international.

For Jason Gillespie, Colonial Stadium in Melbourne was a long, long way from that hospital bed in Colombo.

One irritating factor in our loss was the fact that the match referee, Brian Hastings from New Zealand, took two overs off our run chase, because in his view we had been tardy when bowling our 50 overs during the South African innings. So instead of us facing 50 overs, we were restricted to a maximum of 48.

During our bowling effort, I had checked more than once with the umpires as to our over-rate, and every time the umps told me we were about two overs behind schedule, but that there had been at least five or six minutes' worth of 'deductions' (things such as sawdust being used on the crease, mud being scrapped from the boots of bowlers and fieldsmen, a late start, slow movement of the sightscreens) and consequently we'd be okay. On top of this, because South Africa were around 20 minutes late during the first game and we'd gone well over time in the second, I assumed that, for the sake of consistency, a benevolent attitude would continue in game three. Perhaps there hadn't been as many interruptions during the afternoon of the third game, but I believed there'd still been sufficient stoppages for the match referee to take a lenient view.

The two overs taken from us proved crucial, as it affected our run chase towards the end. With six overs remaining we needed 38 — better than a run a ball — with Shane Lee and Damien Martyn at the crease. If the requirement had been 38 in eight I reckon we would have cruised to victory, but instead our hand was forced and we succumbed. Admittedly, we shouldn't have allowed ourselves to get into this scenario, but I still maintain that the match referee erred in altering the equation in this way.

The South Africans actually took longer to bowl their 48 overs than we did to bowl our 50, which to me just highlighted the farcical nature of the match referee's decision. If penalties such as this are going to be handed out, there is going to be a huge advantage in bowling second in one-day cricket.

This said, we still should have won. Our target was 207 on an excellent batting wicket, but we batted badly, playing some poor shots and not respecting our wickets enough. I reckon we should have only needed around four batsmen to get us home, if we'd been playing at our best. Still, the South Africans played some excellent cricket, and their performance was especially admirable given that they were hindered by injuries to some of their key personnel.

Overall, the matches were a great success. We drew good crowds (25,785 people to game one, then 35,724, and finally 32,769) despite the fact that in the winter outside the AFL finals series should have been taking up much of the local Victorians' sporting interests. The pitches played superbly — a triumph for curator Les Burdett — and while the outfield was a little slippery, the ball was easy to pick up and the atmosphere was vibrant. Innovations such as inviting each cricketer to select a song to be played over the audio as he walked out to bat added to the occasion, but I would have liked it if the heaters had been turned up a fraction — it was at least as cold inside the Stadium as it was outside in the Melbourne night.

There is no doubt in my mind that indoor one-day cricket has a real future. I can see the day in the not-too-distant future when a number of major cricket grounds around the world will have retractable roofs, in the same way that so many international grounds now have floodlights. This series proved that it is possible to create fair-dinkum quality cricket conditions indoors, and by having a roof in place you take out the uncertainty that bad weather can create. With a roof in place, fans will be able to pay their money fully confident that they'll see the entire show, and marketeers and TV programmers can similarly plan their schedules with confidence. And, perhaps most crucially of all, the possibility of important one-day games being decided by the weather will be eliminated.

I am not saying the game should move indoors full-time. My first preference would always be to play with a clear sky overhead, provided the conditions are fair for both sides and top class. But now, I believe, we have started a new tradition. Fifty years from now, I reckon it will be nice to say to people that I was part of the first game of international cricket that was played indoors.

MATCH RECORDS

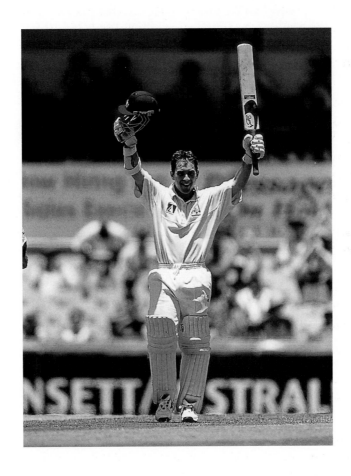

The Tests

Australia in Sri Lanka, 1999

FIRST TEST, AT KANDY, SEPTEMBER 9,10,11 (Toss: Australia)

Australia first innings

MJ Slater	lbw Vaas	0
GS Blewett	lbw Zoysa	0
JL Langer	c de Silva b Vaas	7
ME Waugh	c&b Vaas	6
*SR Waugh	c de Silva b Zoysa	19
RT Ponting	c&b Muralitharan	96
+IA Healy	st Kaluwitharana b Muralitharan	11
SK Warne	c Atapattu b Zoysa	0
JN Gillespie	lbw Muralitharan	41
CR Miller	c Atapattu b Muralitharan	0
GD McGrath	not out	4
Extras	(nb 4)	4
Total	**(all out, 67.1 overs, 264 mins)**	**188**

Fall: 1-0 (Slater, 0.2 ov), 2-4 (Blewett, 1.4 ov), 3-9 (Langer, 6.3 ov), 4-16 (ME Waugh, 8.2 ov), 5-40 (SR Waugh, 18.5 ov), 6-59 (Healy, 23.1 ov), 7-60 (Warne, 24.5 ov), 8-167 (Gillespie, 59.6 ov), 9-171 (Miller, 61.2 ov), 10-188 (Ponting, 67.1 ov).

Bowling: Vaas 16-2-43-3; Zoysa 13-2-38-3; Muralitharan 25.1-4-63-4; Jayasuriya 5-0-5-0; Chandana 8-1-39-0.

Sri Lanka first innings

*ST Jayasuriya	lbw McGrath	18
MS Atapattu	c Langer b Miller	25
RP Arnold	lbw Miller	19
PA de Silva	c Ponting b Warne	78
DPM Jayawardene	c Ponting b Warne	46
A Ranatunga	c Healy b Warne	4
+RS Kaluwitharana	b Miller	9
UDU Chandana	c sub (ML Hayden) b Warne	12
WPUJC Vaas	not out	2
DNT Zoysa	c Miller b Warne	7
M Muralitharan	c McGrath b Miller	0
Extras	(b 4, lb 7, nb 3)	14
Total	**(all out, 66.3 overs, 272 mins)**	**234**

Fall: 1-22 (Jayasuriya, 6.1 ov), 2-69 (Arnold, 20.2 ov), 3-70 (Atapattu, 20.6 ov), 4-177 (Jayawardene, 47.3 ov), 5-181 (Ranatunga, 49.1 ov), 6-197 (Kaluwitharana, 55.1 ov), 7-223 (Chandana, 63.4 ov), 8-226 (de Silva, 65.2 ov), 9-234 (Zoysa, 65.6 ov), 10-234 (Muralitharan, 66.3 ov).

Bowling: McGrath 18-5-66-1; Gillespie 12-2-43-0; Miller 20.3-6-62-4; Warne 16-4-52-5

Australia second innings

GS Blewett	c Atapattu b Muralitharan	14
MJ Slater	lbw Muralitharan	27
JL Langer	lbw Vaas	5
ME Waugh	b Vaas	0
RT Ponting	c Jayasuriya b Chandana	51
+IA Healy	b Muralitharan	3
SK Warne	run out (Jayasuriya)	6
CR Miller	b Vaas	8
GD McGrath	not out	10
*SR Waugh	absent hurt	-
JN Gillespie	absent hurt	-
Extras	(b 6, lb 5, w 1, nb 4)	16
Total	**(all out, 60.2 overs, 233 mins)**	**140**

Fall: 1-37 (Slater, 15.2 ov), 2-49 (Langer, 22.3 ov), 3-49 (ME Waugh, 24.2 ov), 4-49 (Blewett, 27.6 ov), 5-58 (Healy, 33.3 ov), 6-75 (Warne, 37.1 ov), 7-99 (Miller, 46.5 ov), 8-140 (Ponting, 60.2 ov).

Bowling: Vaas 15-7-15-3; Zoysa 10-3-28-0; de Silva 3-0-5-0; Muralitharan 26-5-65-3; Jayasuriya 4-1-7-0; Chandana 2.2-0-9-1.

Sri Lanka second innings

*ST Jayasuriya	c sub (ML Hayden) b Miller	18
MS Atapattu	c Blewett b McGrath	0
+RS Kaluwitharana	b Miller	5
PA de Silva	not out	31
DPM Jayawardene	c Slater b Miller	9
A Ranatunga	not out	19
Extras	(b 8, lb 2, nb 3)	13
Total	**(4 wickets, 26.5 overs, 110 mins)**	**95**

Fall: 1-12 (Atapattu, 2.1 ov), 2-24 (Jayasuriya, 5.2ov), 3-39 (Kaluwitharana, 9.3 ov), 4-60 (Jayawardene, 15.2 ov).

Bowling: McGrath 7-2-19-1; Miller 13-2-48-3; Warne 6.5-3-18-0.

SRI LANKA WON BY SIX WICKETS

* indicates captain
+ indicates wicketkeeper

SECOND TEST, AT GALLE, SEPTEMBER 22,23,24,25,26 (Toss: Sri Lanka)

Sri Lanka first innings

*ST Jayasuriya	c ME Waugh b McGrath	0
MS Atapattu	c Healy b Warne	29
RP Arnold	c Warne b Miller	50
PA de Silva	c SR Waugh b Fleming	64
DPM Jayawardene	c Blewett b Warne	46
A Ranatunga	c Miller b Warne	10
+RS Kaluwitharana	b McGrath	25
WPUJC Vaas	c Ponting b Fleming	41
R Herath	run out (Blewett)	3
DNT Zoysa	c ME Waugh b McGrath	1
M Muralitharan	not out	7
Extras	(b 4, lb 8, nb 8)	20
Total	**(all out, 106.5 overs, 412 mins)**	**296**

Fall: 1-0 (Jayasuriya, 0.1 ov), 2-80 (Atapattu, 28.2 ov), 3-100 (Arnold, 41.3 ov), 4-193 (Jayawardene, 73.5 ov), 5-206 (Ranatunga, 80.1 ov), 6-226 (de Silva, 87.3 ov), 7-262 (Kaluwitharana, 98.3 ov), 8-288 (Vaas, 103.6 ov), 9-288 (Herath, 104.6 ov), 10-296 (Zoysa, 106.5 ov).

Bowling: McGrath 26.5-7-81-3; Fleming 23-6-74-2; Miller 23-1-72-1; Warne 25-11-29-3; Ponting 4-1-7-0; ME Waugh 2-1-9-0; Blewett 3-0-12-0.

Australia first innings

MJ Slater	st Kaluwitharana b Muralitharan	96
GS Blewett	b Muralitharan	62
JL Langer	c Ranatunga b Muralitharan	7
ME Waugh	c Ranatunga b Muralitharan	10
*SR Waugh	c Kaluwitharana b Herath	19
+IA Healy	c Jayawardene b Muralitharan	4
RT Ponting	c Ranatunga b Herath	1
SK Warne	c Atapattu b Herath	0
DW Fleming	b Herath	16
CR Miller	run out (Jayasuriya/Kaluwitharana)	6
GD McGrath	not out	0
Extras	(b 1, lb 4, nb 2)	7
Total	**(all out, 96.3 overs, 346 mins)**	**228**

Fall: 1-138 (Blewett, 55.4 ov), 2-160 (Langer, 67.6 ov), 3-179 (Slater, 77.3 ov), 4-182 (ME Waugh, 79.1 ov), 5-188 (Healy, 81.4 ov), 6-189 (Ponting, 84.4 ov), 7-189 (Warne, 84.6 ov), 8-215 (Fleming, 92.3 ov), 9-228 (Miller, 95.4 ov), 10-228 (SR Waugh, 96.3 ov).

Bowling: Vaas 9-3-31-0; Zoysa 6-1-9-0; Herath 34.3-6-97-4; Muralitharan 38-10-71-5; Jayasuriya 9-1-15-0.

Sri Lanka second innings

*ST Jayasuriya	not out	21
MS Atapattu	not out	28
Extras	(lb 3, nb 3)	6
Total	**(0 wickets, 17.2 overs, 71 mins)**	**55**

Bowling: McGrath 7-2-23-0; Fleming 4-0-15-0; Miller 3-1-9-0; Warne 3.2-1-5-0.

MATCH DRAWN

THIRD TEST, AT SINHALESE SPORTS CLUB GROUND, COLOMBO, SEPTEMBER 30, OCTOBER 1,2,3,4
(Toss: Australia)

Australia first innings

GS Blewett	c Atapattu b Herath	70
MJ Slater	st Kaluwitharanab Arnold	59
JL Langer	c Ranatunga b Muralitharan	32
ME Waugh	c Arnold b Muralitharan	13
*SR Waugh	c Kaluwitharana b Herath	14
RT Ponting	not out	105
+IA Healy	c Jayawardene b Vaas	7
SK Warne	lbw Vaas	0
DW Fleming	c Atapattu b Muralitharan	32
CR Miller	lbw Vaas	0
GD McGrath	c Atapattu b Vaas	0
Extras	(nb 10)	10
Total	**(all out, 136.4 overs)**	**342**

Fall: 1-126 (Slater, 52.4 ov), 2-147 (Blewett, 64.4 ov), 3-182 (ME Waugh, 75.1 ov), 4-183 (Langer, 77.1 ov), 5-221 (SR Waugh, 96.3 ov), 6-253 (Healy, 106.4 ov), 7-255 (Warne, 108.2 ov), 8-335 (Fleming, 133.6 ov), 9-342 (Miller, 136.2 ov), 10-342 (McGrath, 136.4 ov).

Bowling: Vaas 23.4-5-54-4; Zoysa 10-4-23-0; Herath 35-10-98-2; Muralitharan 52-5-150-3; Jayasuriya 9-2-14-0; Arnold 7-4-3-1.

Sri Lanka first innings

*ST Jayasuriya	c Warne b McGrath	0
MS Atapattu	c Healy b Fleming	2
RP Arnold	lbw Fleming	0
PA de Silva	not out	19
DPM Jayawardene	c Healy b Fleming	21
A Ranatunga	not out	1
Extras	(b 8, lb 1, w 5, nb 4)	18
Total	**(4 wickets, 21.5 overs)**	**61**

Did not bat: +RS Kaluwitharana, WPUJC Vaas, R Herath, DNT Zoysa, M Muralitharan.
Fall: 1-0 (Jayasuriya, 0.1 ov), 2-7 (Atapattu, 3.1 ov), 3-10 (Arnold, 5.1 ov), 4-60 (Jayawardene, 21.2 ov).

Bowling: McGrath 10-3-25-1; Fleming 5.5-0-14-3; Warne 5-1-11-0; Miller 1-0-2-0.

MATCH DRAWN

SRI LANKA WON THE SERIES 1-0

ONLY TEST, AT HARARE, OCTOBER 14,15,16,17 (Toss: Zimbabwe)

Zimbabwe first innings

GJ Rennie	c Ponting b McGrath	18
GW Flower	c Ponting b Fleming	1
MW Goodwin	run out (Blewett/Langer)	0
*ADR Campbell	c Slater b Fleming	5
+A Flower	c ME Waugh b McGrath	28
NC Johnson	c ME Waugh b McGrath	75
TR Gripper	lbw Warne	4
HH Streak	c ME Waugh b Warne	3
GJ Whittall	c Healy b Warne	27
BC Strang	run out (Blewett)	17
HK Olonga	not out	0
Extras	(b 2, lb 4, nb 10)	16
Total	**(all out, 85 overs, 343 mins)**	**194**

Fall: 1-6 (GW Flower, 3.1 ov), 2-6 (Goodwin, 3.2 ov), 3-22 (Campbell, 9.5 ov), 4-37 (Rennie, 18.2 ov), 5-107 (A Flower, 48.2 ov), 6-119 (Gripper, 60.1 ov), 7-125 (Streak, 66.5 ov), 8-165 (Whittall, 78.2 ov), 9-190 (Johnson, 82.5 ov), 10-194 (Strang, 84.6 ov).

Bowling: McGrath 23-7-44-3; Fleming 15-6-22-2; Miller 19-6-36-0; Warne 23-2-69-3; Ponting 1-1-0-0; SR Waugh 4-1-17-0.

Zimbabwe second innings

TR Gripper	lbw Miller	60
GW Flower	lbw McGrath	32
MW Goodwin	c SR Waugh b Warne	91
GJ Rennie	c McGrath b Miller	23
*ADR Campbell	run out (Slater/Healy)	1
+A Flower	c Healy b McGrath	0
NC Johnson	c ME Waugh b McGrath	5
GJ Whittall	c ME Waugh b Warne	2
HH Streak	lbw Warne	0
BC Strang	c Langer b Miller	0
HK Olonga	not out	0
Extras	(b 9, lb 2, w 1, nb 6)	18
Total	**(all out, 122.1 overs, 457 mins)**	**232**

Fall: 1-56 (GW Flower, 31.5 ov), 2-154 (Gripper, 77.3 ov), 3-200 (Rennie, 97.2 ov), 4-208 (Campbell, 103.5 ov), 5-211 (A Flower, 108.6 ov), 6-220 (Johnson, 114.2 ov), 7-227 (Whittall, 118.4 ov), 8-227 (Streak, 120.6 ov), 9-232 (Strang, 121.6 ov), 10-232 (Goodwin, 122.1 ov).

Bowling: McGrath 31-12-46-3; Fleming 21-6-31-0; Miller 34-10-66-3; Ponting 1-1-0-0; Warne 30.1-11-68-3; Blewett 5-1-10-0.

Australia first innings

MJ Slater	c A Flower b Strang	4
GS Blewett	c Campbell b Streak	1
JL Langer	run out (Olonga)	44
ME Waugh	c&b GW Flower	90
*SR Waugh	not out	151
RT Ponting	c Johnson b Streak	31
+IA Healy	c A Flower b Strang	5
SK Warne	c A Flower b Streak	6
DW Fleming	lbw Streak	65
CR Miller	c Johnson b Streak	2
GD McGrath	c Johnson b Whittall	13
Extras	(lb 5, w 4, nb 1)	10
Total	**(all out, 139.4 overs, 544 mins)**	**422**

Fall: 1-6 (Blewett, 3.3 ov), 2-7 (Slater, 4.2 ov), 3-96 (Langer, 29.3 ov), 4-174 (ME Waugh, 56.5 ov), 5-253 (Ponting, 83.4 ov), 6-275 (Healy, 94.1 ov), 7-282 (Warne, 97.1 ov), 8-396 (Fleming, 131.3 ov), 9-398 (Miller, 131.6 ov), 10-422 (McGrath, 139.4 ov).

Bowling: Olonga 17-1-83-0; Streak 34-8-93-5; Strang 44-14-96-2; Johnson 2-0-14-0; Whittall 21.4-3-74-1; GW Flower 18-3-38-1; Gripper 3-0-19-0.

Australia second innings

GS Blewett	not out	4
MJ Slater	not out	0
Extras	(w 1)	1
Total	**(0 wickets, 0.3 overs, 2 mins)**	**5**

Bowling: Strang 0.3-0-5-0.

AUSTRALIA WON BY 10 WICKETS

FIRST TEST, AT BRISBANE, NOVEMBER 5,6,7,8,9 (Toss: Australia)

Pakistan first innings

Saeed Anwar	c ME Waugh b Warne	61
Mohammad Wasim	c Gilchrist b Fleming	18
Ijaz Ahmed	c Warne b Fleming	0
Inzamam-ul-Haq	lbw McGrath	88
Yousuf Youhana	c Gilchrist b Fleming	95
Azhar Mahmood	c Slater b McGrath	13
Mushtaq Ahmed	c Gilchrist b Fleming	0
Abdur Razzaq	c ME Waugh b Muller	11
+Moin Khan	run out (Ponting/Gilchrist)	61
*Wasim Akram	c&b Muller	9
Shoaib Akhtar	not out	0
Extras	(b 4, lb 2, nb 5)	11
Total	**(all out, 117.1 overs, 464 mins)**	**367**

Fall: 1-42 (Mohammad Wasim, 16.2 ov), 2-42 (Ijaz Ahmed, 16.5 ov), 3-113 (Saeed Anwar, 33.2 ov), 4-265 (Inzamam-ul-Haq, 84.6 ov), 5-280 (Yousuf Youhana, 89.2 ov), 6-280 (Mushtaq Ahmed, 91.1 ov), 7-288 (Azhar Mahmood, 96.2 ov), 8-334 (Abdur Razzaq, 110.1 ov), 9-356 (Wasim Akram, 114.4 ov), 10-367 (Moin Khan, 117.1 ov).

Bowling: McGrath 28-4-116-2; Fleming 31-5-65-4; Muller 19-4-72-2; Warne 28.1-11-73-1; Blewett 5-1-22-0; Ponting 5-1-12-0; SR Waugh 1-0-1-0.

Pakistan second innings

Saeed Anwar	c Gilchrist b McGrath	119
Mohammad Wasim	lbw Fleming	0
Ijaz Ahmed	c Gilchrist b McGrath	5
Inzamam-ul-Haq	c Ponting b Fleming	12
Yousuf Youhana	c ME Waugh b Muller	75
Abdur Razzaq	c Ponting b Warne	2
+Moin Khan	c Muller b Fleming	17
Azhar Mahmood	st Gilchrist b Warne	0
*Wasim Akram	b Fleming	28
Mushtaq Ahmed	not out	1
Shoaib Akhtar	b Fleming	5
Extras	(b 6, lb 6, nb 5)	17
Total	**(all out, 74.1 overs, 315 mins)**	**281**

Fall: 1-3 (Mohammad Wasim, 1.4 ov), 2-8 (Ijaz Ahmed, 2.1 ov), 3-37 (Inzamam-ul-Haq, 9.5 ov), 4-214 (Yousuf Youhana, 50.2 ov), 5-223 (Abdur Razzaq, 53.1 ov), 6-225 (Saeed Anwar, 60.5 ov), 7-227 (Azhar Mahmood, 63.2 ov), 8-273 (Wasim Akram, 72.1 ov), 9-276 (Moin Khan, 72.6 ov), 10-281 (Shoaib Akhtar, 74.1 ov).

Bowling: McGrath 21-9-63-2; Fleming 14.1-2-59-5; Muller 10-1-55-1; Warne 25-8-80-2; Ponting 4-0-12-0.

Australia first innings

MJ Slater	c Y. Youhana b Azhar Mahmood	169
GS Blewett	lbw Mushtaq Ahmed	89
JL Langer	c Abdur Razzaq b Mushtaq Ahmed	1
ME Waugh	c Wasim Akram b Mushtaq Ahmed	100
*SR Waugh	c Moin Khan b Shoaib Akhtar	1
RT Ponting	lbw Shoaib Akhtar	0
+AC Gilchrist	b Shoaib Akhtar	81
SK Warne	c Mushtaq Ahmed b Wasim Akram	86
DW Fleming	lbw Shoaib Akhtar	0
GD McGrath	c Yousuf Youhana b Wasim Akram	1
SA Muller	not out	6
Extras	(b 3, lb 12, nb 26)	41
Total	**(all out, 139.1 overs, 607 mins)**	**575**

Fall: 1-269 (Blewett, 71.3 ov), 2-272 (Langer, 73.3 ov), 3-311 (Slater, 83.5 ov), 4-328 (SR Waugh, 88.5 ov), 5-342 (Ponting, 92.2 ov), 6-465 (ME Waugh, 117.6 ov), 7-485 (Gilchrist, 122.1 ov), 8-486 (Fleming, 122.3 ov), 9-489 (McGrath, 123.6 ov), 10-575 (Warne, 139.1 ov).

Bowling: Wasim Akram 31.1-6-87-2; Shoaib Akhtar 32-2-153-4; Abdur Razzaq 17-3-66-0; Azhar Mahmood 19-2-52-1; Mushtaq Ahmed 38-3-194-3; Ijaz Ahmed 2-0-8-0.

Australia second innings

GS Blewett	not out	40
MJ Slater	not out	32
Extras	(lb 2)	2
Total	**(0 wickets, 14.2 overs, 56 mins)**	**74**

Bowling: Wasim Akram 4-0-14-0; Shoaib Akhtar 5-0-25-0; Azhar Mahmood 3.2-0-13-0; Mushtaq Ahmed 2-0-20-0

AUSTRALIA WON BY 10 WICKETS

SECOND TEST, AT HOBART, NOVEMBER 18,19,20,21,22 (Toss: Australia)

Pakistan first innings

Saeed Anwar	c Warne b McGrath	0
Mohammad Wasim	c Gilchrist b Muller	91
Ijaz Ahmed	c Slater b McGrath	6
Inzamam-ul-Haq	b Muller	12
Yousuf Youhana	c ME Waugh b Fleming	17
Azhar Mahmood	b Warne	27
+Moin Khan	c McGrath b Muller	1
*Wasim Akram	c Gilchrist b Warne	29
Saqlain Mushtaq	lbw Warne	3
Waqar Younis	not out	12
Shoaib Akhtar	c Gilchrist b Fleming	5
Extras	(b 10, lb 6, w 3)	19
Total	**(all out, 72.5 overs, 283 mins)**	**222**

Fall: 1-4 (Saeed Anwar, 2.1 ov), 2-18 (Ijaz Ahmed, 10.2 ov), 3-71 (Inzamam-ul-Haq, 23.4 ov), 4-120 (Yousuf Youhana, 35.2 ov), 5-148 (Mohammad Wasim, 44.1 ov), 6-153 (Moin Khan, 44.6 ov), 7-188 (Azhar Mahmood, 57.2 ov), 8-198 (Saqlain Mushtaq, 65.2 ov), 9-217 (Wasim Akram, 71.5 ov), 10-222 (Shoaib Akhtar, 72.5 ov).

Bowling: McGrath 18-8-34-2; Fleming 24.5-7-54-2; Muller 12-0-68-3; Warne 16-6-45-3; Blewett 2-1-5-0.

Pakistan second innings

Saeed Anwar	b Warne	78
Mohammad Wasim	c McGrath b Muller	20
Saqlain Mushtaq	lbw Warne	8
Ijaz Ahmed	c SR Waugh b McGrath	82
Inzamam-ul-Haq	c ME Waugh b Warne	118
Yousuf Youhana	c Ponting b Fleming	2
Azhar Mahmood	lbw Warne	28
+Moin Khan	c Gilchrist b Fleming	6
*Wasim Akram	c Blewett b Warne	31
Waqar Younis	run out (Gilchrist)	0
Shoaib Akhtar	not out	5
Extras	(lb 6, w 1, nb 7)	14
Total	**(all out, 128.5 overs, 521 mins)**	**392**

Fall: 1-50 (Mohammad Wasim, 18.6 ov), 2-100 (Saqlain Mushtaq, 41.1 ov), 3-122 (Saeed Anwar, 47.4 ov), 4-258 (Ijaz Ahmed, 82.1 ov), 5-263 (Yousuf Youhana, 85.2 ov), 6-320 (Azhar Mahmood, 101.5 ov), 7-345 (Moin Khan, 110.5 ov), 8-357 (Inzamam-ul-Haq, 115.3 ov), 9-358 (Waqar Younis, 116.4 ov), 10-392 (Wasim Akram, 128.5 ov).

Bowling: McGrath 27-8-87-1; Fleming 29-5-89-2; Warne 45.5-11-110-5; Muller 17-3-63-1; SR Waugh 4-1-19-0; ME Waugh 2-0-6-0; Ponting 2-1-7-0; Blewett 2-0-5-0.

Australia first innings

MJ Slater	c Ijaz Ahmed b Saqlain Mushtaq	97
GS Blewett	c Moin Khan b Azhar Mahmood	35
JL Langer	c M. Wasim b Saqlain Mushtaq	59
ME Waugh	lbw Waqar Younis	5
*SR Waugh	c Ijaz Ahmed b Wasim Akram	24
RT Ponting	b Waqar Younis	0
+AC Gilchrist	st Moin Khan b Saqlain Mushtaq	6
SK Warne	b Saqlain Mushtaq	0
DW Fleming	lbw Saqlain Mushtaq	0
GD McGrath	st Moin Khan b Saqlain Mushtaq	7
SA Muller	not out	0
Extras	(b 2, lb 6, nb 5)	13
Total	**(all out, 80 overs, 355 mins)**	**246**

Fall: 1-76 (Blewett, 28.4 ov), 2-191 (Slater, 59.5 ov), 3-206 (ME Waugh, 64.5 ov), 4-206 (Langer, 65.3 ov), 5-213 (Ponting, 68.1 ov), 6-236 (Gilchrist, 75.1 ov), 7-236 (Warne, 75.2 ov), 8-236 (Fleming, 75.6 ov), 9-246 (SR Waugh, 78.6 ov), 10-246 (McGrath, 79.6 ov).

Bowling: Wasim Akram 20-4-51-1; Shoaib Akhtar 17-2-69-0; Waqar Younis 12-1-42-2 Saqlain Mushtaq 24-8-46-6; Azhar Mahmood 7-1-30-1.

Australia second innings

GS Blewett	c Moin Khan b Azhar Mahmood	29
MJ Slater	c Azhar Mahmood b Shoaib Akhtar	27
JL Langer	c Inzamam b Saqlain Mushtaq	127
ME Waugh	lbw Azhar Mahmood	0
*SR Waugh	c&b Saqlain Mushtaq	28
RT Ponting	lbw Wasim Akram	0
+AC Gilchrist	not out	149
SK Warne	not out	0
Extras	(b 1, lb 4, nb 4)	9
Total	**(6 wickets, 113.5 overs, 503 mins)**	**369**

Fall: 1-39 (Slater, 16.4 ov), 2-81 (Blewett, 32.3 ov), 3-81 (ME Waugh, 32.4 ov), 4-125 (SR Waugh, 53.3 ov), 5-126 (Ponting, 54.4 ov), 6-364 (Langer, 113.3 ov).

Bowling: Wasim Akram 18-1-68-1; Waqar Younis 11-2-38-0; Shoaib Akhtar 23-4-85-1; Saqlain Mushtaq 44.5-9-130-2; Azhar Mahmood 17-3-43-2.

AUSTRALIA WON BY FOUR WICKETS

THIRD TEST, AT PERTH, NOVEMBER 26,27,28 (Toss: Pakistan)

Pakistan first innings

Saeed Anwar	c Ponting b McGrath	18
Wajahatullah Wasti	c Ponting b McGrath	5
Ijaz Ahmed	b Fleming	1
Inzamam-ul-Haq	c SR Waugh b Kasprowicz	22
Yousuf Youhana	c Gilchrist b McGrath	18
Azhar Mahmood	c Warne b Fleming	39
+Moin Khan	c&b Fleming	28
*Wasim Akram	not out	5
Saqlain Mushtaq	c Blewett b Kasprowicz	7
Shoaib Akhtar	b Kasprowicz	0
Mohammad Akram	c ME Waugh b Kasprowicz	0
Extras	(lb 4, nb 8)	12
Total	**(all out, 52 overs, 224 mins)**	**155**

Fall: 1-18 (Wajahatullah, 4.3 ov), 2-26 (Ijaz Ahmed, 9.3 ov), 3-26 (Saeed Anwar, 10.4 ov), 4-51 (Yousuf Youhana, 18.4 ov), 5-83 (Inzamam-ul-Haq, 26.1 ov), 6-135 (Azhar Mahmood, 39.4 ov), 7-142 (Moin Khan, 41.6 ov), 8-155 (Saqlain Mushtaq, 51.3 ov), 9-155 (Shoaib Akhtar, 51.5 ov), 10-155 (Mohammad Akram, 51.6 ov).

Bowling: McGrath 19-3-44-3; Fleming 19-7-48-3; Kasprowicz 12-2-53-4; Warne 2-0-6-0.

Australia first innings

MJ Slater	lbw Wasim Akram	0
GS Blewett	c Inzamam b Mohammad Akram	11
JL Langer	c Moin Khan b Shoaib Akhtar	144
ME Waugh	c sub (Ghulam Ali) b M. Akram	0
*SR Waugh	c Yousuf Youhana b M. Akram	5
RT Ponting	c Ijaz Ahmed b Azhar Mahmood	197
+AC Gilchrist	b Mohammad Akram	28
SK Warne	c Moin Khan b Saqlain Mushtaq	13
MS Kasprowicz	not out	9
DW Fleming	lbw Saqlain Mushtaq	0
GD McGrath	c Azhar Mahmood b M. Akram	0
Extras	(b 9, lb 9, nb 26)	44
Total	**(all out, 110.5 overs, 517 mins)**	**451**

Fall: 1-0 (Slater, 0.2 ov), 2-28 (Blewett, 5.4 ov), 3-48 (ME Waugh, 9.5 ov), 4-54 (SR Waugh, 11.2 ov), 5-381 (Langer, 96.2 ov), 6-424 (Gilchrist, 102.6 ov), 7-424 (Ponting, 103.2 ov), 8-448 (Warne, 107.6 ov), 9-450 (Fleming, 109.3 ov), 10-451 (McGrath, 110.5 ov).

Bowling: Wasim Akram 17-2-55-1; Mohammad Akram 27.5-1-138-5; Shoaib Akhtar 16-2-74-1; Azhar Mahmood 23-2-91-1; Saqlain Mushtaq 26-7-75-2; Wajahatullah 1-1-0-0.

Pakistan second innings

Saeed Anwar	c Gilchrist b Fleming	6
Wajahatullah Wasti	c Fleming b McGrath	7
Ijaz Ahmed	c Slater b Kasprowicz	115
Saqlain Mushtaq	lbw Kasprowicz	12
Inzamam-ul-Haq	c ME Waugh b McGrath	8
Yousuf Youhana	c SR Waugh b McGrath	0
Azhar Mahmood	b Warne	17
+Moin Khan	c Gilchrist b McGrath	26
*Wasim Akram	c McGrath b Kasprowicz	52
Shoaib Akhtar	c Warne b Fleming	8
Mohammad Akram	not out	10
Extras	(lb 6, nb 9)	15
Total	**(all out, 69.4 overs, 295 mins)**	**276**

Fall: 1-15 (Saeed Anwar, 5.6 ov), 2-25 (Wajahatullah, 8.6 ov), 3-53 (Inzamam-ul-Haq, 18.3 ov), 4-56 (Yousuf Youhana, 24.1 ov), 5-114 (Azhar Mahmood, 35.6 ov), 6-168 (Moin Khan, 52.1 ov), 7-230 (Ijaz Ahmed, 60.6 ov), 8-256 (Saqlain Mushtaq, 66.4 ov), 9-261 (Wasim Akram, 68.1 ov), 10-276 (Shoaib Akhtar, 69.4 ov).

Bowling: McGrath 21-5-49-4; Fleming 19.4-3-86-2; Kasprowicz 16-3-79-3; Warne 13-1-56-1.

AUSTRALIA WON BY AN INNINGS AND 20 RUNS

AUSTRALIA WON THE SERIES 3-0

Australia v India

FIRST TEST, AT ADELAIDE, DECEMBER 10,11,12,13,14 (Toss: Australia)

Australia first innings

GS Blewett	c MSK Prasad b Srinath	4
MJ Slater	c Ramesh b Ganguly	28
JL Langer	lbw BKV Prasad	11
ME Waugh	c MSK Prasad b BKV Prasad	5
*SR Waugh	c MSK Prasad b Agarkar	150
RT Ponting	run out (Agarkar/MSK Prasad)	125
+AC Gilchrist	c&b Agarkar	0
SK Warne	lbw Kumble	86
MS Kasprowicz	b Kumble	4
DW Fleming	not out	12
GD McGrath	c MSK Prasad b BKV Prasad	4
Extras	(b 1, lb 5, nb 6)	12
Total	**(all out, 125.3 overs, 512 mins)**	**441**

Fall: 1-8 (Blewett, 2.2 ov), 2-29 (Langer, 9.6 ov), 3-45 (Slater, 14.4 ov), 4-52 (ME Waugh, 17.3 ov), 5-291 (Ponting, 87.4 ov), 6-298 (Gilchrist, 90.1 ov), 7-406 (SR Waugh, 115.5 ov), 8-417 (Kasprowicz, 118.4 ov), 9-424 (Warne, 120.6 ov), 10-441 (McGrath, 125.3 ov).

Bowling: Srinath 29-3-117-1; Agarkar 26-5-86-2; BKV Prasad 24.3-4-83-3; Ganguly 7-1-34-1; Kumble 34-1-101-2; Tendulkar 2-0-12-0; Laxman 3-1-2-0.

India first innings

DJ Gandhi	c Kasprowicz b McGrath	4
S Ramesh	run out (Blewett)	2
VVS Laxman	c SR Waugh b McGrath	41
R Dravid	c Langer b Warne	35
*SR Tendulkar	c Langer b Warne	61
SC Ganguly	st Gilchrist b Warne	60
+MSK Prasad	b Warne	14
AB Agarkar	b Fleming	19
J Srinath	c SR Waugh b Fleming	11
A Kumble	not out	17
BKV Prasad	lbw Fleming	0
Extras	(lb 1, w 1, nb 19)	21
Total	**(all out, 113.4 overs, 464 mins)**	**285**

Fall: 1-7 (Ramesh, 2.1 ov), 2-9 (Gandhi, 4.1 ov), 3-90 (Laxman, 30.1 ov), 4-107 (Dravid, 45.1 ov), 5-215 (Tendulkar, 73.5 ov), 6-229 (Ganguly, 87.1 ov), 7-240 (MSK Prasad, 91.5 ov), 8-266 (Srinath, 103.1 ov), 9-275 (Agarkar, 109.4 ov), 10-285 (BKV Prasad, 113.4 ov).

Bowling: McGrath 30-13-49-2; Fleming 24.4-7-70-3; Kasprowicz 11-2-62-0; Warne 42-12-92-4; Blewett 6-1-11-0.

Australia second innings

MJ Slater	c Ganguly b Srinath	0
GS Blewett	b Agarkar	88
JL Langer	c Gandhi b Kumble	38
ME Waugh	c Laxman b Agarkar	8
*SR Waugh	c MSK Prasad b Agarkar	5
RT Ponting	c MSK Prasad b BKV Prasad	21
+AC Gilchrist	c Laxman b Srinath	43
SK Warne	c Dravid b Srinath	0
MS Kasprowicz	not out	21
Extras	(b 3, lb 8, w 2, nb 2)	15
Total	**(8 wickets dec, 89.5 overs, 386 mins)**	**239**

Fall: 1-1 (Slater, 2.2 ov), 2-65 (Langer, 26.5 ov), 3-95 (ME Waugh, 41.5 ov), 4-113 (SR Waugh, 49.2 ov), 5-153 (Ponting, 67.5 ov), 6-204 (Blewett, 81.2 ov), 7-205 (Warne, 82.2 ov), 8-239 (Gilchrist, 89.5 ov).

Bowling: Srinath 21.5-4-64-3; Agarkar 18-6-43-3; BKV Prasad 18-5-48-1; Kumble 32-9-73-1.

India second innings

DJ Gandhi	c Gilchrist b McGrath	0
S Ramesh	lbw Warne	28
VVS Laxman	b Fleming	0
R Dravid	c Gilchrist b Warne	6
*SR Tendulkar	lbw McGrath	0
SC Ganguly	c Gilchrist b Fleming	43
+MSK Prasad	c Langer b Fleming	11
AB Agarkar	c SR Waugh b Fleming	0
J Srinath	c Slater b McGrath	11
A Kumble	b Fleming	3
BKV Prasad	not out	2
Extras	(lb 1, nb 5)	6
Total	**(all out, 38.1 overs, 177 mins)**	**110**

Fall: 1-0 (Gandhi, 0.6 ov), 2-3 (Laxman, 1.3 ov), 3-24 (Dravid, 7.3 ov), 4-27 (Tendulkar, 8.3 ov), 5-48 (Ramesh, 15.2 ov), 6-93 (Ganguly, 30.3 ov), 7-93 (Agarkar, 30.4 ov), 8-102 (MSK Prasad, 34.3 ov), 9-108 (Srinath, 37.4 ov), 10-110 (Kumble, 38.1 ov).

Bowling: McGrath 12-2-35-3; Fleming 9.1-2-30-5; Warne 10-6-21-2; Kasprowicz 6-0-23-0; ME Waugh 1-1-0-0.

AUSTRALIA WON BY 285 RUNS

SECOND TEST, AT MELBOURNE, DECEMBER 26,27,28,29,30 (Toss: India)

Australia first innings

GS Blewett	b Srinath	2
MJ Slater	c Srinath b BKV Prasad	91
JL Langer	lbw Srinath	80
ME Waugh	lbw Agarkar	41
*SR Waugh	c MSK Prasad b BKV Prasad	32
RT Ponting	lbw Srinath	67
+AC Gilchrist	c Ganguly b Agarkar	78
SK Warne	c MSK Prasad b Agarkar	2
DW Fleming	not out	31
B Lee	c&b Srinath	27
GD McGrath	run out (Kanitkar)	1
Extras	(b 1, lb 9, w 1, nb 14)	25
Total	**(all out, 118.1 overs, 526 mins)**	**405**

Fall: 1-4 (Blewett, 2.2 ov), 2-28 (Langer, 10.2 ov), 3-123 (ME Waugh, 38.4 ov), 4-192 (Slater, 62.4 ov), 5-197 (SR Waugh, 64.4 ov), 6-341 (Gilchrist, 96.4 ov), 7-343 (Ponting, 97.6 ov), 8-345 (Warne, 98.6 ov), 9-404 (Lee, 116.6 ov), 10-405 (McGrath, 118.1 ov).

Bowling: Srinath 33.1-7-130-4; Agarkar 28-7-76-3; BKV Prasad 26-6-101-2; Ganguly 2-0-10-0; Kumble 29-3-78-0.

Australia second innings

MJ Slater	lbw Agarkar	3
GS Blewett	c Ganguly b Kumble	31
JL Langer	c MSK Prasad b Agarkar	9
+AC Gilchrist	c Srinath b Kumble	55
ME Waugh	not out	51
*SR Waugh	lbw Agarkar	32
RT Ponting	not out	21
Extras	(lb 2, w 1, nb 3)	6
Total	**(5 wickets dec, 59 overs, 263 mins)**	**208**

Fall: 1-5 (Slater, 3.2 ov), 2-32 (Langer, 13.2 ov), 3-91 (Blewett, 31.2 ov), 4-109 (Gilchrist, 35.3 ov), 5-167 (SR Waugh, 48.2 ov).

Bowling: Srinath 14-0-45-0; Agarkar 17-3-51-3; BKV Prasad 10-0-38-0; Kumble 18-3-72-2.

India first innings

VVS Laxman	c ME Waugh b McGrath	5
S Ramesh	b Lee	4
R Dravid	c Gilchrist b Lee	9
*SR Tendulkar	c Langer b Fleming	116
SC Ganguly	c ME Waugh b McGrath	31
HH Kanitkar	lbw Warne	11
+MSK Prasad	b Lee	6
AB Agarkar	lbw Lee	0
J Srinath	c ME Waugh b Lee	1
A Kumble	not out	28
BKV Prasad	c ME Waugh b McGrath	10
Extras	(lb 8, nb 9)	17
Total	**(all out, 76.1 overs, 346 mins)**	**238**

Fall: 1-11 (Ramesh, 5.4 ov), 2-11 (Laxman, 6.4 ov), 3-31 (Dravid, 18.2 ov), 4-108 (Ganguly, 44.6 ov), 5-138 (Kanitkar, 51.6 ov), 6-167 (MSK Prasad, 58.1 ov), 7-167 (Agarkar, 58.2 ov), 8-169 (Srinath, 58.6 ov), 9-212 (Tendulkar, 69.1 ov), 10-238 (BKV Prasad, 76.1 ov).

Bowling: McGrath 18.1-3-39-3; Fleming 15-0-62-1; Lee 18-2-47-5; Warne 24-5-77-1; ME Waugh 1-0-5-0.

India second innings

VVS Laxman	c McGrath b Fleming	1
S Ramesh	retired hurt	26
R Dravid	c Gilchrist b Lee	14
*SR Tendulkar	lbw Warne	52
SC Ganguly	b Blewett	17
HH Kanitkar	lbw Fleming	45
+MSK Prasad	c Warne b ME Waugh	13
AB Agarkar	c Blewett b ME Waugh	0
A Kumble	run out (SR Waugh/Fleming)	13
J Srinath	c Warne b Lee	1
BKV Prasad	not out	6
Extras	(lb 4, nb 3)	7
Total	**(all out, 89.3 overs, 371 mins)**	**195**

Fall: 1-5 (Laxman, 3.5 ov), 2-72 (Dravid, 42.2 ov), 3-110 (Ganguly, 55.5 ov), 4-133 (Tendulkar, 61.6 ov), 5-162 (MSK Prasad, 72.3 ov), 6-162 (Agarkar, 72.4 ov), 7-184 (Kanitkar, 81.1 ov), 8-185 (Srinath, 82.1 ov), 9-195 (Kumble, 89.3 ov).

Bowling: McGrath 17-8-22-0; Fleming 21.3-7-46-2; Warne 26-7-63-1; Lee 19-6-31-2; Blewett 3-1-17-1; ME Waugh 3-0-12-2.

AUSTRALIA WON BY 180 RUNS

THIRD TEST, AT SYDNEY, JANUARY 2,3,4 (Toss: India)

India first innings

+MSK Prasad	c ME Waugh b McGrath	5
VVS Laxman	c Slater b Lee	7
R Dravid	c Ponting b McGrath	29
*SR Tendulkar	lbw McGrath	45
SC Ganguly	c SR Waugh b Blewett	1
HH Kanitkar	c Gilchrist b Lee	10
R Vijay Bharadwaj	c Gilchrist b Lee	6
A Kumble	c Langer b McGrath	26
AB Agarkar	c ME Waugh b Lee	0
J Srinath	c Ponting b McGrath	3
BKV Prasad	not out	1
Extras	(lb 12, w 1, nb 4)	17
Total	**(all out, 67.5 overs, 295 mins)**	**150**

Fall: 1-10 (MSK Prasad, 10.5 ov), 2-27 (Laxman, 22.2 ov), 3-68 (Dravid, 34.1 ov), 4-69 (Ganguly, 35.1 ov), 5-95 (Tendulkar, 40.6 ov), 6-118 (Kanitkar, 54.1 ov), 7-119 (Vijay Bharadwaj, 56.1 ov), 8-119 (Agarkar, 56.2 ov), 9-126 (Srinath, 61.5 ov), 10-150 (Kumble, 67.5 ov).

Bowling: McGrath 18.5-7-48-5; Fleming 13-7-24-0; Lee 21-9-39-4; Warne 12-4-22-0; Blewett 3-2-5-1.

Australia first innings

GS Blewett	b BKV Prasad	19
MJ Slater	c MSK Prasad b Srinath	1
JL Langer	c BKV Prasad b Tendulkar	223
ME Waugh	b Ganguly	32
*SR Waugh	lbw Srinath	57
RT Ponting	not out	141
+AC Gilchrist	not out	45
Extras	(b 2, lb 21, nb 11)	34
Total	**(5 wickets dec, 140.2 overs, 608 mins)**	**552**

Did Not Bat: SK Warne, DW Fleming, B Lee, GD McGrath.

Fall: 1-9 (Slater, 4.3 ov), 2-49 (Blewett, 19.5 ov), 3-146 (ME Waugh, 42.1 ov), 4-267 (SR Waugh, 80.1 ov), 5-457 (Langer, 122.5 ov).

Bowling: Srinath 28-4-105-2; Agarkar 19-3-95-0; BKV Prasad 28-10-86-1; Kumble 33.2-6-126-0; Ganguly 12-1-46-1; Vijay Bharadwaj 12-1-35-0; Tendulkar 7-0-34-1; Kanitkar 1-0-2-0.

India second innings

VVS Laxman	c Gilchrist b Lee	167
+MSK Prasad	c ME Waugh b McGrath	3
R Dravid	c Warne b McGrath	0
*SR Tendulkar	c Langer b Fleming	4
SC Ganguly	c ME Waugh b McGrath	25
HH Kanitkar	c Slater b Lee	8
A Kumble	c Ponting b McGrath	15
AB Agarkar	c Gilchrist b McGrath	0
J Srinath	not out	15
BKV Prasad	run out (Gilchrist)	3
R Vijay Bharadwaj	absent injured	–
Extras	(b 4, lb 2, w 1, nb 14)	21
Total	**(all out, 58 overs, 260 mins)**	**261**

Fall: 1-22 (MSK Prasad, 4.3 ov), 2-26 (Dravid, 6.4 ov), 3-33 (Tendulkar, 7.4 ov), 4-101 (Ganguly, 24.5 ov), 5-145 (Kanitkar, 30.6 ov), 6-234 (Kumble, 50.1 ov), 7-234 (Agarkar, 50.3 ov), 8-258 (Laxman, 57.1 ov), 9-261 (BKV Prasad, 57.6 ov).

Bowling: McGrath 17-1-55-5; Fleming 13-2-47-1; Lee 11-2-67-2; Blewett 2-0-16-0; Warne 13-1-60-0; Ponting 1-0-8-0; Slater 1-0-2-0.

AUSTRALIA WON BY AN INNINGS AND 141 RUNS

AUSTRALIAN WON THE SERIES 3-0

Australia in New Zealand, 2000

FIRST TEST, AUCKLAND, MARCH 11,12,13,14,15 (Toss: Australia)

Australia first innings

MJ Slater	b Cairns	5
GS Blewett	c Astle b Wiseman	17
JL Langer	st Parore b Wiseman	46
ME Waugh	not out	72
*SR Waugh	c Spearman b Vettori	17
DR Martyn	c Astle b Vettori	17
+AC Gilchrist	lbw Wiseman	7
SK Warne	c Fleming b Vettori	7
B Lee	c Parore b Vettori	6
CR Miller	b Cairns	0
GD McGrath	c Spearman b Vettori	8
Extras	(b 7, lb 4, nb 1)	12
Total	**(all out, 71 overs, 286 mins)**	**214**

Fall: 1-10 (Slater, 4.5 ov), 2-77 (Langer, 19.5 ov), 3-78 (Blewett, 21.6 ov), 4-114 (SR Waugh, 32.2 ov), 5-138 (Martyn, 40.2 ov), 6-161 (Gilchrist, 49.6 ov), 7-184 (Warne, 56.4 ov), 8-192 (Lee, 60.3 ov), 9-193 (Miller, 61.2 ov), 10-214 (McGrath, 70.6 ov).

Bowling: Cairns 18-0-71-2; Doull 14-6-21-0; Vettori 25-8-62-5; Wiseman 14-3-49-3.

Australia second innings

GS Blewett	c Spearman b Vettori	8
MJ Slater	c Horne b Cairns	6
JL Langer	c Astle b Vettori	47
ME Waugh	c Parore b Vettori	25
*SR Waugh	c&b Wiseman	10
DR Martyn	b Vettori	36
+AC Gilchrist	c Fleming b Vettori	59
SK Warne	c Wiseman b Vettori	12
B Lee	not out	6
CR Miller	st Parore b Vettori	8
GD McGrath	lbw Wiseman	1
Extras	(b 7, lb 4)	11
Total	**(all out, 77.5 overs, 291 mins)**	**229**

Fall: 1-7 (Slater, 2.5 ov), 2-46 (Blewett, 18.3 ov), 3-67 (Langer, 26.3 ov), 4-81 (SR Waugh, 31.1 ov), 5-107 (ME Waugh, 44.5 ov), 6-174 (Martyn, 66.6 ov), 7-202 (Warne, 70.5 ov), 8-214 (Gilchrist, 74.3 ov), 9-226 (Miller, 76.2 ov), 10-229 (McGrath, 77.5 ov).

Bowling: Cairns 4-1-13-1; Wiseman 33.5-6-110-2; Vettori 35-11-87-7; Doull 5-1-8-0.

New Zealand first innings

MJ Horne	c Blewett b McGrath	3
CM Spearman	c Martyn b Lee	12
MS Sinclair	lbw Warne	8
PJ Wiseman	b Lee	1
*SP Fleming	st Gilchrist b Miller	21
NJ Astle	c ME Waugh b Warne	31
CD McMillan	lbw Warne	6
CL Cairns	c Gilchrist b McGrath	35
+AC Parore	c Gilchrist b McGrath	11
DL Vettori	not out	15
SB Doull	c Lee b McGrath	12
Extras	(b 4, lb 1, nb 3)	8
Total	**(all out, 62.1 overs, 240 mins)**	**163**

Fall: 1-4 (Horne, 6.2 ov), 2-25 (Sinclair, 13.2 ov), 3-25 (Spearman, 14.2 ov), 4-26 (Wiseman, 16.6 ov), 5-80 (Astle, 31.5 ov), 6-80 (Fleming, 32.2 ov), 7-102 (McMillan, 41.4 ov), 8-134 (Cairns, 54.4 ov), 9-143 (Parore, 60.1 ov), 10-163 (Doull, 62.1 ov).

Bowling: McGrath 11.1-2-33-4; Miller 22-8-38-1; Warne 22-4-68-3; Lee 7-4-19-2.

New Zealand second innings

MJ Horne	c Langer b Miller	11
CM Spearman	lbw McGrath	4
MS Sinclair	lbw Miller	6
*SP Fleming	c Gilchrist b Miller	8
NJ Astle	b Warne	35
CD McMillan	c Warne b Lee	78
CL Cairns	c SR Waugh b Miller	20
+AC Parore	c SR Waugh b Lee	26
DL Vettori	c Warne b Miller	0
SB Doull	not out	5
PJ Wiseman	c Gilchrist b Warne	9
Extras	(b 7, lb 7, nb 2)	16
Total	**(all out, 73.3 overs, 290 mins)**	**218**

Fall: 1-15 (Horne, 7.4 ov), 2-25 (Sinclair, 11.1 ov), 3-25 (Spearman, 12.1 ov), 4-43 (Fleming, 17.5 ov), 5-121 (Astle, 35.2 ov), 6-151 (Cairns, 49.5 ov), 7-195 (Parore, 66.6 ov), 8-204 (McMillan, 68.6 ov), 9-204 (Vettori, 69.4 ov), 10-218 (Wiseman, 73.3 ov).

Bowling: McGrath 23-8-33-1; Lee 12-4-36-2; Miller 18-5-55-5; Warne 20.3-4-80-2.

AUSTRALIA WON BY 62 RUNS

SECOND TEST, AT WELLINGTON, MARCH 24,25,26,27 (Toss: New Zealand)

New Zealand first innings

MJ Horne	c Warne b Lee	4
CM Spearman	c Gilchrist b Lee	4
MS Sinclair	lbw Miller	4
*SP Fleming	c Miller b Warne	16
NJ Astle	c ME Waugh b Warne	61
CL Cairns	c Blewett b Miller	109
+AC Parore	c Gilchrist b Blewett	46
DL Vettori	c Langer b Warne	27
SB Doull	c Slater b Warne	12
SB O'Connor	not out	2
Extras	(b 1, lb 8, nb 3)	12
Total	**(all out, 80.5 overs, 335 mins)**	**298**

Fall: 1-4 (Spearman, 1.3 ov), 2-9 (Horne, 3.5 ov), 3-18 (Sinclair, 9.6 ov), 4-53 (Fleming, 19.5 ov), 5-66 (McMillan, 24.3 ov), 6-138 (Astle, 38.4 ov), 7-247 (Parore, 69.1 ov), 8-282 (Cairns, 77.1 ov), 9-287 (Vettori, 78.5 ov), 10-298 (Doull, 80.5 ov).

Bowling: McGrath 17-4-60-0; Lee 17-2-49-3; Miller 20-2-78-2; Warne 14.5-1-68-4; Blewett 8-1-24-1; SR Waugh 4-0-10-0.

Australia first innings

MJ Slater	c Parore b McMillan	143
GS Blewett	c Astle b Doull	0
SK Warne	lbw Vettori	7
JL Langer	c Parore b Cairns	12
ME Waugh	c Sinclair b Cairns	3
*SR Waugh	not out	151
DR Martyn	c Parore b McMillan	78
+AC Gilchrist	c Parore b O'Connor	3
B Lee	lbw O'Connor	0
CR Miller	c&b McMillan	4
GD McGrath	c&b Cairns	14
Extras	(lb 1, nb 3)	4
Total	**(all out, 120.3 overs, 476 mins)**	**419**

Fall: 1-8 (Blewett, 3.3 ov), 2-29 (Warne, 6.6 ov), 3-47 (Langer, 12.6 ov), 4-51 (ME Waugh, 14.3 ov), 5-250 (Slater, 71.3 ov), 6-364 (Martyn, 101.2 ov), 7-375 (Gilchrist, 108.3 ov), 8-375 (Lee, 110.3 ov), 9-386 (Miller, 111.5 ov), 10-419 (McGrath, 120.3 ov).

Bowling: Cairns 26.3-2-110-3; Doull 19-3-78-1; Vettori 15-1-50-1; O'Connor 26-2-78-2; Astle 11-2-45-0; McMillan 23-10-57-3.

New Zealand second innings

MJ Horne	b Lee	14
CM Spearman	c Langer b Miller	38
MS Sinclair	b Lee	0
*SP Fleming	c Blewett b Miller	60
NJ Astle	b Warne	14
CD McMillan	c ME Waugh b Warne	0
CL Cairns	lbw McGrath	69
+AC Parore	run out (Blewett)	33
DL Vettori	c SR Waugh b Lee	8
SB Doull	c SR Waugh b Warne	40
SB O'Connor	not out	4
Extras	(b 3, lb 8, nb 3)	14
Total	**(all out, 96.2 overs, 398 mins)**	**294**

Fall: 1-46 (Horne, 22.1 ov), 2-46 (Sinclair, 22.4 ov), 3-69 (Spearman, 30.5 ov), 4-88 (Astle, 37.1 ov), 5-88 (McMillan, 37.2 ov), 6-198 (Cairns, 64.2 ov), 7-205 (Fleming, 71.4 ov), 8-222 (Vettori, 78.4 ov), 9-276 (Doull, 89.3 ov), 10-294 (Parore, 96.2 ov).

Bowling: McGrath 22.2-11-35-1; Lee 23-6-87-3; Miller 21-5-54-2; Warne 27-7-92-3; Blewett 3-0-15-0.

Australia second innings

MJ Slater	st Parore b Vettori	12
GS Blewett	b Cairns	25
JL Langer	c Spearman b O'Connor	57
ME Waugh	not out	44
*SR Waugh	c Fleming b O'Connor	15
DR Martyn	not out	17
Extras	(b 2, lb 2, w 3)	7
Total	**(4 wickets, 54.1 overs, 225 mins)**	**177**

Fall: 1-22 (Slater, 9.1 ov), 2-83 (Blewett, 32.2 ov), 3-110 (Langer, 40.2 ov), 4-144 (SR Waugh, 46.4 ov).

Bowling: Cairns 13-2-45-1; O'Connor 11-3-42-2; Vettori 8-1-19-1; Doull 10-2-35-0; McMillan 2-0-13-0; Astle 10.1-4-19-0.

AUSTRALIA WON BY SIX WICKETS

THIRD TEST, AT HAMILTON, MARCH 31, APRIL 1,2,3 (Toss: Australia)

New Zealand first innings

MJ Horne	c Gilchrist b McGrath	12
CM Spearman	c Gilchrist b McGrath	12
MS Sinclair	c Warne b Lee	19
*SP Fleming	lbw Lee	30
NJ Astle	lbw Lee	0
CD McMillan	c Gilchrist b Lee	79
CL Cairns	c Martyn b Lee	37
+AC Parore	not out	12
PJ Wiseman	b Warne	1
DR Tuffey	c Gilchrist b McGrath	3
SB O'Connor	c Gilchrist b McGrath	0
Extras	(b 5, lb 7, w 2, nb 13)	27
Total	**(all out, 82.5 overs, 359 mins)**	**232**

Fall: 1-22 (Spearman, 8.5 ov), 2-42 (Horne, 14.4 ov), 3-53 (Sinclair, 18.4 ov), 4-53 (Astle, 18.6 ov), 5-131 (Fleming, 44.4 ov), 6-208 (McMillan, 66.4 ov), 7-212 (Cairns, 72.6 ov), 8-224 (Wiseman, 77.1 ov), 9-227 (Tuffey, 80.5 ov), 10-232 (O'Connor, 82.5 ov).

Bowling: McGrath 21.5-8-58-4; Lee 23-8-77-5; Warne 20-5-45-1; Miller 11-4-28-0; Martyn 7-4-12-0.

Australia first innings

ML Hayden	c Parore b O'Connor	2
MJ Slater	lbw O'Connor	2
SK Warne	lbw O'Connor	10
JL Langer	b Cairns	4
ME Waugh	c Sinclair b Wiseman	28
*SR Waugh	c Fleming b Cairns	3
DR Martyn	not out	89
+AC Gilchrist	c Horne b Wiseman	75
B Lee	c McMillan b Cairns	8
GD McGrath	b O'Connor	7
CR Miller	c Tuffey b O'Connor	2
Extras	(b 4, lb 6, nb 12)	22
Total	**(all out, 61.5 overs, 268 mins)**	**252**

Fall: 1-3 (Hayden, 3.5 ov), 2-16 (Slater, 9.1 ov), 3-17 (Warne, 9.3 ov), 4-25 (Langer, 10.4 ov), 5-29 (SR Waugh, 12.2 ov), 6-104 (ME Waugh, 26.5 ov), 7-223 (Gilchrist, 49.3 ov), 8-233 (Lee, 54.2 ov), 9-248 (McGrath, 59.4 ov), 10-252 (Miller, 61.5 ov).

Bowling: Cairns 22-7-80-3; O'Connor 15.5-5-51-5; Tuffey 9-0-75-0; Astle 4-3-5-0; Wiseman 11-3-31-2.

New Zealand second innings

MJ Horne	run out (Miller)	0
CM Spearman	c Gilchrist b Lee	35
MS Sinclair	lbw Miller	24
*SP Fleming	c Gilchrist b Miller	2
NJ Astle	c Gilchrist b Warne	26
CD McMillan	c ME Waugh b Warne	30
CL Cairns	b McGrath	71
+AC Parore	c Gilchrist b McGrath	16
PJ Wiseman	c Gilchrist b Lee	16
DR Tuffey	not out	1
SB O'Connor	lbw Lee	0
Extras	(lb 4, nb 4)	8
Total	**(all out, 86.4 overs, 345 mins)**	**229**

Fall: 1-3 (Horne, 2.2 ov), 2-49 (Sinclair, 22.5 ov), 3-53 (Fleming, 24.6 ov), 4-71 (Spearman, 35.5 ov), 5-111 (Astle, 49.3 ov), 6-130 (McMillan, 57.6 ov), 7-165 (Parore, 68.3 ov), 8-220 (Wiseman, 84.2 ov), 9-228 (Cairns, 85.4 ov), 10-229 (O'Connor, 86.4 ov).

Bowling: McGrath 20-7-50-2; Lee 18.4-2-46-3; Miller 20-5-58-2; Warne 25-11-61-2; SR Waugh 3-0-10-0.

Australia second innings

MJ Slater	lbw O'Connor	9
ML Hayden	c Spearman b Wiseman	37
JL Langer	not out	122
ME Waugh	c Sinclair b Wiseman	18
*SR Waugh	retired hurt	18
DR Martyn	lbw O'Connor	4
+AC Gilchrist	not out	0
Extras	(lb 1, nb 3)	4
Total	**(4 wickets, 41.3 overs, 179 mins) 212**

Fall: 1-13 (Slater, 3.3 ov), 2-96 (Hayden, 17.6 ov), 3-124 (ME Waugh, 25.1 ov), 4-190 (Martyn, 37.6 ov).

Bowling: Cairns 10-1-60-0; O'Connor 11-1-53-2; Wiseman 9-1-42-2; Tuffey 11-1-52-0; McMillan 0.3-0-4-0.

AUSTRALIA WON BY SIX WICKETS

AUSTRALIAN WON THE SERIES 3-0

STEVE WAUGH

Australian Test Averages

AUSTRALIA IN SRI LANKA, 1999 — TEST AVERAGES

Australia Batting and Fielding

Name	Mat	I	NO	Runs	HS	Ave	100	50	Ct	St
RT Ponting	3	4	1	253	105*	84.33	1	2	3	-
MJ Slater	3	4	0	182	96	45.50	-	2	1	-
JN Gillespie	1	1	0	41	41	41.00	-	-	-	-
GS Blewett	3	4	0	146	70	36.50	-	2	2	-
DW Fleming	2	2	0	48	32	24.00	-	-	-	-
SR Waugh	3	3	0	52	19	17.33	-	-	1	-
GD McGrath	3	4	3	14	10*	14.00	-	-	1	-
JL Langer	3	4	0	51	32	12.75	-	-	1	-
ME Waugh	3	4	0	29	13	7.25	-	-	2	-
IA Healy	3	4	0	25	11	6.25	-	-	4	-
CR Miller	3	4	0	14	8	3.50	-	-	2	-
SK Warne	3	4	0	6	6	1.50	-	-	2	-

Australia Bowling

Name	Mat	O	M	R	W	Ave	Best	5	10
SK Warne	3	56.1	20	115	8	14.37	5-52	1	-
DW Fleming	2	32.5	6	103	5	20.60	3-14	-	-
CR Miller	3	60.3	10	193	8	24.12	4-62	-	-
GD McGrath	3	68.5	19	214	6	35.66	3-81	-	-
RT Ponting	3	4	1	7	0	-	-	-	-
ME Waugh	3	2	1	9	0	-	-	-	-
GS Blewett	3	3	0	12	0	-	-	-	-
JN Gillespie	1	12	2	43	0	-	-	-	-

AUSTRALIA IN ZIMBABWE, 1999

Australia Batting and Fielding

Name	Mat	I	NO	Runs	HS	Ave	100	50	Ct	St
ME Waugh	1	1	0	90	90	90.00	-	1	5	-
DW Fleming	1	1	0	65	65	65.00	-	1	-	-
JL Langer	1	1	0	44	44	44.00	-	-	1	-
RT Ponting	1	1	0	31	31	31.00	-	-	2	-
GD McGrath	1	1	0	13	13	13.00	-	-	1	-
SK Warne	1	1	0	6	6	6.00	-	-	-	-
GS Blewett	1	2	1	5	4*	5.00	-	-	-	-
IA Healy	1	1	0	5	5	5.00	-	-	2	-
MJ Slater	1	2	1	4	4	4.00	-	-	1	-
CR Miller	1	1	0	2	2	2.00	-	-	-	-
SR Waugh	1	1	1	151	151*	-	1	-	1	-

Australia Bowling

Name	Mat	O	M	R	W	Ave	Best	5	10
GD McGrath	1	54	19	90	6	15.00	3-44	-	-
SK Warne	1	53.1	13	137	6	22.83	3-68	-	-
DW Fleming	1	36	12	53	2	26.50	2-22	-	-
CR Miller	1	53	16	102	3	34.00	3-66	-	-
RT Ponting	1	2	2	0	0	-	-	-	-
GS Blewett	1	5	1	10	0	-	-	-	-
SR Waugh	1	4	1	17	0	-	-	-	-

PAKISTAN IN AUSTRALIA, 1999–2000

Australia Batting and Fielding

Name	Mat	I	NO	Runs	HS	Ave	100	50	Ct	St
AC Gilchrist	3	4	1	264	149*	88.00	1	1	12	1
JL Langer	3	4	0	331	144	82.75	2	1	-	-
MJ Slater	3	5	1	325	169	81.25	1	1	3	-
GS Blewett	3	5	1	204	89	51.00	-	1	2	-
RT Ponting	3	4	0	197	197	49.25	1	-	5	-
SK Warne	3	4	1	99	86	33.00	-	1	4	-
ME Waugh	3	4	0	105	100	26.25	1	-	7	-
SR Waugh	3	4	0	58	28	14.50	-	-	3	-
GD McGrath	3	3	0	8	7	2.66	-	-	3	-

Name	Mat	I	NO	Runs	HS	Ave	Best	5	10	Ct	St
DW Fleming	3	3	0	0	0	0.00	-	-	-	2	-
MS Kasprowicz	1	1	1	9	9*	-	-	-	-	-	-
SA Muller	2	2	2	6	6*	-	-	-	-	2	-

Australia Bowling

Name	Mat	O	M	R	W	Ave	Best	5	10
MS Kasprowicz	1	28	5	132	7	18.85	4-53	-	-
DW Fleming	3	137.4	29	401	18	22.27	5-59	1	-
GD McGrath	3	134	37	393	14	28.07	4-49	-	-
SK Warne	3	129.5	36	370	12	30.83	5-110	1	-
SA Muller	2	58	8	258	7	36.85	3-68	-	-
ME Waugh	3	2	0	6	0	-	-	-	-
SR Waugh	3	5	1	20	0	-	-	-	-
RT Ponting	3	11	2	31	0	-	-	-	-
GS Blewett	3	9	2	32	0	-	-	-	-

INDIA IN AUSTRALIA, 1999–2000

Australia Batting and Fielding

Name	Mat	I	NO	Runs	HS	Ave	100	50	Ct	St
RT Ponting	3	5	2	375	141*	125.00	2	1	3	-
JL Langer	3	5	0	289	223	57.80	1	-	6	-
AC Gilchrist	3	5	1	221	78	55.25	-	2	9	1
SR Waugh	3	5	0	276	150	55.20	1	1	4	-
ME Waugh	3	5	1	137	51*	34.25	-	1	8	-
SK Warne	3	3	0	88	86	29.33	-	1	3	-
GS Blewett	3	5	0	144	88	28.80	-	1	1	-
B Lee	2	1	0	27	27	27.00	-	-	-	-
MS Kasprowicz	1	2	1	25	21*	25.00	-	-	1	-
MJ Slater	3	5	0	123	91	24.60	-	1	3	-
GD McGrath	3	2	0	5	4	2.50	-	-	1	-
DW Fleming	3	2	2	43	31*	-	-	-	-	-

Australia Bowling

Name	Mat	O	M	R	W	Ave	Best	5	10
ME Waugh	3	5	1	17	2	8.50	2-12	-	-
GD McGrath	3	113	34	248	18	13.77	5-48	2	1
B Lee	2	69	19	184	13	14.15	5-47	1	-
DW Fleming	3	96.2	25	279	12	23.25	5-30	1	-
GS Blewett	3	14	4	49	2	24.50	1-5	-	-
SK Warne	3	127	35	335	8	41.87	4-92	-	-
MJ Slater	3	1	0	2	0	-	-	-	-
RT Ponting	3	1	0	8	0	-	-	-	-
MS Kasprowicz	1	17	2	85	0	-	-	-	-

AUSTRALIA IN NEW ZEALAND, 2000

Australia Batting and Fielding

Name	Mat	I	NO	Runs	HS	Ave	100	50	Ct	St
DR Martyn	3	6	2	241	89*	60.25	-	2	2	-
JL Langer	3	6	1	288	122*	57.60	1	1	3	-
SR Waugh	3	6	2	214	151*	53.50	1	-	4	-
ME Waugh	3	6	2	190	72*	47.50	-	1	4	-
AC Gilchrist	3	5	1	144	75	36.00	-	2	17	1
MJ Slater	3	6	0	177	143	29.50	1	-	1	-
ML Hayden	1	2	0	39	37	19.50	-	-	-	-
GS Blewett	2	4	0	50	25	12.50	-	-	3	-
SK Warne	3	4	0	36	12	9.00	-	-	4	-
GD McGrath	3	4	0	30	14	7.50	-	-	-	-
B Lee	3	4	1	20	8	6.66	-	-	1	-
CR Miller	3	4	0	14	8	3.50	-	-	1	-

Australia Bowling

Name	Mat	O	M	R	W	Ave	Best	5	10
B Lee	3	100.4	26	314	18	17.44	5-77	1	-
GD McGrath	3	115.2	40	269	12	22.41	4-33	-	-
CR Miller	3	112	29	311	12	25.91	5-55	1	-
SK Warne	3	129.2	32	414	15	27.60	4-68	-	-
GS Blewett	2	11	1	39	1	39.00	1-24	-	-
DR Martyn	3	7	4	12	0	-	-	-	-
SR Waugh	3	7	0	20	0	-	-	-	-

The One-day Internationals

- Figures in square brackets indicate number of balls faced for batsmen and number of overs bowled for bowlers.
- 'MOM' indicates Man of the Match.
- 'SR' indicates Strike rate (ie. Runs per 100 balls for batsmen and balls per wicket for bowlers).
- 'Econ' indicates Economy Rate (ie. Runs per over).

Australia in Sri Lanka, 1999

At Galle, August 22 (Aiwa Cup, Game One)
Australia 9-206 (43 overs: MG Bevan 44* [44]; ST Jayasuriya 5-28 [9]) **defeated Sri Lanka** 160 (37.4 overs: JN Gillespie 3-26 [6]) by 46 runs. MOM: JN Gillespie.

At Galle, August 23 (Aiwa Cup, Game Two)
India 7-151 (38 overs: RR Singh 38 [52]; TM Moody 2-25 [8]) **lost to Australia** 2-159 (29.1 overs: AC Gilchrist 68 [92], A Symonds 68* [68]) by eight wickets. MOM: A Symonds.

At R. Premadasa Stadium, Colombo, August 26 (Aiwa Cup, Game Four)
Australia 9-241 (50 overs: AC Gilchrist 38 [50], ME Waugh 84 [94]; UDU Chandana 3-35 [10], M Muralitharan 3-50 [10]) **defeated Sri Lanka** 214 (47.1 overs: RP Arnold 41 [62], LPC Silva 55 [85]) by 27 runs. MOM: ME Waugh

At Sinhalese Sports Club Ground, Colombo, August 28 (Aiwa Cup, Game Five)
Australia 8-252 (50 overs: AC Gilchrist 77 [84], A Symonds 45 [60]) **defeated India** 211 (48.3 overs: S Ramesh 71 [123], RR Singh 75 [105]; JN Gillespie 4-26 [9]) by 41 runs. MOM: AC Gilchrist.

At R. Premadasa Stadium, Colombo, August 31 (Aiwa Cup Final)
Australia 202 (50 overs: SR Waugh 43 [68]) lost to **Sri Lanka 2-208** (39.3 overs: RS Kaluwitharana 95* [117], RP Arnold 47 [57]) by eight wickets. MOM: RS Kaluwitharana; Sri Lanka won the Aiwa Cup. Player of the Series: AC Gilchrist.

LEADING AUSTRALIAN AVERAGES

Batting and Fielding

Name	Mat	I	NO	Runs	HS	Ave	SR	100	50	Ct	St
A Symonds	5	5	2	157	68*	52.33	83.51	-	1	2	-
AC Gilchrist	5	5	0	231	77	46.20	84.61	-	2	8	3
ME Waugh	5	5	0	174	84	34.80	79.45	-	1	1	-
RT Ponting	5	5	1	102	37	25.50	53.96	-	-	2	-
MG Bevan	5	4	1	74	44*	24.66	83.14	-	-	1	-

Bowling

Name	Mat	O	M	R	W	Ave	Best	4w	SR	Econ
JN Gillespie	4	32	2	119	10	11.90	4-26	1	19.2	3.71
DS Lehmann	5	8.4	0	41	3	13.66	2-4	-	17.3	4.73
TM Moody	3	25	5	74	3	24.66	2-25	-	50.0	2.96
SK Warne	5	40	1	213	6	35.50	2-36	-	40.0	5.32
GD McGrath	3	27	0	154	4	38.50	2-52	-	40.5	5.70

Australia in Zimbabwe, 1999

At Bulawayo, October 21
Australia 6-303 (50 overs: ME Waugh 106 [97], RT Ponting 67 [90], DR Martyn 57* [38]) **defeated Zimbabwe 220** (43.4 overs: NC Johnson 110 [124]: DW Fleming 3-33 [8], A Symonds 3-52 [8]) by 83 runs. MOM: ME Waugh.

At Harare, October 23
Zimbabwe 116 (37.3 overs: DW Fleming 3-14 [10], AC Dale 2-24 [9], DR Martyn 2-21 [8]) **lost to Australia 1-117** (28.3 overs: ME Waugh 54* [95]) by nine wickets. MOM: DW Fleming.

At Harare, October 24
Zimbabwe 9-200 (50 overs: A Flower 99* [111]; GD McGrath 2-18 [10]) **lost to Australia** (RT Ponting 87 [110], MG Bevan 77 [107]) by nine wickets. MOM: A Flower. Australia won series 3-0.

LEADING AUSTRALIAN AVERAGES

Batting and Fielding

Name	Mat	I	NO	Runs	HS	Ave	SR	100	50	Ct	St
RT Ponting	3	3	2	185	87*	185.00	75.20	-	2	4	-
ME Waugh	2	2	1	160	106	160.00	83.33	1	1	4	-
MG Bevan	3	2	1	102	77*	102.00	75.00	-	1	1	-
DR Martyn	3	1	1	57	57*	-	150.00	-	1	2	-
AC Gilchrist	3	3	0	60	28	20.00	82.19	-	-	6	1

Bowling

Name	Mat	O	M	R	W	Ave	Best	4w	SR	Econ
DW Fleming	2	18	5	47	6	7.83	3-14	-	18.0	2.61
GD McGrath	2	16.4	4	39	3	13.00	2-18	-	33.3	2.34
SK Warne	3	19	1	82	4	20.50	2-40	-	28.5	4.31
TM Moody	3	22	3	89	4	22.25	2-25	-	33.0	4.04
A Symonds	3	19.3	0	127	5	25.40	3-52	-	23.4	6.51

India and Pakistan in Australia, 1999–2000

At Brisbane, January 9 (World Series Game One)
Pakistan 8-184 (50 overs: Wasim Akram 35 [61], Saqlain Mushtaq 37* [46]; A Symonds 3-34 [10]) **defeated Australia 139** (39 overs: MG Bevan 31* [76]; Shoaib Akhtar 3-31 [7], Abdur Razzaq 4-23 [8]) by 45 runs. MOM: Abdur Razzaq.

At Melbourne Cricket Ground, Melbourne, January 12 (World Series Game Three)
Australia 7-269 (50 overs: RT Ponting 115 [121], MG Bevan 41 [54]) **defeated India 6-241** (50 overs: SC Ganguly 100 [127], R Dravid 60 [85]) by 28 runs. MOM: RT Ponting.

At Sydney, January 14 (World Series Game Four)
India 100 (36.3 overs: GD McGrath 4-8 [10], A Symonds 4-11 [3.3]) **lost to Australia 5-101** (26.5 overs: AC Gilchrist 37 [51], A Symonds 28* [32]) by five wickets. MOM: A Symonds.

At Melbourne Cricket Ground, Melbourne, January 16 (World Series Game Five)
Pakistan 9-176 (41 overs: Saeed Anwar 49 [67], Abdur Razzaq 51*; S Lee 3-24 [8]) **lost to Australia 4-177** (SR Waugh 81* [92], DR Martyn 39* [61]) by six wickets. MOM: SR Waugh.

At Sydney, January 19 (World Series Game Six)
Australia 286 (49.4 overs: ME Waugh 43 [71], MG Bevan [97], DR Martyn 50 [56], A Symonds 47 [26], S Lee 26 [13]; Wasim Akram 3-40 [9]) **defeated Pakistan 205** (45.2 overs: Abdur Razzaq 40 [38]; SCG MacGill 4-19 [10]) by 81 runs. MOM: SCG MacGill.

At Melbourne Cricket Ground, Melbourne, January 23 (World Series Game Eight)
Australia 9-260 (50 overs: RT Ponting 53 [64], MG Bevan 83 [101]) **defeated Pakistan 245** (48.5 overs: Ijaz Ahmed 85 [104]; S Lee 4-37 [8.5]) by 15 runs. MOM: MG Bevan.

At Adelaide, January 26 (World Series Game 10)
Australia 5-329 (50 overs: AC Gilchrist 92 [102], ME Waugh 116 [131], RT Ponting 43 [33]) **defeated India 177** (46.5 overs: R Dravid 63 [82]; B Lee 5-27 [8.5]) by 152 runs. MOM: ME Waugh.

At Perth, January 30 (World Series Game 12)
India 6-226 (50 overs: R Dravid 65 [106], RR Singh 45 [51]) **lost to Australia 6-230** (49.3 overs: ME Waugh 40 [63], MG Bevan 71 [92]) by four wickets. MOM: MG Bevan.

At Melbourne Cricket Ground, Melbourne, February 2 (World Series First Final)
Pakistan 154 (47.2 overs: Moin Khan 47 [48]; GD McGrath 3-17 [9], B Lee 3-18 [8.2]) **lost to Australia 4-155** (42.4 overs: RT Ponting 50 [75], MG Bevan 54 [102]; Shoaib Akhtar 2-26 [7]) by six wickets. MOM: GD McGrath.

At Sydney, February 4 (World Series Second Final)
Australia 7-337 (50 overs: ME Waugh 53 [73], AC Gilchrist 51 [42], RT Ponting 78 [80], A Symonds 45 [45], SR Waugh 37 [30]) **defeated Pakistan 185** (36.3 overs: Yousuf Youhana 41 [73]; GD McGrath 5-48 [9.3], B Lee 3-51 [9]) by 152 runs. MOM: RT Ponting. Australia won Finals 2-0. Player of the World Series: Abdur Razzaq.

STEVE WAUGH

LEADING AUSTRALIAN AVERAGES

Batting and Fielding

Name	Mat	I	NO	Runs	HS	Ave	SR	100	50	Ct	St
DR Martyn	9	9	6	194	50	64.66	71.58	-	1	7	-
MG Bevan	10	10	2	388	83	48.50	65.65	-	4	3	-
RT Ponting	10	10	0	404	115	40.40	87.06	1	3	1	-
A Symonds	9	7	1	184	47	30.66	115.72	-	-	2	-
ME Waugh	10	10	0	305	116	30.50	67.03	1	1	6	-
AC Gilchrist	10	10	0	272	92	27.20	85.26	-	2	18	-
SR Waugh	10	9	2	195	81*	27.85	73.86	-	1	5	-

Bowling

Name	Mat	O	M	R	W	Ave	Best	4w	SR	Econ
GD McGrath	9	79.3	14	291	19	15.31	5-49	1	25.1	3.66
A Symonds	9	51.5	2	203	12	16.91	4-11	1	25.9	3.91
SCG MacGill	3	30	4	105	6	17.50	4-19	1	30.0	3.50
S Lee	9	73.5	2	293	16	18.31	4-37	1	27.6	3.96
B Lee	9	81.1	4	320	16	20.00	5-27	-	30.4	3.94

Australia in New Zealand, 2000

At Wellington, February 17
Australia 1-119 (ME Waugh 45 [68], ML Hayden 64 [68]). Game **abandoned** due to rain.

At Auckland, February 19
New Zealand 122 (30.1 overs: GD McGrath 3-33 [8.1], B. Lee 3-21 [7]) **lost to Australia 5-123** (24.4 overs: ML Hayden 50 [49]) by five wickets. MOM: B Lee.

At Dunedin, February 23
Australia 4-310 (50 overs: AC Gilchrist 77 [65], ME Waugh 75 [109], MG Bevan 52 [50], SR Waugh 43 retired hurt [32], A Symonds 34 [13]) defeated New Zealand 260 (45 overs: NJ Astle 81 [83], RG Twose 62 [61]) by 50 runs. MOM: AC Gilchrist.

At Christchurch, February 26
Australia 6-349 (50 overs: ME Waugh 70 [88], AC Gilchrist 128 [98], SR Waugh 54 [44], MG Bevan 37 [33], DR Martyn 29* [14]) defeated New Zealand 9-301 (50 overs: SP Fleming 82 [88], CZ Harris 59* [52]; DW Fleming 3-58 [10], SK Warne 3-50 [9]) by 48 runs. MOM: AC Gilchrist.

At Napier, March 1
New Zealand 9-243 (50 overs: NJ Astle 104 [128]; DW Fleming 4-41 [8]) **lost to Australia 5-245** (45.4 overs: ML Hayden 57 [67], MG Bevan 107 [141], SR Waugh 43* [34]) by five wickets. MOM: MG Bevan.

LEADING AUSTRALIAN AVERAGES

Batting and Fielding

Name	Mat	I	NO	Runs	HS	Ave	SR	100	50	Ct	St
SR Waugh	6	5	3	145	54	72.50	108.20	-	1	2	-
ML Hayden	5	5	1	191	64*	47.75	85.26	-	3	3	-
AC Gilchrist	6	6	0	251	128	41.83	112.05	1	1	7	-
MG Bevan	6	5	0	206	107	41.20	78.32	1	1	-	-
ME Waugh	6	6	1	206	75	41.20	66.23	-	2	3	-
DR Martyn	6	5	5	158	116*	-	94.04	1	-	1	-

Australia Bowling

Name	Mat	O	M	R	W	Ave	Best	4w	SR	Econ
DW Fleming	3	24	0	141	9	15.66	4-41	1	16.0	5.87
GD McGrath	5	33.1	4	158	8	19.75	3-33	-	24.8	4.76
SK Warne	6	49	4	194	9	21.55	3-50	-	32.6	3.95
S Lee	5	22	2	109	4	27.25	2-27	-	33.0	4.95
B Lee	5	33	1	170	5	34.00	3-21	-	39.6	5.15

Australia in South Africa, 2000

At Durban, April 12
Australia 9-240 (50 overs: AC Gilchrist 51 [40], DR Martyn 74 [91]; M Ntini 4-56 [10]) **lost to South Africa 4-241** (48 overs: G Kirsten 97 [126], JH Kallis 61 [88], JN Rhodes 46* [40]; GD McGrath 2-21 [9]) by six wickets. MOM: G Kirsten.

At Cape Town, April 14
South Africa 9-144 (50 overs: GD McGrath 1-13 [10], B Lee 3-32 [10], SK Warne 1-21 [10]) **lost to Australia 5-145** (24.3 overs: DR Martyn 50 [32]; JH Kallis 3-40 [6]) by five wickets. MOM: DR Martyn.

At Johannesburg, April 16
Australia 205 (49.5 overs: SR Waugh 51 [86], IJ Harvey 38 [45]; SM Pollock 4-37 [9.5]) **lost to South Africa 6-209** (47.5 overs: MV Boucher 55 [89], L Klusener 52 [50]; B Lee 3-32 [10]) by four wickets. MOM: L Klusener. South Africa won series 2-1. Player of the Series: L Klusener.

LEADING AUSTRALIAN AVERAGES

Batting and Fielding

Name	Mat	I	NO	Runs	HS	Ave	SR	100	50	Ct	St
IJ Harvey	2	2	1	49	38	49.00	87.50	-	-	-	-
DR Martyn	3	3	0	130	74	43.33	97.01	-	2	1	-
MG Bevan	3	3	0	103	39	34.33	60.58	-	-	-	-
SR Waugh	3	2	0	53	51	26.50	54.63	-	1	1	-
B Lee	3	2	1	25	24*	25.00	73.52	-	-	-	-
AC Gilchrist	3	3	0	69	51	23.00	116.94	-	1	7	-

Bowling

Name	Mat	O	M	R	W	Ave	Best	4w	SR	Econ
GD McGrath	3	28	4	71	5	14.20	2-13	-	33.6	2.53
B Lee	3	30	4	121	8	15.12	3-32	-	22.5	4.03
SK Warne	3	28	3	98	3	32.66	2-30	-	56.0	3.50
S Lee	2	14	1	66	2	33.00	2-19	-	42.0	4.71
A Symonds	3	11	0	47	1	47.00	1-15	-	66.0	4.27

South Africa in Australia, 2000

At Colonial Stadium, Melbourne, August 16
Australia 5-295 (50 overs: MG Bevan 106 [125], SR Waugh 114 [103]) **defeated South Africa 7-201** (50 overs: G Kirsten 43 [69], JH Kallis 42 [66]; IJ Harvey 3-41 [10]) by 94 runs. MOM: SR Waugh.

At Colonial Stadium, Melbourne, August 18
South Africa 8-226 (50 overs: AJ Hall 37 [59], JN Rhodes 54 [53], MV Boucher 51 [63]; JN Gillespie 3-40 [10]) **tied with Australia 9-226** (50 overs: ME Waugh 48 [64], RT Ponting 39 [61]; N Boje 2-33 [10], AJ Hall 2-8 [3]). MOM: AJ Hall.

At Colonial Stadium, Melbourne, August 20
South Africa 7-206 (50 overs: ND McKenzie 45 [93], L Klusener 49 [74]; GD McGrath 3-26 [10], B Lee 3-56 [10]) **defeated Australia 9-198** (48 overs: AC Gilchrist 63 [67]; N Boje 2-29 [10]) by eight runs, after Australia was 'fined' two overs for having a slow over-rate during the South African innings. MOM: N. Boje. Series tied 1-1. Player of the Series: N. Boje

LEADING AUSTRALIAN AVERAGES

Batting and Fielding

Name	Mat	I	NO	Runs	HS	Ave	SR	100	50	Ct	St
SR Waugh	3	3	1	161	114*	80.50	99.38	1	-	-	-
MG Bevan	3	3	0	142	106	47.33	66.04	1	-	1	-
AC Gilchrist	3	3	0	101	63	33.66	73.18	-	1	3	1
DR Martyn	3	2	0	49	31	24.50	66.21	-	-	1	-
ME Waugh	3	3	0	66	48	22.00	64.70	-	-	4	-

Bowling

Name	Mat	O	M	R	W	Ave	Best	4w	SR	Econ
IJ Harvey	2	20	1	84	5	16.80	3-41	-	24.0	4.20
GD McGrath	3	30	6	101	4	25.25	3-26	-	45.0	3.36
JN Gillespie	2	20	1	79	3	26.33	3-40	-	40.0	3.95
B Lee	2	20	1	107	3	35.66	3-56	-	40.0	5.35
SK Warne	3	30	2	101	2	50.50	2-38	-	90.0	3.36

Appendix: The Winning Streaks

Tests

In winning 10 consecutive Test matches, the Australian team built the second longest such winning streak in Test history. The list of most consecutive Test wins is as follows:

Wins	Team	Start	End
11	West Indies	Bridgetown, 1984	Adelaide, 1984-85
10*	**Australia**	**Harare, 1999**	**Hamilton, 2000**
8	Australia	Sydney, 1920-21	Leeds, 1921
7	England	Melbourne, 1884-85	Sydney, 1887-88
7	England	Lord's, 1928	Adelaide 1928-29
7	West Indies	Bridgetown, 1985	St John's, 1986
7	West Indies	Lord's 1988	Melbourne 1988-89
6	England	The Oval, 1888	The Oval, 1890
6	England	Leeds, 1957	Manchester, 1958
6	West Indies	Port-of-Spain, 1962	Manchester, 1963

* This table is correct as at September 1, 2000. The Australian streak remains unbroken. Their next Test match will be against the West Indies in Brisbane in November 2000.

Clean sweeps

Australia's effort in sweeping each of the series against Pakistan, India and New Zealand was the 18th, 19th and 20th instances of a team winning all three Tests in a three-match series. There have been seven instances of teams winning all five Tests in a series, and two instances of a team winning all four Tests. The Australian examples are:

Tests	Season	Venue	Opponent
5	1920-21	Australia	England
5	1931-32	Australia	South-Africa
4	1967-68	Australia	India
3	1972-73	Australia	Pakistan
3	1979-80	Australia	England
3	1995-96	Australia	Sri Lanka
3	**1999-00**	**Australia**	**Pakistan**
3	**1999-00**	**Australia**	**India**
3	**1999-00**	**New Zealand**	**New Zealand**

Most wins in an Australian season

The 1999-00 Australians' effort in winning six Tests in one Australian home summer was unprecedented. The list of most wins in an Australian season is as follows:

Season	Team	Opponent(s)	Wins (series result)
1999-00	**Australia**	**Pakistan, India**	**6 (3-0, 3-0)**
1920-21	Australia	England	5 (5-0)
1931-32	Australia	South Africa	5 (5-0)
1975-76	Australia	West Indies	5 (5-1)
1978-79	England	Australia	5 (5-1)
1995-96	Australia	Pakistan, Sri Lanka	5 (2-1, 3-0)
1897-98	Australia	England	4 (4-1)
1901-02	Australia	England	4 (4-1)
1907-07	Australia	England	4 (4-1)
1910-11	Australia	South Africa	4 (4-1)
1911-12	England	Australia	4 (4-1)
1924-25	Australia	England	4 (4-1)
1928-29	England	Australia	4 (4-1)
1930-31	Australia	West Indies	4 (4-1)
1932-33	England	Australia	4 (4-1)
1947-48	Australia	India	4 (4-0)
1950-51	Australia	England	4 (4-1)
1951-52	Australia	West Indies	4 (4-1)
1958-59	Australia	England	4 (4-0)
1967-68	Australia	India	4 (4-0)
1974-75	Australia	England	4 (4-1)
1991-92	Australia	India	4 (4-0)

One-Day Internationals

During 1999-00, Australia created a new world record for most consecutive wins in one-day international cricket. The streak began with the second game of the World Series on January 12 and ended when Australia were defeated by New Zealand in Auckland on March 3. The list of most consecutive wins by teams in one-day international cricket is as follows:

Wins	Team	Start	End
13*	Australia	v India, 12.1.00	v New Zealand, 26.2.00
11	West Indies	v England, 4.6.84	v Sri Lanka, 2.2.85
11	England	v West Indies, 23.5.91	v South Africa, 12.3.92
10	West Indies	v India, 5.1.88	v Pakistan, 30.3.88
10	Australia	v Pakistan, 23.2.90	v Sri Lanka, 2.5.90
10	Pakistan	v India, 27.4.90	v West Indies, 13.11.90
10	South Africa	v England, 13.1.96	v Holland, 5.3.96
10+	Australia	v Bangladesh, 27.5.99	v India, 28.8.99

This figure does not include the abandoned match between Australia and New Zealand on 17.1.00
+ *This figure does not include the tied World Cup semi-final between Australia and South Africa on 17.6.99.*
This streak stretched from Australia's fourth group match of the 1999 World Cup until Australia's final preliminary game of the 1999 Aiwa Cup in Sri Lanka.

Photography Credits

COLOUR

Allsport: pages 34 (top), 35, 38 (bottom two), 40 (top), 58 (both), 62 (bottom), 97 (both), 98 (both), 100 (both), 101, 102 (both), 103 (both), 104, 137, 139 (both), 140 (top), 141 (both), 142 (top left, bottom), 143 (both), 144, 177 (bottom), 178 (top), 179 (both), 180, 181, 182 (top), 183, 217, 218 (bottom), 219, 220 (bottom), 221 (both), 223, 224 (both).

Steve Waugh: pages 34 (bottom two), 36 (both), 37 (both), 38 (top), 39 (both), 40 (bottom), 57 (all), 59 (all), 60 (both), 61 (all), 62 (top), 63 (all), 64 (top), 99 (all), 138 (both), 140 (bottom), 142 (top right), 177 (top), 178 (bottom), 182 (bottom), 184 (all), 218 (top and middle), 220 (top), 222 (all).

BLACK AND WHITE

Allsport: pages 13, 15, 16, 22, 23, 24, 26 (both), 30 (both), 47, 48, 53, 67, 68, 77, 78, 80, 82, 84 (bottom), 86, 88 (both), 89, 90, 93(both), 96 (bottom), 109, 111, 113, 115, 117 (all), 118, 121, 122, 123, 125, 127 (both), 136 (bottom), 147, 148, 151, 153, 156 (both), 158, 160 (both), 161, 162, 163 (both), 165, 167, 169 (both), 172, 173 (both), 175, 187, 192 (all), 195, 197, 201 (all), 202, 207, 225, 229, 233, 235.

Steve Waugh: pages 14, 19, 20, 28, 41 (both), 42, 44, 45, 50 (both), 51, 52, 54, 55, 56, 65, 70, 74, 75, 84 (top), 85, 92, 94, 96 (top), 107 (all), 124, 128 (both), 130 (all), 131, 132, 133, 136 (top), 145, 150, 176, 185 (both), 190, 199, 200 (both), 204 (both), 210 (both), 213, 215, 216, 226.

CHAPTER TITLE PAGES

Page 13: Steve Waugh leaves the field after colliding with Jason Gillespie, Kandy, September 1999.
Page 53: Steve Waugh during his century against Zimbabwe, one-off Test in Harare, October 1999.
Page 77: Steve Waugh modelling his 'Trumper cap', Sydney, January 2000.
Page 151: Ricky Ponting, after scoring a century during the World Series, Melbourne, January 2000.
Page 175: Shane Warne, immediately after taking his 356th Test wicket, Auckland, March 2000.
Page 213: Andrew Symonds on Table Mountain, Cape Town, April 2000.
Page 229: The toss at cricket's first indoor international match, Melbourne, August 2000.
Page 235: Justin Langer, after reaching his century against Pakistan, Perth, November 1999